Published in 2012 by

Laurence King Publishing Ltd
361–373 City Road
London EC1V 1LR
United Kingdom
Tel: +44 20 7841 6900
Fax: +44 20 7841 6910
email: enquiries@laurenceking.com
www.laurenceking.com

A catalogue record for this book is available from the British Library.

ISBN 978-1-85669-821-4

Book and cover design: & SMITH
www.andsmithdesign.com

Commissioning Editor: Jo Lightfoot
Senior Editor: Melissa Danny

Printed in Hong Kong

Front cover: Sony Bravia, Balls (Fallon, 2005/Photo Peter Funch/ see pp. 172–177)

Back cover: Carlton Draught, Big Ad (George Patterson Partners, 2005/ see pp. 56–61)

Pages 4–5: Cadbury's Dairy Milk, Eyebrows (Fallon, 2009/ see pp. 36–43)

HOW 30 GREAT ADS WERE MADE

FROM IDEA TO CAMPAIGN

ELIZA WILLIAMS

LAURENCE KING PUBLISHING

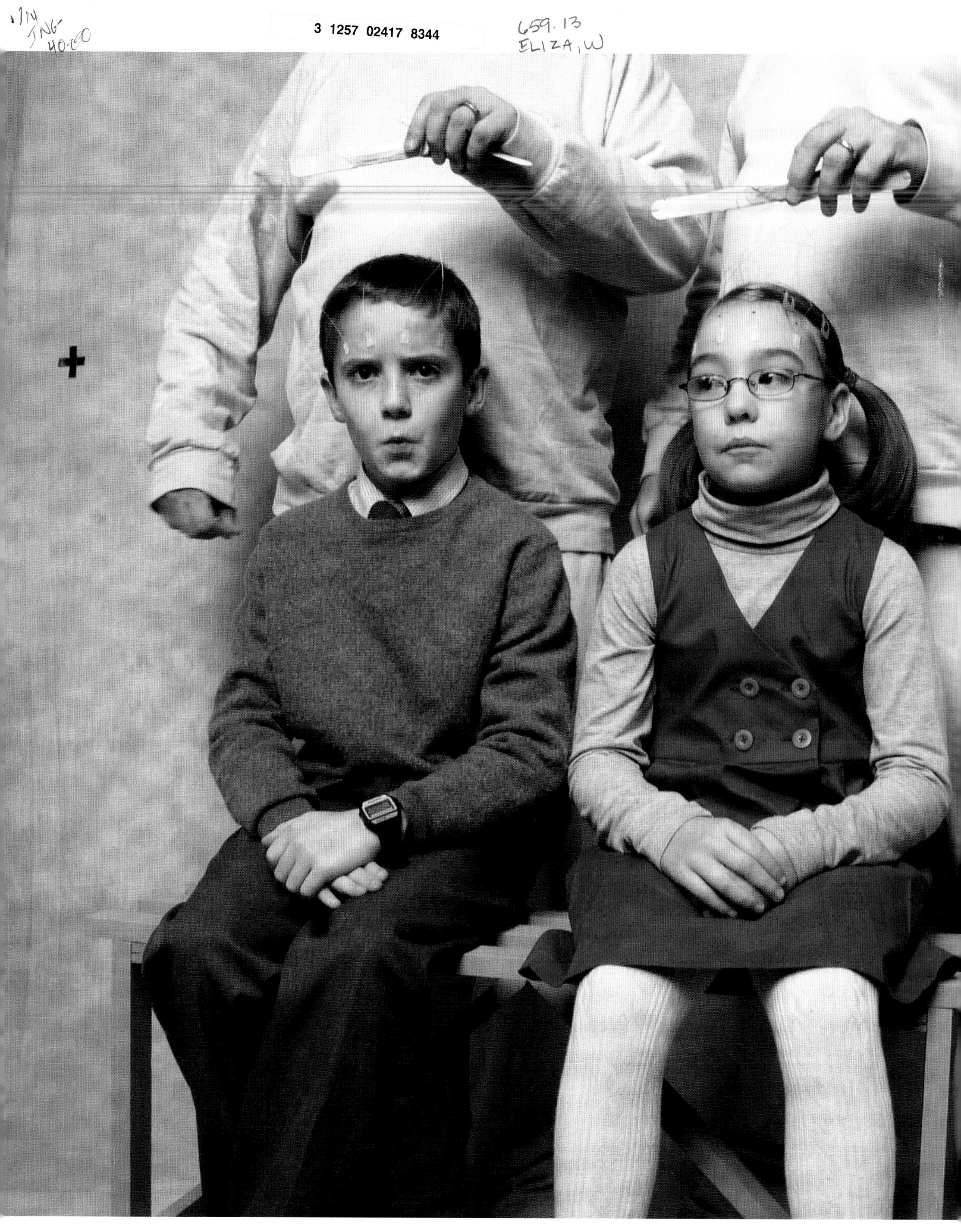

Contents

Introduction

30 Great Ads

A great piece of advertising can inspire conversation, newspaper headlines and a viral response. It can be a cultural event, become symbolic of a certain era. It can take you back in time. For this book, I have gathered together 30 such ads that were created in the first decade of the new millennium, the 2000s. I have chosen ads that are highly creative, successful and have an unusual story behind their making. I've also picked work that offers an overview of the decade in advertising, which saw massive changes occur in the industry.

It was during this period that digital media really took hold – a force that proved immensely disruptive to the rather conservative working methods of the ad industry. Prior to the rise of the internet, television and print advertising were king and queen; they were the only media that mattered. Suddenly in the 2000s, brands and ad agencies were forced to explore different ways of talking to their customers, via digital means.

Despite this digital explosion, fantastic TV ads continued to be made throughout the decade, many of which enjoyed more of a life online than off, as viewers watched and shared the most imaginative pieces of work via the internet. The success of these ads proves that while television's prominence may be on the wane, a great piece of film can still bring people together.

Looking at the TV ads, certain themes of the decade emerge. The most obvious is a preoccupation with craft. After the rise of computer-generated effects in advertising in the 1990s, the 2000s brought a desire for imagery rooted in reality. The commercials had to be as visually impressive as the CGI ads, but it was all the more exciting if they were real. Honda's ad Cog arguably began this trend, with its stunning chain reaction of car parts. It was quickly followed by a succession of ads based on real events, including Sony's famous bouncing balls and exploding paint, and Skoda's car made of cake. CGI didn't disappear completely of course, and in fact the Guinness noitulovE ad, in which a group of three Guinness-drinking friends travel back through time, supposedly contained the widest range of visual effects ever seen in a commercial.

Another theme of the decade – and an enduring motif throughout the history of advertising – was the use of humour to reach consumers. In a series of hugely successful spots, Budweiser created a cultural phenomenon around the use of the word 'Wassup', while Cadbury's Dairy Milk used surreal humour to sell its chocolate bars. Carlton Beer in Australia sent up some of the more pompous elements of the ad industry to massive success, and Coke charmed audiences with ads that mixed stunning visuals and gentle wit.

The first major advertising success for a brand online was also rooted in a wicked sense of humour. Subservient Chicken, a website created in the U.S. for Burger King, allowed users to command a man dressed as a chicken to act out their every whim. Millions flocked to the site to play, proving that, with the right approach, the internet can prove as powerful a tool for advertising as TV.

Further online inventiveness followed, albeit slowly. Uniqlo created another worldwide phenomenon with its clock widget, Uniqlock, while U.S. pay-per-view channel HBO created a live event followed by an elaborate web experience to prove its prowess at storytelling. Other brands used the internet to introduce longer format ads and films to its audiences, hoping that these would go viral and be shared with friends via social media sites and blogs. The most surprising projects became successful online: Johnnie Walker's film The Man Who Walked Around The World, which stars Scottish actor Robert Carlyle delivering a six-minute monologue about the whisky brand, was originally intended purely as an internal staff film, but proved so popular when leaked to the wider world via the web, it was later formally released online.

Innovation occurred in other ad mediums too: Johannesburg-based agency TBWA\Hunt\Lascaris created a poster campaign for The Zimbabwean newspaper using worthless Zimbabwean trillion dollar bank notes, viscerally highlighting the state of the economy in the country under Robert Mugabe's regime; while a more light-hearted, though equally dynamic, campaign in the U.S. saw New York street musicians launch Oasis's new album instead of the band themselves.

Each ad featured in this book comes with a multitude of images to show how it was developed, including storyboards, production photographs and other behind-the-scenes shots. The tale of the making of each ad is then told by the main protagonists involved in its creation. Struggles are uncovered, and enduring industry myths are unravelled as these hidden stories are revealed.

Looking at the work collected here, it might be imagined that it is possible to glean a magic formula for making a great ad. This, sadly, remains elusive. A great many of those I interviewed for the book talked about 'stars aligning' when they created their work, implying that it was fate that brought everything together. Commonalities in approach can be ascertained, however – virtually every ad featured here had a creative team behind it with tenacity and a determination to make something extraordinary, along with a brave client who was willing to take some risks. The ads were then dosed with a certain degree of luck, that ambiguous quality that can turn a good piece of creative work into an exceptional one.

What is certain is that it's incredibly difficult to make a brilliant piece of advertising, as hard as it is to create any piece of amazing creative work. Those that do manage to achieve it should be applauded, as their work serves to show that advertising, so ubiquitous in our lives, doesn't just have to be about selling a product but can also serve to make our visual and cultural landscape that little bit more interesting too.

01/

adidas Originals
House Party

Sid Lee

In 2009, adidas Originals turned 60. Reaching such a landmark age surely deserves a party, and for its first major television commercial for the Originals brand, adidas threw an epic one, with guests including David Beckham, Katy Perry, Method Man and The Ting Tings. The idea came from Montreal-based advertising agency Sid Lee, who realized that a house party could be the perfect vehicle to bring together all the disparate groups connected to the Originals brand. 'When we started studying adidas Originals, and seeing what they'd done in the last 60 years, we realized that no other brand has as much breadth and depth. They touch everyone from the punk to the skateboard kid, to the electro guy to the jock,' says Kris Manchester, the agency's creative director.

'We had this epiphany that a house party was the perfect device to tell this story.'

01 Dancers at the adidas Originals house party, an ad campaign created to celebrate the brand's 60th birthday. This image was one of a series of print ads that formed part of the campaign, alongside a 60-second commercial.

02

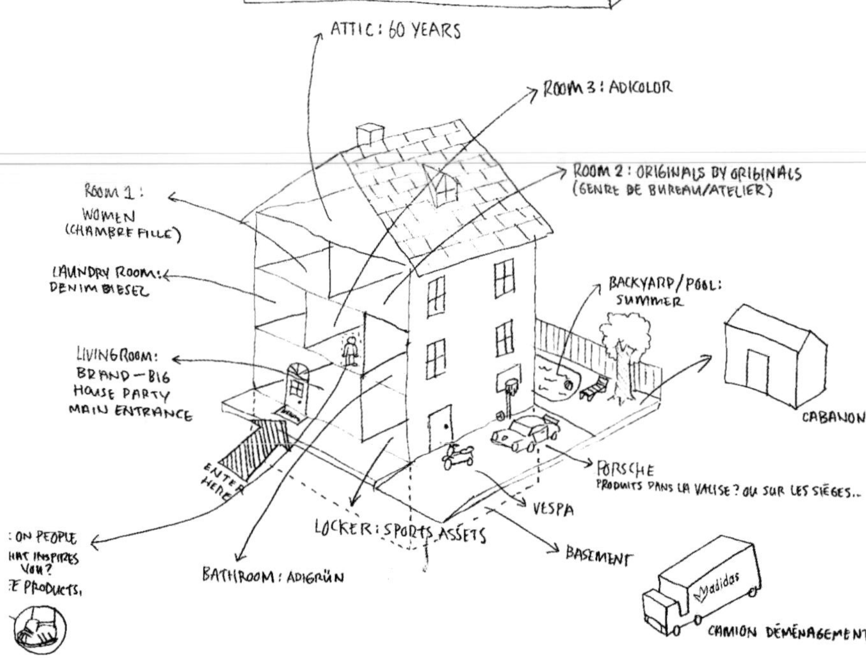

03

04-06

'We realized that the idea of a house party itself is open to a diverse audience. I remember when I was a kid at an open house party you'd have different crews there, all mixing up. You'd have the goth kids, you'd have the sports guys, you'd have the punk band and so on.... So we had this epiphany that a house party was the perfect device to tell this story,' Manchester continues.

Initially, the idea was to focus just on these varying groups of kids, but as the creatives expanded the idea, they proposed including celebrities at the party. Although the brand has been involved in tie-ins with celebrities before, this was quite an unusual proposition for Originals, as Tom Ramsden, global director of communications at the company, explains. 'The star thing came about later on in the development,' he says. 'adidas Originals has worked in entertainment for 30 years or so – we've had placements on Baywatch and with Run DMC – but never in a way where we've worked with people for a television commercial, or any overt commercial stuff. So it came about fairly organically; Sid Lee was brainstorming ideas, and it came to them saying, "Oh, you can imagine Will Ferrell doing this, or The Ting Tings"; or "What would happen if these people turned up?" Those things were thrown at us and we said, "Well, actually, we kind of know those people, we've got good relationships with them." Not to sound too much of a cliché, but it was like inviting people to a house party – saying "we're doing a TV commercial, it's a house party, do you want to come?" And it really didn't take much more of a sell-in than that on a lot of occasions.'

A major part of the ad's charm is in the handling of these huge names, who are incorporated into the scenes at the party in a very natural way, rather than being given any obvious star treatment. We see Missy Elliott dancing in the living room, while

02-03 Drawing for a possible invite to the adidas party and a sketch by the ad agency showing a loose plan of how different areas in the house might be used on the shoot.

04-06 Sketches of possible scenes at the party, including a pool jump, a DJ entertaining the crowd, and lots of adidas shoes being thrown up in the air.

07-09 The ad brought together the different adidas 'tribes', from punk kids to jocks, who were all shown partying together. Also invited were several big name celebrities, including David Beckham, who mingled with the crowd.

10 More storyboard sketches revealing other ideas for the shoot.

07

'After many, many storyboards it ended up being something else when we were on the spot. It's basically composing with what you have at hand. It's sort of like documenting a live event. I think magic came out of that.'

08

09

10

David Beckham shares a joke on the sofa. Many of the celebrities are incorporated so subtly that they are easy to miss, though other moments, such as a flirtatious scene featuring Katy Perry, are less disguised. Sid Lee felt this naturalness was central to the spot, so hired a director – Nima Nourizadeh – who would be able to pull this off. 'I think that ends up being the big idea, to be quite honest,' says Manchester. 'The big idea is the way we shot the celebrities; the way we positioned them; the way we showed them with just normal kids, as anybody else.... We didn't want this to be a traditional spot. We had planned for it just to be a video clip, and that's why Nima came on board. He had a huge amount of music video experience and had never really done a TV spot before.... He just got the brief from us and from adidas that this had to be the most authentic party ever.'

'The style in which it was made was what made it exciting,' agrees Nourizadeh. 'From the start I wanted it to be something that downplayed the whole celebrity scene. It was shot in a very documentary style. Even the house wasn't something that was flash, where you'd normally see parties like this, with loads of celebrities. We were looking at the kind of house where we'd all been to parties – kind of run-down, not that exciting. Okay, it's got a pool in the back garden, but it's still not a really big, flash party. That just made it more exciting, more surprising, when you saw the faces – you know, you had Run DMC DJing, that was cool, Beckham pops his head out, that was cool. We just shot it in a very real way.'

When watching the film, it might be easy to assume that the director simply set up a party and then sat back and let the cameras roll, capturing the action. In fact, the shoot took place over six days in Los Angeles, in different locations, and required an inordinate amount of organization, especially when it came to the celebrities.

'The big idea is the way we shot the celebrities; the way we positioned them; the way we showed them with just normal kids, as anybody else.'

'It was the most insane schedule,' comments Nourizadeh. 'We had scenes that we had to shoot with certain celebrities, but their schedules dictated when we could shoot them. It was really difficult – for example, the idea might have been to shoot Beckham at night, but he was only available in the morning. There was a scene where Young Jeezy was playing poker with Kevin Garnett, but they couldn't make the same time so we had to use body doubles. It was a real nightmare scheduling-wise.'

In order to provoke exciting footage, the team developed situations and activities for the celebrities. These all had to be approved, although they were often changed at the last minute due to timings, or the celebrity's whim on the day. 'It was such a special shoot; it was very spontaneous,' says Manchester. 'We'd never know who we were shooting with when and where – there was a lot of trust on the client side, because after many, many storyboards it ended up being something else when we were on the spot. It's basically composing with what you have at hand. It's sort of like documenting a live event. I think magic came out of that; it doesn't feel like a normal commercial, it feels as if we were documenting this thing happening, which was half true.'

'We had one day that was such a great day,' continues Nourizadeh. 'We had so many challenges – this was our big, scary day where we had eight or nine big people to shoot and it turned out to be our best day. We had Missy, who we'd allowed four hours in make-up for, and she had seven, so we couldn't do the scene we wanted to do with her. So we ended up putting her in the scene with DMC, who's DJing, and that turned out to be one of the best scenes for me, where they do that exchange at the decks.'

'That was the same day we had Redman and Method Man as well. With them, I went into their trailer, and said "this is the idea, we want you to do this," and they both just looked at me and there was silence. So I said, "okay guys, you don't have to do that, I'll figure something else out". And I walked out and was like "get me a leaf blower,

'I don't know if we were really lucky, or if we created something amazing, but people were just right on pretty much all of the time. There was never really a problem with anybody.'

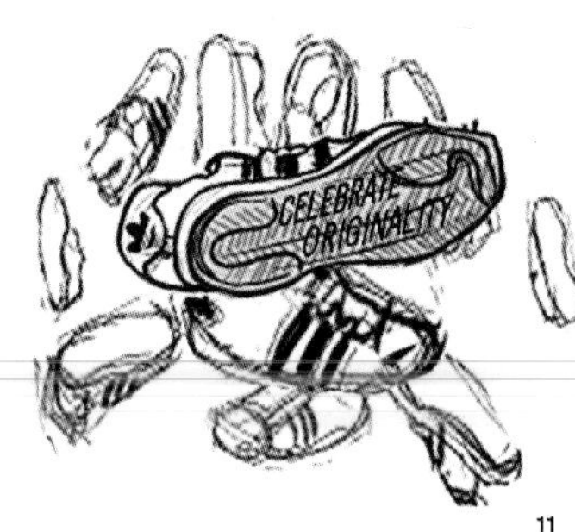

11

12

get me some party stuff, get me some silly string" – I literally on the spot gave them two things, and as soon as Method Man had the leaf blower, he didn't put it down, he was going round blowing in everyone's faces. And it was for real – we actually gave him something he wanted to have fun with. And Redman had the silly string, and he was spraying and totally covering people in it. There are moments in it like that where I had a great time.'

While the shoot was taking place, word got around LA, and Nourizadeh found himself taking calls from other celebrities who wanted to be part of it. 'It was quite nuts,' he remembers. 'I was on the phone with Anthony Kiedis at one point – I was in the middle of the shoot, stressed – and he wanted to be in a scene with Kevin Garnett. I told him, "that sounds wicked, but we've already shot the scene with Kevin Garnett... is there a way we can still get you in it?" He said, "I'll get back to you", and I didn't hear from him again.'

Such a full-on shooting experience did allow the agency and directors a certain flexibility to experiment with ideas that the client may not have approved in a normal, tightly organized set-up. For example, adidas was initially unimpressed with the idea of shooting a shoe sinking in the swimming pool – an image that became the final shot of the finished ad, offering a moment of reflection after the frenzy of the party scenes. The loose structure of the shoot meant that the team got the shot regardless, and then persuaded adidas of its value later on.

'These are the kinds of discussions you have with the client where you say, "let's just try it",' comments Manchester. 'Even if you don't believe it, let's try it anyway. This is the shot that's the poetic ending to the big bang. This is the kind of stuff you have to go above and beyond people's levels to get, because you never know when you'll need it. I would say the same thing with Method Man and Redman when they play with the leaf blower – you can imagine the number of hours of trying to sell in this comedic moment and in the client's mind when you sketch that out or you talk about it, it sounds stupid. Then when you end up doing that and putting it in there, opinions change.'

At the end of the shoot, the team had 27 hours of footage, which had to be edited down to just a 60-second spot (plus some extra films for the web). Nourizadeh and the editors spent three months refining the film to produce the final ad. 'That's where Nima's craftsmanship really came out,' says Manchester. 'You see him shoot and you think, "okay, the guy's good", but when you see the number of hours he spent with the editor to get the crystal, that's where I'm the most impressed.'

One of the major decisions made at this time was the soundtrack. Beggin', a cover of a Four Seasons song by Norwegian hip-hop group Madcon, was chosen, and provides the perfect blend of contemporary cool and retro to the spot. 'It seems to resonate with everyone,' says Nourizadeh. 'The kids loved it, and I played it to my parents and my Dad was asking "what's that song?".'

The ad itself strikes a similar crossover note, with the infectious atmosphere appealing to people across different generations and different tastes. It proves that taking a loose approach to making an ad – unusual in the industry today – can result in gold, and also that working with celebrities can be fun rather than arduous.

'You'd plan until the nth degree, then as soon as it started you were just rolling with punches and everyone's doing what they can,' remembers Tom Ramsden. 'There were always simultaneous things happening. In that respect it was like a real house party – you were swapping stories about your version of events that day.... From my perspective, it was the first time I worked with a lot of names in one place. I was blown away by it – everyone was so friendly, amicable, up for it, patient. I don't know if we were really lucky, or if we created something amazing, but people were just right on pretty much all of the time. There was never really a problem with anybody.'

11-12 Ideas sketched by the ad agency of typical party scenes that might be recreated on the shoot. While the agency and director devised a lot of scenarios in advance, many more were created spontaneously on set.

13

14

15

13-15 The TV commercial was shot over six days in Los Angeles. By the time it was finished, the team had over 27 hours of footage that had to be edited down to just a 60-second spot. Photographs taken during the shoot were also used in a print campaign.

02/

Axe Dark Temptation Chocolate Man

Ponce Buenos Aires

With its Chocolate Man spot for Axe deodorant, Argentinean agency Ponce Buenos Aires gave a familiar ad campaign a surreal twist. When the spot was released, a global ad campaign for Axe (also branded as Lynx) had been running for some time, based on the notion that the anti-perspirant spray made users magnetically attractive to women. The spot for the Dark Temptation scent in 2007 continued this proposition, drawing on a long-established symbol for female desire as its inspiration. 'We started with a question,' explain Mario Crudele, copywriter, and Jose Silva, producer of the ad. 'What's one of the most irresistible things for women? And we realized that chocolate is one of them.'

'We thought that a man who becomes chocolate would be desirable not only for women but for men too,' they continue. 'We thought every man could fantasize about being treated as chocolate.' The spot opens to reveal an average-looking guy in the bathroom, spraying himself with Axe. As he puts down the deodorant, we can see he has been transformed, and is now entirely made of chocolate. We then follow him as he strolls around the town, reducing women to a barely contained frenzy as he passes. They nibble on him, dip strawberries into his chocolate belly button, and bite him lasciviously on the bottom. At one point he makes hot chocolate for a bevy of beautiful women by melting down his own arm. The entire ad is firmly tongue-in-cheek, and the chocolate man maintains a maniacal grin throughout.

'What's one of the most irresistible things for women? We realized that chocolate is one of them.'

01-03 Photographs taken during the shoot for the Axe Dark Temptation commercial. The premise of the ad is that the deodorant turns its wearer into chocolate, making him devastatingly attractive to women.

01-03

04

'It was the kind of commercial where the character is everything. If the chocolate man didn't look right, the whole ad would have failed.'

08

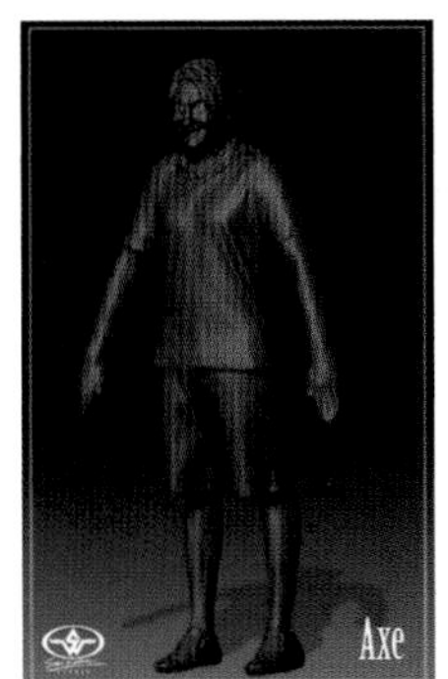

05-07

04-07 The team experimented with a number of different facial expressions for the character. Director Tom Kuntz was inspired by the faces of chocolate Easter bunnies, and this look was incorporated into the final design.

08-10 Photographs taken during the shoot for the Chocolate Man commercial, which took place in Los Angeles.

09

10

11

12

11 The Chocolate Man actor reveals his true features while relaxing on set.

12-15 Photographs from the shoot. Rather than use CGI effects, a suit was created for the Chocolate Man actor to wear. Unfortunately, the suit was very difficult to take on and off and was extremely hot. The only way to fan the actor within was via his mouth, as shown in image 12.

'We found some inconveniences due to the nature of the suit. It was not easy to put on or take off. The weather was very hot and since the only place to fan some cool air into the suit was the mouth, the guy in the suit didn't have the best of times.'

13

The spot's director, Tom Kuntz, devised this expression, along with the overall look of the chocolate man. 'A large part of the early development was simply figuring out how literal or abstract we would go with what this boy turned into,' he explains. 'We eventually arrived at the idea of making him look like chocolate the way that Easter bunnies are made to look like chocolate. There was one bunny I found that had bright white eyes, which I found very funny, so we embraced that in our design.'

14

'It was the kind of commercial where the character is everything,' agree Crudele and Silva. 'If the chocolate man didn't look right, the whole ad would have failed. So we went through many different stages until it was right. We discussed things that might not seem important, but everything adds up in the end – for example, what tonality should the brown paint used to colour the suit be? Facial expression was very important too. We even discussed whether the chocolate man should have teeth.'

Rather than use CGI to create the chocolate man, the creatives and director decided to make a suit that could be worn by an actor. The suit was created by Stan Winston Studios (now Legacy Effects), and was laborious to make. 'The actor had to come in and get a full body scan that perfectly charted the contours of his body so that the suit was carved to fit him like a glove,' says Kuntz. 'From there we did a ton of face experiments, working hard to get the eyes and the smile to be absurd and funny.'

Despite this careful planning, the suit proved to be problematic when it came to the shoot, which took place in Los Angeles. 'We found some inconveniences due to the nature of the suit,' say Crudele and Silva. 'It was not easy to put on or take off.

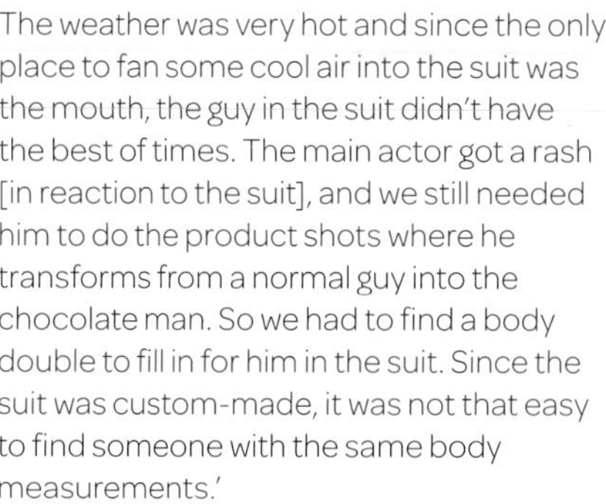

The weather was very hot and since the only place to fan some cool air into the suit was the mouth, the guy in the suit didn't have the best of times. The main actor got a rash [in reaction to the suit], and we still needed him to do the product shots where he transforms from a normal guy into the chocolate man. So we had to find a body double to fill in for him in the suit. Since the suit was custom-made, it was not that easy to find someone with the same body measurements.'

Regardless of these problems, the shoot went relatively smoothly, and the ad required little post-production, despite many viewers believing that the chocolate man in the final ad was entirely created in post. 'Post was mainly used to clean up the suit,' explain Crudele and Silva. 'Seams and a few joints in the suit were erased in post, and post was also used to enhance the melted arm and add melted chocolate drops in the hot chocolate scene.'

Chocolate and humour are a deadly combination in advertising, so unsurprisingly the spot proved an immediate success on release. Its target audience also snapped up the Dark Temptation scent, leading it to become the brand's most popular variety worldwide.

15

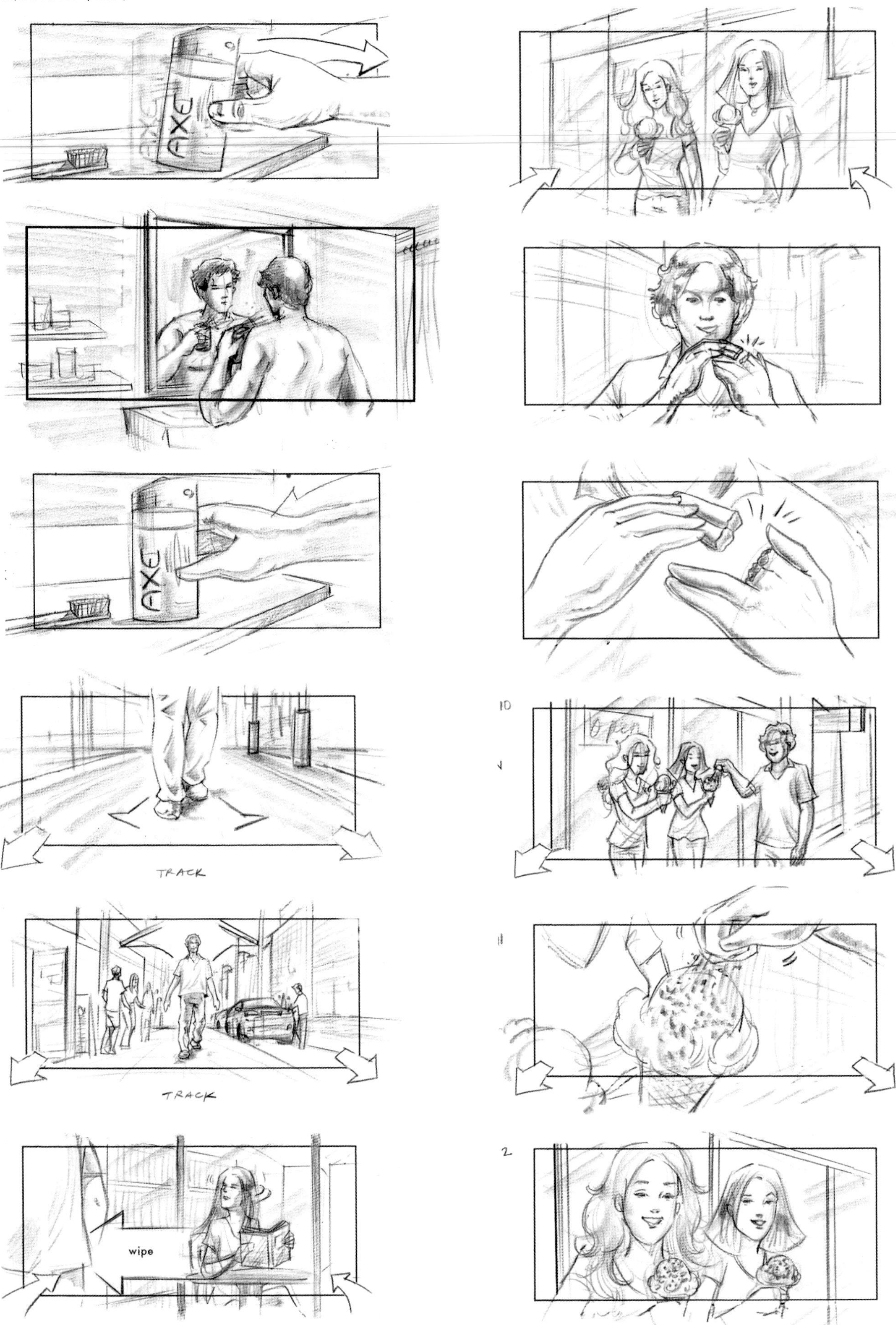
AXE
AXE
TRACK
TRACK
wipe
10
Open
11
2

16

16-17 Storyboards were used to plan each shot in the commercial. A selection of the sketches are shown here alongside stills from the finished ad.

17

03/

Budweiser Wassup

DDB Chicago

'Wasssssuuuuupppppp' is a word that defines an era. To a certain demographic, the sound of it immediately provokes a smile. The expression came to prominence in True, a series of U.S. TV ads for Budweiser. The ads star a group of friends hanging out and chatting on phones, all of whom greet each other with the word 'Wassup'. It's a simple premise that produced a set of films that are charming, warm and funny. The first spot aired on Christmas Eve in 1999, but the ad truly took off when it was shown during the Superbowl (an event that is watched keenly for its ads as well as the football, with brands seeing the game's massive audience as an excellent opportunity to launch major new campaigns) in January 2000.

The concept had been in gestation long before then, however, as Wassup's director, Charles Stone III, first conceived it as a short film back in the mid-1990s. Stone had carved out a career directing music videos, but was keen to move into feature films; he began writing short film ideas to help make this happen. All in the Family, which became the first Budweiser ad, was Stone's first narrative film with dialogue. Written in 1995, it was shot towards the end of 1997, but wasn't finished until 1998, when he sent it to various short film festivals. The film immediately caused a stir, and off the back of its success Stone was signed up to direct his first feature, Paid In Full. It was at this point that Budweiser became interested.

'While I was in production for Paid In Full, in the fall of 1999, I had a call from my commercials rep, who said that DDB Chicago had seen my short and wanted to turn it into a commercial campaign,' says Stone. 'At first I was really reluctant, because I figured they'd dilute it, and would want to change the cast. Then my lawyer said, "If you don't do it, then they're probably going to try and do it anyway, and make something worse than what you've created." So I agreed to come on board with the stipulation that I direct all the spots, and I consult on the scripts. Budweiser paid me a flat fee for owning the idea for five years.'

'We shot five spots in the fall of 1999,' Stone continues. 'It was a really fast turnaround. We did a 60-second version, three 30-second ones and one 15-second spot. The 60-second spot was a replica of the short film; the only thing that was different is when the guys in the Budweiser spot say, "Yo, what's up, D?", and he replies

'At first I was really reluctant, because I figured they'd dilute it, and want to change the cast. Then my lawyer said, "If you don't do it, then they're probably going to try and do it anyway, and make something worse than what you've created."'

01 **All in the Family**
Love
In The House

Characters:

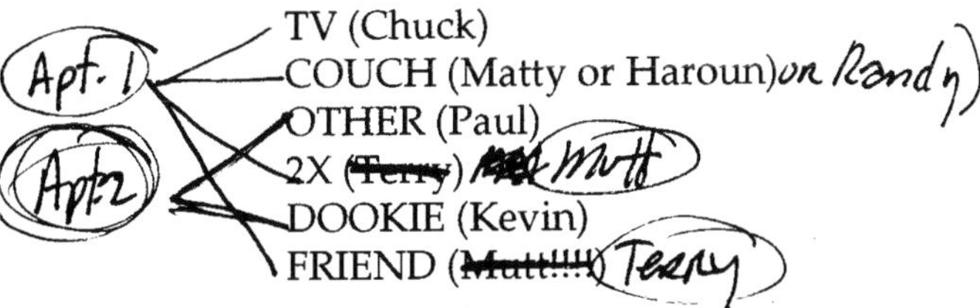
TV (Chuck)
COUCH (Matty or Haroun) or Randy
OTHER (Paul)
2X (~~Terry~~) Matt
DOOKIE (Kevin)
FRIEND (~~Matt!!!!~~) Terry

02-03

Two guys sit on the couch watching television. One of the guys looks like he's comatose. The phone rings. The other guy picks up the phone.

TV (CHUCK)
"Hullo?"

In another apartment a young man lies on a couch watching television with the phone to his ear.

OTHER (PAUL)
"Yo-whassup?"

TV
"Wassup Yo. Whatchoo doin."

OTHER
"Nutin, just chillin."

TV
"Word?"

OTHER
"Word. Wassup widtchoo?"

TV
"Nutin....Chillin."

OTHER
"True."

01 Page from the script for All in the Family, the short film by director Charles Stone III which inspired the Budweiser Wassup ad. The script features notes by Stone.

02-03 Stills from All in the Family. The same actors went on to appear in the Budweiser ads, including the director, Charles Stone III, shown top.

andrea fontaine : script notes
tel/fax: 914.699.5863

C & C Films/Storm Films : charles stone
Budweiser
"Whats Up Bud"
#91201

04

101
RAY ON SOFA picks up phone.
Ray: HULLO?
(caller: yo, wasup... what'chdoin?)
ray: NUTIN B. JUST WATCHIN' AGAME. HAVINABUD. WASSUPWITCHOO?
(caller: nutin... watchinagam. Havinabud)
ray: TRUE.... TRUE...
fred enters bg, hands in air
fred: WHATSSSSAAAHHHHHPPP!!!!
Ray: WHATSSSAAAAHHHHHH!!!

05

Camera; roll 1. 18mm. 24fps. T2.8.1/3. Approx 30"
Sound: roll 1

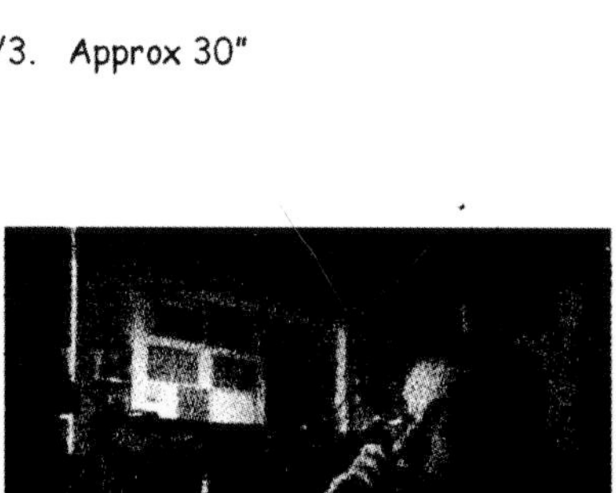

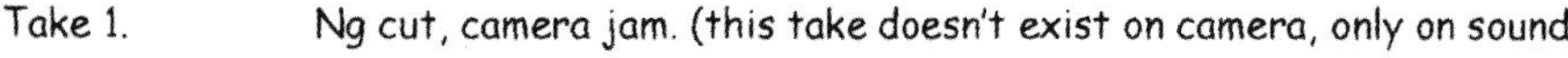

Take 1. Ng cut, camera jam. (this take doesn't exist on camera, only on sound)
Take 2. 20'" to end.
Take 3. Again
Take 4. 1st: ng incomplete.
2nd: 21.5. again. Fred too loud?
Take 5. Again
Take 6. Ng cut. Fred late
Take 7. Okay, again
Take 8. Oka
Take 9. (already on phone) 1st: no fred
2nd: from notin'b..... (bangs on sound)
Take 10. (no "b")
Take 11. (no "b")
Take 12. (no "b") fred seems to interrupt him?

06

'Even though I owned the idea, there were still those wonderfully, sometimes ridiculously, absurd little pointers and suggestions and concerns that the client will have.'

"nothing, just watching a game, having a Bud". In the original, he said "nothing, just chilling".'

As Stone had feared, initially the agency wanted to explore using a different cast for the ad version of the film. The original, all-black, cast consisted of a group of friends of Stone's, as well as the director himself. 'The casting process in the beginning was very funny,' he remembers. 'We did three days of looking at everybody and anybody under the sun. Obviously, the quiet mandate came down that we should open it up culturally and put some white folks in there – usually it's the other way around.... But we did, we looked at a lot of folks; we probably saw over 300 guys. On the last day it was suggested that the original cast come in, so we could see what the difference was. So they came in, and I sat in with them, just because I was there. We did it, and immediately the agency responded, "We should just stick with the original cast, the chemistry is obviously there, and anybody else feels like they're forcing it." And I thought, "yeah, no shit".'

Despite being reunited with the original cast, the experience of shooting the ad proved to be slightly different to that of the short. 'When you're shooting with your buddies, when it's just your film and you don't have clients and everyone around, it's easier,' says Stone. 'You can breathe creatively. Even in this situation, regardless of me owning the idea, there were still those wonderfully, sometimes ridiculously, absurd little pointers and suggestions and concerns that the client will have. A good one is that in the original film I'm lying down on the bed watching television, and the only light that's illuminating my face is the TV light. One of their concerns was that the room should be bright, because the idea of you in a dark room watching television connotes that you have a drinking problem and you're depressed. Then it was, "You shouldn't really be lying down, because that could suggest you're drunk; you should be sitting upright." These were some of the concerns that made the process a little more stiff. But for the most part it worked out fine.'

Once the ads broke, the cast, including Stone, became famous. This led to some bizarre occurrences for the director, including having Dustin Hoffman call him up to congratulate him on the ad, and making appearances on the Oprah Winfrey Show, Jay Leno's show, and the Today Show. 'We hit all the major Americana benchmarks of pop art,' says Stone. Not all the attention was quite so welcome, though. 'I had to avoid going to sports bars and events because people would scream that thing at me. Literally, people would drive by in a car and scream it. It's not like women were screaming because I'm a sexy man, or

04 Script for one of the Budweiser ads, titled What's Up Bud, showing notes for the director. The script features photocopied stills from the ad.

05-06 Stills from All in the Family, Charles Stone III's short film that inspired the Budweiser campaign.

07

08

SHORT

Charles sits on a couch in an apartment where there is nothing left except for a small-ass TV (whose form is just peaking into the frame) and a few boxes. It looks like someone's moving out.

Charles has a deadening expression of depression on his face as he watches TV (Senator McCain explain that "the fundamentals of the economy are sound.") and nurses a beverage.

The composition looks familiar like maybe this is that "Whassup" guy.

His cell phone rings. With lack luster enthusiasm, he searches for the cheap gadget and answers it.

Me: *"Hullo..."*

Paul dressed in full-on "operation Iraqi freedom" army fatigues, is calling from a pay phone in the middle of a firefight in Baghdad. The shooting is sporatic and loud. He cups one ear (despite having a helmet on) as he yells into the phone.

Paul: *"YO WASSUP, B?!"*

still out of a job what's up with you?

10 **Charles**: (a sad, unfazed pause) *"...Nutin, just watchin the country fall apart, havin a... (looks down at his beverage) ...a water. What's up with you?"*

Paul: *"Still in Iraq, watchin my ass!"*

Charles: *"True, true..."*

Fred walks delicately into the background as if he's got eggs balancing on top of his head. His neck is wrapped in a cheap white foam brace. He struggles to pick up one of the many moving boxes. He suddenly bumps into the counter.

Fred: *"Aaaaaaahhhkkk!!"*

Paul: *"WHO'S THAT?!"*

Charles: *"Hold on.* (turns to Fred.) *Yo, pick up the phone!"*

prescription drugs? painkillers?

Fred: *"Fuck the phone, I need pain killers! You got money for pain killers!"*

Fred picks up the phone anyway. "Hullo?"

Paul: Wassaahh!

~~Fred: Who... aaahh!~~ "

09

'Because these guys are as Americana as apple pie or baseball, it's funny to be able to use them to make a political statement on change. It's personally gratifying to me on that level.'

people were cheering me on because I won the World Series, it's people yelling "Wassup!" at me. It was a very bizarre form of adulation.'

Riding on the success of the campaign, Budweiser and DDB Chicago continued to produce more spots in the series, with Stone's approval and involvement. However, the concept eventually began to be drained dry. The major turning point for Stone was when the agency proposed a set of scripts featuring aliens and talking animals saying 'Wassup'. 'At that point I had a conference call with the agency and Budweiser and said, "I think what we're doing here is making it into something that it's not",' Stone says. 'I said, if you want to do that, do that with Bud Lite, but this whole True campaign has got its own charm.' The agency went ahead regardless without Stone's involvement, and then the campaign eventually petered out.

For most ads, this would be the end of the story. Yet the short film that Stone had first created in 1995 ended up having a third lease of life in 2008. While people had suggested that the director resurrect the idea in some form over the years, he was reluctant until Barack Obama began his presidency run. 'I knew I wanted to do something,' Stone says. 'I wanted to make a film, but I also knew that whatever I was going to do couldn't get lost in the ether of the internet – it had to be something identifiable. That's when I knew I should just bring back the Wassup guys and use that.'

Stone brainstormed with a group of friends to define what the new film's storyline should be. The final film closely echoes the original short and the True campaign, but reflects life in America at the end of George W. Bush's presidency. The actors all came back to star in it once more, but this time, rather than being a group of carefree friends, they are used as props to reflect some of the crises of the era: one character calls in from Iraq, where he is stationed as a soldier; another is shown in the midst of a hurricane, reminiscent of Katrina; a third is shown watching an ever-tumbling stock market on a laptop. The camaraderie and humour remain, but the 'Wassup' is more a cry for help than of greeting. The spot ends with B, Stone's character, watching Obama appear on the television, and delivers the altered endline: 'Change. That's what's up'. Due to Stone's initial contract with Budweiser, the rights to the story and characters had reverted to him, allowing him to make the new film, though he was careful to include an end panel to state that Anheuser-Busch, who own the Budweiser brand, had no involvement in it.

The Obama Change film was a huge success online, and completed a circle in the life of the original short film for Stone. 'It maintained the truth of the spot,' says Stone. 'People could say that I sold out because I did this whole thing to promote beer, and that's very true. But when the Obama thing happened, that's what compelled me to resurrect it. I felt 100 per cent compelled to make a short with these guys for this cause. And the thing that was really magical about it was that it was literally eight years later – meaning the Bush period of the presidency. It was "okay, where are these guys now?". It made total sense, and because these guys are as Americana as apple pie or baseball, it's funny to be able to use them to make a political statement on change. It's personally gratifying to me on that level.'

07-09 Stills from the Obama Change film, directed by Charles Stone III. The film showed the characters from the Budweiser Wassup ads eight years later, and in a far bleaker situation. Stone retained the rights to the characters in the ads, so was able to use them in the political film without facing opposition from Budweiser.

10 Page from the script for the Obama Change film, featuring notes by Stone.

04/

Burger King
Subservient Chicken

Crispin Porter + Bogusky

Burger King's Subservient Chicken website was launched in 2004, and immediately caused an internet storm, receiving millions of hits in a matter of days. Its impact on the advertising industry as a whole was equally seismic – prior to Subservient Chicken, agencies and brands had been tiptoeing around using the internet, uncertain of how it could be useful to them, and viewing it more as a threat than an opportunity. Subservient Chicken showed that brands could use the web to be playful, to be risqué, and, most of all, to interact with their audiences.

Initially, the campaign had been all about TV. Burger King had wanted to bring back the tagline 'have it your way' in its marketing, so when working on a brief for the TenderCrisp chicken sandwich, U.S. ad agency Crispin Porter + Bogusky came up with the concept of a giant chicken-man being instructed to perform various tasks at the whim of its owners. A set of television ads were created, all with a cheeky tone reminiscent of the website, although these have now been largely forgotten. 'We actually shot the spots and they ran,' says Jeff Benjamin, partner/chief creative officer at CP+B, 'but now nobody really remembers them, they just remember the website. I think this is a great example of how you can have a great idea, but you also have to find the right medium for that idea.'

The website was a last-minute add-on to the campaign, but gave the opportunity of taking the TV idea to a much higher level, and of inviting the audience to join in. The concept was simple – place the giant BK chicken from the ads in a room with a webcam, and allow visitors to the site to type in a command, which the chicken would then act out. The chicken would appear to be reacting live to the commands, but in fact the site was pre-programmed to respond to hundreds of instructions. 'Originally it was going to be more of a PR thing,' says Benjamin, 'where for one day people could tell the chicken what to do. But we had recently stumbled on some technology for a campaign for another client, where we did a banner where you could just put in a sentence and it would pick up keywords and then trigger an animation. So with that fresh in mind, and looking at the TV campaign, it brought about the idea for the website.

'We wrote up the idea on a Word doc,' Benjamin continues, 'and I remember going over to the client's house and pitching it to her, and they bought it. It was one of those ideas where we thought, "Oh my God, we sold it!" We were a little scared, because

'It was a cool idea, and we took it way too far, and that's why it worked.'

01 The Subservient Chicken warms up in the apartment where the website footage was shot.

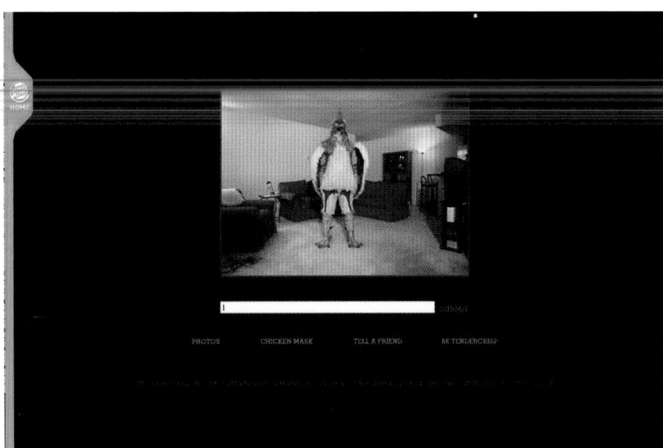
PHOTOS
CHICKEN MASK
TELL A FRIEND
BK TENDERCRISP

02-07

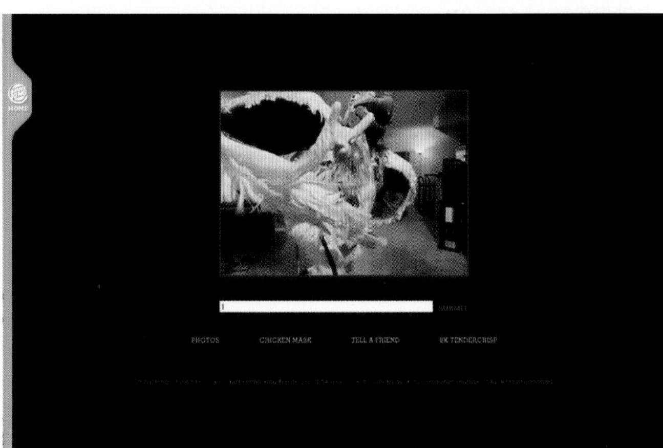
PHOTOS
CHICKEN MASK
TELL A FRIEND
BK TENDERCRISP

PHOTOS
CHICKEN MASK
TELL A FRIEND
BK TENDERCRISP

Get chicken just the way you like it. Type in your command here.
PHOTOS
CHICKEN MASK
TELL A FRIEND
BK TENDERCRISP

PHOTOS
CHICKEN MASK
TELL A FRIEND
BK TENDERCRISP

08

when we'd tried something similar with the technology, it was on a much smaller scale. We were freaked out, and there were days when we wanted to go back to just doing it for one day... but every time we thought, "no, we've got to do this!" At that point we connected with the Barbarian Group; they started helping us with the technology and how to do it, and that gave us more confidence in the idea.'

Rather than feature just a few simple commands, the creative team wanted it to be rigorous, to make it impossible for users to crack. So they turned to the whole agency for help. 'We made a fake website, just for the agency internally,' says Benjamin. 'I Photoshopped a picture of one of the creative directors and put it on a guy in the chicken suit, and there was a form field at the bottom where we said, "if this website were real, and you could ask the chicken to do anything, what would you ask it?" We had 200 people at that point and we collected all the actions people were asking the chicken to do. We got thousands and thousands. Then we went through them and from those thousands we gleaned a couple of hundred unique actions, because people would ask the same things over and over again. So we started with our list of those couple of hundred and then added a day to the TV shoot. We set up in one of the camera guys' apartments and just shot the chicken for the whole day. At the end of the day we had about 500 actions.'

'It was a cool idea, and we took it way too far, and that's why it worked,' says Benjamin Palmer, co-founder and CEO at the Barbarian Group. 'We could have just shot a few videos, but we shot hundreds and hundreds of clips. We did everything in a day on the shoot, and the code to do the artificial intelligence stuff was maybe a couple of days' programming. There's not really a lot of technology in there, but we did spend a month and a half writing 25,000 different keywords into the database, in three different languages, with all sorts of slang, and then beta-tested it. No matter who was using it, it was magic; you would just say, "how did it know that?" You played with it saying, "I'm going to stump this thing," and then you totally couldn't.'

The range of commands that the chicken responds to is phenomenal, from simple suggestions such as 'swim' or 'sit' to more obscure instructions including 'riverdance', 'walk like an Egyptian', or 'do the YMCA'. The look of the website is deliberately lo-fi, almost dingy, but despite its seedy surroundings, the chicken is surprisingly moral, responding with a scolding finger to the camera if the

'It just exploded instantly. It travelled like a piece of news, and the news was that a big brand that we've never heard a peep from before had made this really weird thing.'

09

02-07 Stills from the Burger King Subservient Chicken website, showing the chicken performing various different commands submitted by visitors online.

08 Promotional materials for the Subservient Chicken campaign.

09 A cut-out-and-keep Subservient Chicken mask, used to help promote the TV campaign and the website.

10

11

'It was a pain in the ass because everybody in every meeting after that would say, "give me a chicken". We got calls for three years straight about that. But at the same time it helped everyone who wanted to do something new.'

instructions become too explicit. The chicken also knows which brand it is marketing – if a user suggests that it eats a McDonald's, it places a finger down its throat. Unsurprisingly, a lot of fun was had on the shoot: 'Another funny thing is that originally the website was going to have sound, but we were laughing so loud in the background, we had to take it out,' says Jeff Benjamin. 'But it's probably better without sound.'

The release of the site was fairly loose. 'We just posted it on some of our blogs...,' says Benjamin Palmer. 'It was early days, so Boing Boing picked it up, people picked it up organically from us. We sent out some links and we had 100,000 visitors in a day, which was completely insane. Then it just exploded instantly. It travelled like a piece of news, and the news was that a big brand that we've never heard a peep from before had made this really weird thing.'

Subservient Chicken is very much of its time, and was successful in part because no one had done anything like it for a brand before. It was one of the first online ad campaigns to go truly viral, and it demonstrated that, if the idea is appealing enough, people will interact with brands online and tell all their friends about them too. 'It legitimized our approach,' says Palmer. 'We had done other stuff, and tried to pitch things that were pushing clients a lot further than they felt comfortable going, and we hadn't had a huge success yet, so that legitimized that approach. The chicken was pure branding; it didn't really tell you anything about the product. It was the internet version of a big fancy TV branding ad, and nobody had ever done that. It was a pain in the ass because everybody in every meeting after that would say, "give me a chicken". We got calls for three years straight about that. But at the same time it helped everyone who wanted to do something new.'

12

'Another funny thing is that originally the website was going to have sound, but we were laughing so loud in the background, we had to take it out.'

10-12 Photographs of the Subservient Chicken taken during the shoot for the Burger King television campaign and website. The campaign became famous as a website, though it originally began as an idea for TV, and a series of commercials were made featuring characters ordering the chicken to perform certain tasks. These ads have been largely forgotten now though, while the website continues to be popular years after it was first released.

05/

Cadbury's Dairy Milk Eyebrows

Fallon

The Cadbury's Eyebrows commercial in 2009 was the third in a series for the chocolate brand that saw its advertising take the guise of entertainment, rather than straightforward marketing. Titled A Glass and a Half Productions (which alludes to the quantity of milk in a Cadbury's Dairy Milk bar), the series began, infamously, with a drumming gorilla, a creature that caused delight and bafflement in equal measure. Shown performing a euphoric accompaniment to the Phil Collins track In The Air Tonight, the gorilla charmed viewers but divided commentators. Some pronounced it the future of advertising; others wondered just where the link to chocolate was.

While primarily a television spot, the ad benefited from the internet, with millions of viewers watching, sharing and discussing it online, before creating their own versions to put on YouTube. However divisive the gorilla may have been, as the numbers watching it steadily increased it was clear that Fallon in London, the agency behind the spot, were onto something.

After all the hype that had surrounded Gorilla, the second ad in the series, Trucks, was something of a disappointment. Featuring a race between mini airport trucks, the idea was cute but the finished ad lacked the weirdness and surprise of Gorilla, and proved less compelling to viewers. So when it came to creating a third ad, the agency knew they needed something special.

'Trucks had been met with mixed reviews,' agrees Richard Flintham, executive creative director at Fallon at the time, 'but we didn't think about that too much. It's just about trying to find another one. There were hundreds and hundreds and hundreds of ideas. Everyone was working on it. We were quite straight with Cadbury's when we started the whole process. It's about joy, glass-and-a-half full, let's judge it as if we are kids. Let's try not to have too many meetings or words beyond three syllables. It was waiting for one of those ideas that would do that to us, waiting for some little giggle, or some little naughtiness to come out of a script.'

In the end though, it wasn't a script that prompted the Eyebrows spot, but a photograph. 'It was really late at night,'

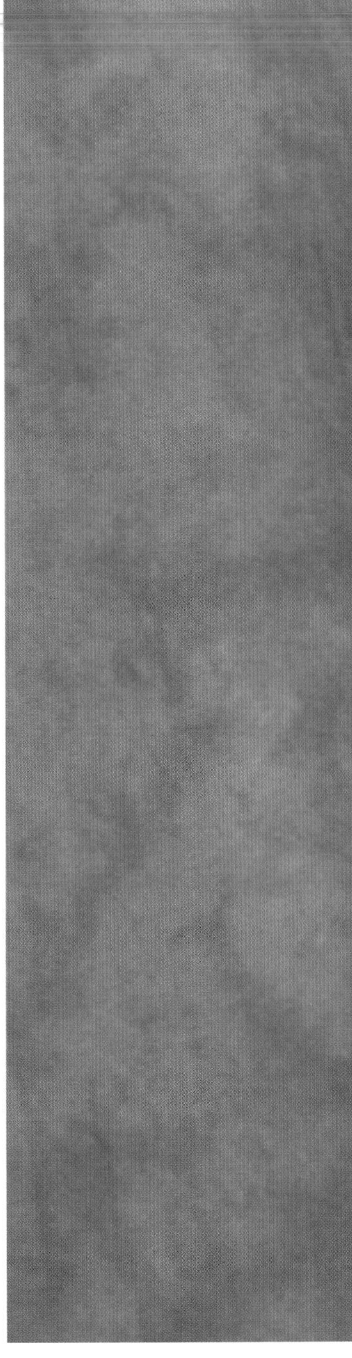

01

01 The Cadbury's Eyebrows commercial starred two children with an unusual gift for eyebrow dancing, which they revealed while waiting to have their school photo taken.

02

'Joy comes from within and it had to feel like that, it couldn't feel like a surface layer. It had to feel like the muscles behind the eyebrows were doing it.'

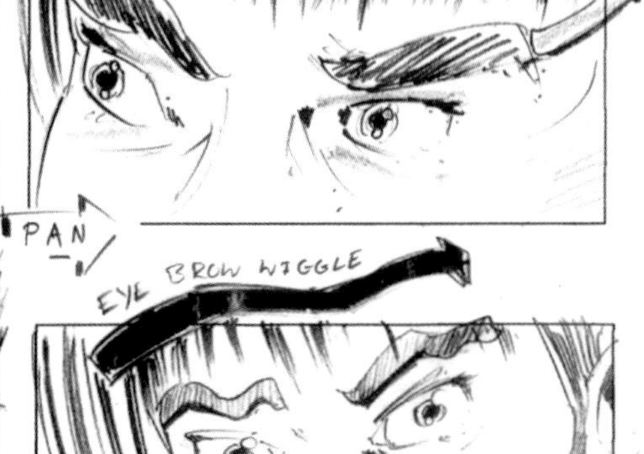

remembers Flintham, 'and we'd gone through all of the stuff, and I think it was down to four people. We were just trying to work it out and Nils-Petter [Lovgren, the copywriter on the spot] showed me a portrait of a young girl and boy in a school picture, and talked about whether their eyebrows could dance.' The idea wasn't an immediate hit with the team, however. 'Even then we thought, "okay, let's see if that's good",' says Flintham, 'rather than, "that's it!"'

The worry was whether the idea was funny enough to sustain the entire length of a commercial. At this stage, Lovgren made the excellent suggestion of using the retro song 'Don't Stop The Rock' by Freestyle as a soundtrack to the piece, but even that didn't entirely assuage concerns. 'We talked about how to do it, and he quickly followed that up with the track, which I thought was a brilliant, brilliant decision by him,' says Flintham. 'Then we asked "how would you do it? How much would the children be aware of doing it? Are they being naughty? Where's the peak?" We wanted to make sure there was a peak moment. I think if we were to look at Trucks, was there a release moment or a peak? We don't always have to have that, but I think that was probably a bit of baggage, to make sure there's a joyous moment in it.'

The team commissioned Tom Kuntz to direct the ad. Kuntz already had a long-established track record of creating bizarre but hilarious advertising and music videos, and he introduced the idea of using multiple camera angles to sustain the action. In the finished spot, however, a humble balloon provides the elusive peak moment.

The ad opens with the two kids in a photographer's studio, waiting for their portrait to be taken. The photographer is

03

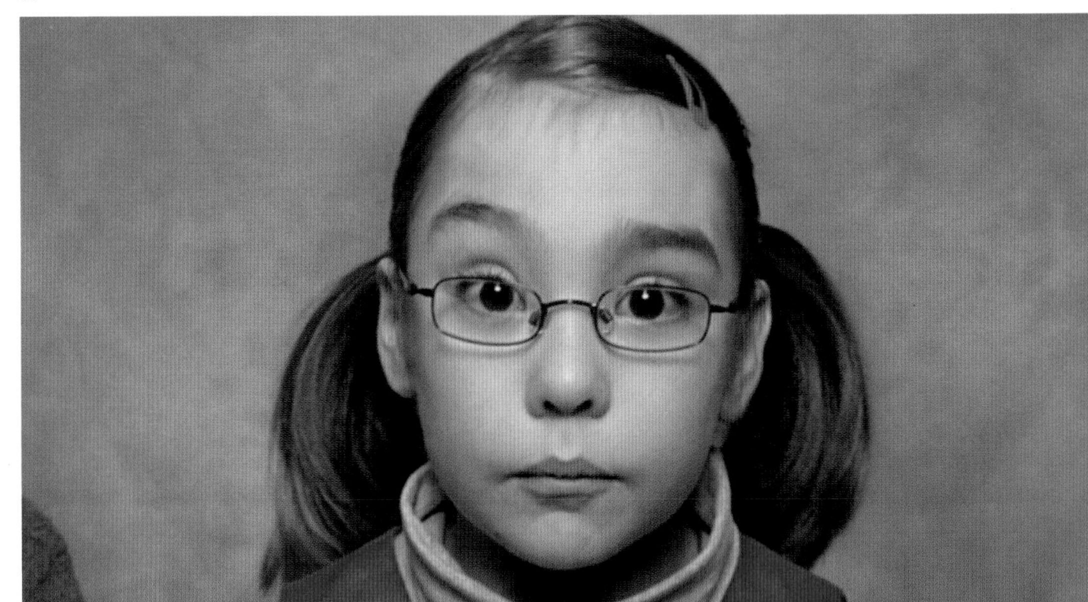

02 Each shot in the ad was carefully planned in advance using detailed storyboards, some of which are shown here alongside stills from the ad.

03 A close up still of the girl from the final advert.

04 An image from the casting for the boy in the ad, which shows the actor who went on to win the part trying out his facial expressions.

05 Another still from the final advert showing the young actors.

06 More storyboard sketches revealing the concept for the shoot.

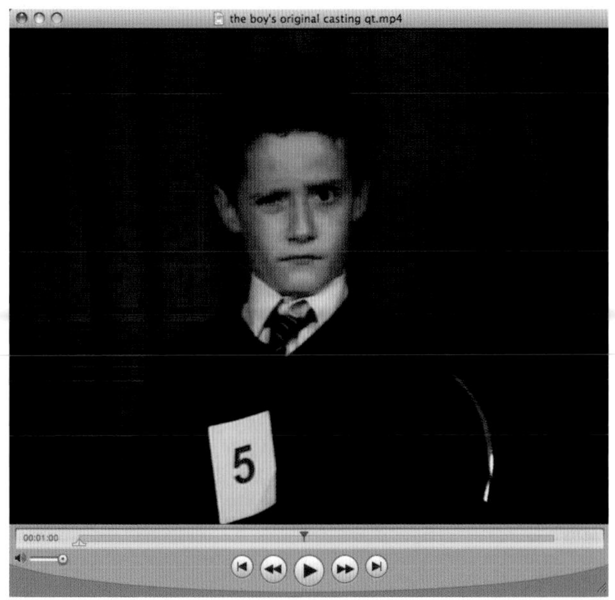

04

05

06

'We were quite straight with Cadbury's when we started the whole process. It's about joy, glass-and-a-half full, let's judge it as if we are kids. Let's try not to have too many meetings or words beyond three syllables.'

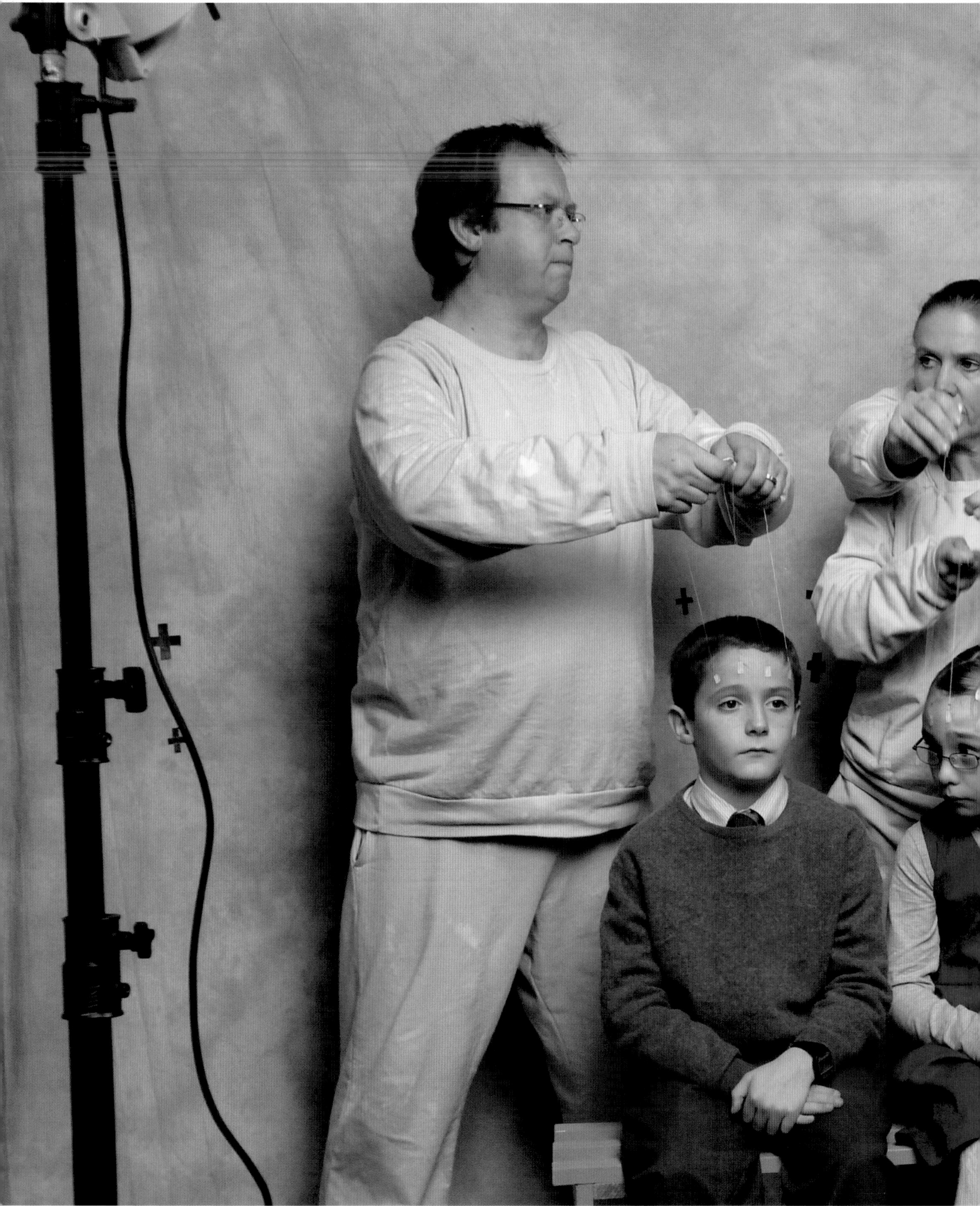

'Tom brilliantly said, "I'm going to puppeteer them." So it's just theatrical tape above and at the side of the eyebrows, and string.'

distracted by a phone call, and they are left alone. With a quick glance at one another, they begin their eyebrow dance, initially to the tinny tune on the boy's digital watch. The main soundtrack then kicks in, and the eyebrow moves become more extreme, as the kids, with earnest, deadpan expressions, perform for the camera. Finally, with their eyebrows almost out of control, the girl breaks out the balloon, using its squeak to accompany the song's bongo solo.

The charm of the ad lies in its simplicity. It uses a scene recognizable to adults and children alike – the tedium of the school portrait – and turns it into something surreal yet familiar. This mixture of the real and the ridiculous also gives the ad its talking point – were the kids really making their eyebrows dance? If not, how did they do it?

From the moment the idea was first mooted, the team at Fallon knew that they couldn't use CGI to create the facial effects. 'A lot of our conversations with Nils were about how, if we had to use post [production], then we didn't want to do it,' says Flintham. 'Because we didn't think it would have the innocence.... That's false. Joy comes from within and it had to feel like that, it couldn't feel like a surface layer. It had to feel like the muscles behind the eyebrows were doing it. If we'd had had to do it that way, then we wouldn't have done it. That was the late-night conversation.'

In the end the solution was surprisingly old-fashioned, with the children's faces animated by puppeteers, rather than technological wizardry. 'What always seems to go wrong when people try and mess around with face stuff in post is you don't get the surrounding ripples or creases correct – a wiggly nose will not be supported by pinched cheeks, for example,' Flintham continues. 'Tom brilliantly said, "I'm going to puppeteer them." So it's just theatrical tape above and at the side of the eyebrows, and string.'

07

With the puppeteers and their tools then removed in post, the ad is left with a look and feel that seems possible to replicate. And viewers certainly tried to. Within days of airing, kids were imitating the eyebrow dance across playgrounds. Fans put films of themselves on YouTube, and pop musician Lily Allen performed her own spoof of it on TV. As with the Cadbury's Gorilla, the Eyebrows spot had entered popular culture.

For Flintham, the massive response the ad received is down to this basis in reality. 'If you give yourself the freedom to go completely artificial,' he says, 'would we have gone an inch too far? It would have been something that's just not possible – therefore no Lily Allen spoof, nobody trying to do it and nearly doing it.... Just because you can, it doesn't mean that you should.'

07 The two children in more demure mode in a publicity photograph for the campaign.

08 Further storyboards for the ad.

09-10 The creative team at the ad agency was keen to avoid using CGI effects to make the children's eyebrows dance. Tom Kuntz, the director, came up with the idea to manipulate their faces using string instead. The puppeteers are shown on set here during the shoot.

11-12 Stills from the finished commercial.

08

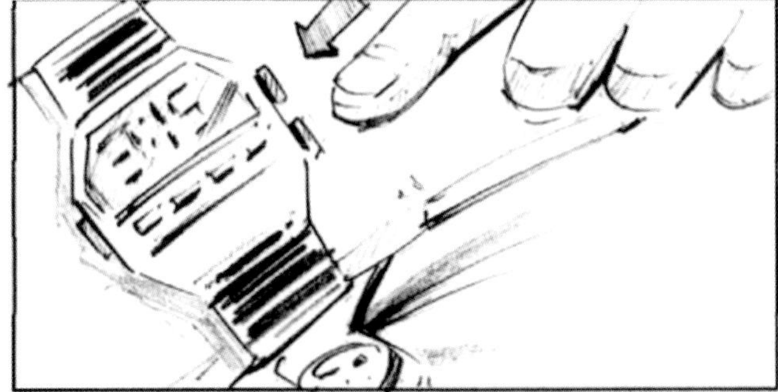

09-10

11-12

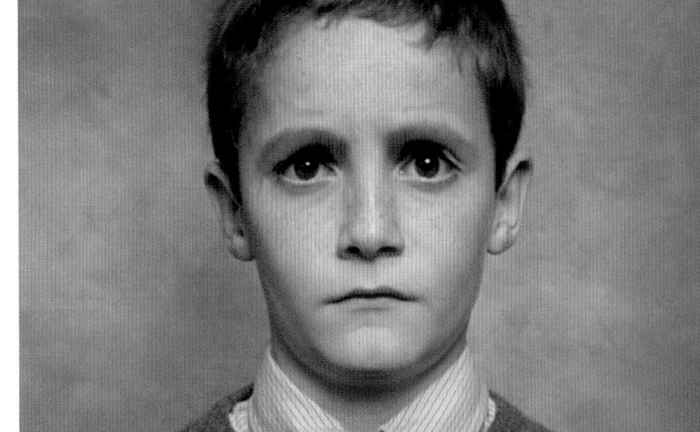

06/

California Milk Processor Board
Get The Glass

Goodby, Silverstein & Partners

When we think of website design, we often presume that everything is created digitally – computer-generated graphics and imagery used in place of the hands-on tools of the analogue world. This is not always true, however, with many websites featuring handcrafted elements at the core of their aesthetic. This was very much the case for the website that Swedish digital creative agency North Kingdom constructed as part of a campaign for the California Milk Processor Board.

01-02 At the centre of the Get The Glass website was an island; this was built by hand by the production team at North Kingdom and then shot for the website. These images show the model of the island during the photo shoot.

01-02

The main campaign in 2007, by Goodby, Silverstein & Partners in San Francisco, was called Get The Glass, and aimed to highlight the health benefits that milk has to offer, which include healthy hair, help with insomnia, and strong teeth. Rather than take a conventional teaching style approach to impart this information, the agency wanted to create something fun. They came up with a family of characters, the Adachi family, who all suffered from ailments that could be cured if they could only get a glass of milk. A series of TV spots was created, which then drove viewers to an interactive board game online.

'In the television ads, it was the Adachis' milk deficiencies that undermined their various attempts to get the glass,' explains GS&P's creative director on the project, Will McGinness. 'In the online board game, we challenged users to aid the Adachis to break into "Fort Fridge" to get the coveted glass of milk by helping them make their way through five regions [each emphasizing one benefit of milk] while being chased by Fort Fridge security.' The first 4,000 players to complete the game (and avoid being incarcerated in 'Milkatraz') won a specially designed glass as a prize.

No matter how well they are designed, it is difficult to get an audience to visit a micro-site for a brand, let alone stay long enough to explore it. Games are one of the few proven solutions to this problem, and can be a clever way of hooking a visitor in long enough to deliver some brand information along the way. To give added charm to their website, and appeal to a family audience, GS&P decided to base their site on the classic board game model.

'We knew we wanted to bring the world of the Adachi family online and help tell the milk story in an engaging way,' continues McGinness. 'Suffice to say, most people aren't terribly interested in learning about milk. We knew we needed to create an experience that held the user's attention long enough to teach them about the health benefits of milk. We primarily wanted to capture a younger demographic, but the hope was that we could do something that could potentially engage the entire family. The classic board game seemed like a perfect fit. It's something that everyone can understand and relate to – everyone is familiar with the basic rules of board games. You roll dice, move your game piece and encounter challenges or questions along the way.'

03-04

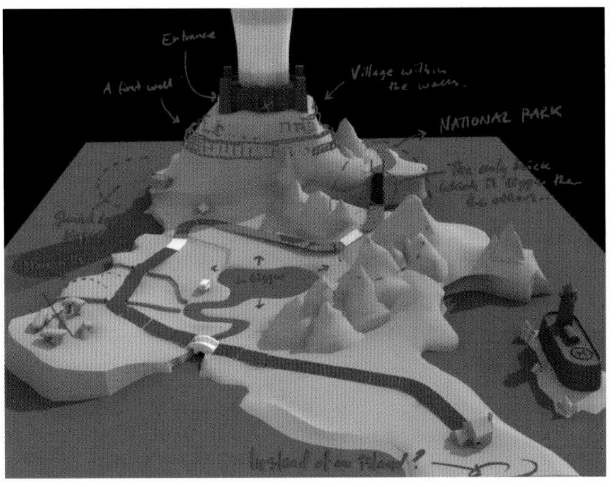

05

'We primarily wanted to capture a younger demographic, but the hope was that we could do something that could potentially engage the entire family. The classic board game seemed like a perfect fit.'

06

03-06 The production team began by planning the design for the island in Photoshop (shown in image 05). They then built the large island model in their studio, drawing on references such as the movie Beetlejuice and the 1970s Swedish TV show Vilse i pannkakan to devise its look.

The creatives reacquainted themselves with other board games in order to flesh out the narrative of their own online game. 'Figuring out the game play was a bit of a challenge,' admits McGinness. 'We basically went out and bought every classic board game we could think of and had a games night. We started mapping out board game conventions and thought about our story and how we'd fold it into the experience. Then we created a few crude prototypes out of foam core and cardboard. We played them repeatedly and made adjustments until the game play seemed to make sense. Granted, we could have spent six months trying to figure this out, but this loose crash course in board game methodology seemed to work pretty well.'

At this stage, North Kingdom became involved. 'Generally, we concept and design our interactive work in-house, and then work with one of our production partners to execute the project,' explains McGinness of the working process. 'Our best vendors will use the work that we do as a springboard and work with us to take the project to a new level. In the case of Get The Glass, we knew we wanted to create an experience that relied heavily on 3D. So we focused our work on that idea – the general game-play mechanics and design direction. Then we worked closely with North Kingdom in executing the experience. So our role in this particular project ended up being a lot more directional, as they brought the experience to new heights with their design and execution. They were instrumental in the success of the project.'

From early on, North Kingdom was keen to create the island at the centre of the game as a physical model, rather than use digital 3D modelling software. They began by using a computer, however, first mapping out the island in Photoshop before designing a rough 3D version on screen. Then they began the laborious process of building a large island in their studio that would be filmed for the site. They used a number of visual references as inspiration for the island's look. 'To find good references is a very important part of the work,' says Roger Stighall, co-founder of North Kingdom. 'We found stuff like the physical worlds of [model train sets] Märklin Trains, movies like Beetlejuice, and Vilse i pannkakan, a 1970s

GET THE
GLASS
got milk?
POINTS
LIFE
TIME

GET THE
GLASS
got milk?
FORTUNE
The basketball coach gives Tad a backpack on wheels to carry his books because Tad doesn't have milk to help his muscles rebuild after practice.
Move ahead one space.
1
CONTINUE

ADACHI HOME
360 DEGREE
EXPLORE
BOARD
GET THE GLASS
PLAY
THE GAME

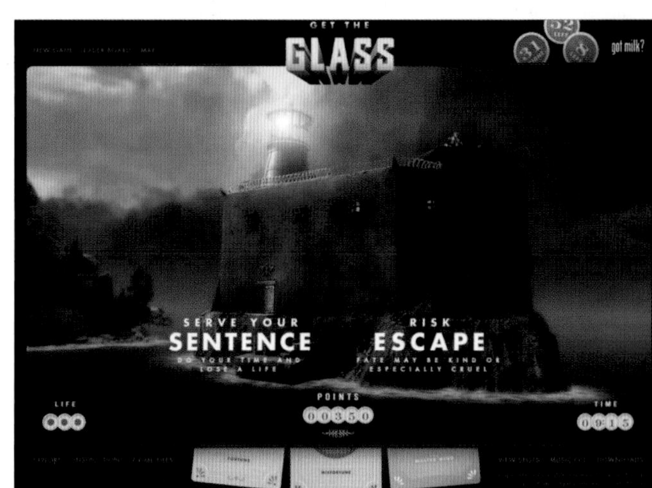
GET THE
GLASS
got milk?
SERVE YOUR
SENTENCE
DO YOUR TIME AND LOSE A LIFE
RISK
ESCAPE
FATE MAY BE KIND OR ESPECIALLY CRUEL
LIFE
POINTS
00350
TIME
0915

GET THE
GLASS
got milk?
START
POINTS
00000
TIME

GET THE
GLASS
got milk?
POINTS
00500
TIME

08

'As an art director, you work with so many different 3D artists, model builders, character designers and graphic designers on a project that you never know in the beginning exactly what it will look like in the end. You have to be able to see the beauty in the different parts and hold on to that.'

Swedish children's TV programme. But the style itself mostly came naturally. As an art director, you work with so many different 3D artists, model builders, character designers and graphic designers on a project that you never know in the beginning exactly what it will look like in the end. You have to be able to see the beauty in the different parts and hold on to that, and get the other visual parts to merge together.'

North Kingdom worked closely and successfully with GS&P on the project, though, despite this close collaboration, last-minute adaptations to the narrative proved stressful. One such change was the decision to alter the look of the major building on the model, a castle. 'The television commercial hadn't been shot when we were building our island, so we just had some references of how the main building would look, which at the time was a big castle,' explains Stighall. 'Three days before the shooting, which we could not move at all, we had a call from our client, saying "the castle is no longer a castle...". Our client had at this point got footage of how the "castle" would look in the TV commercial [which was quite different]. However, the new style turns out to be much better, I think; it gave the whole island a totally new character.'

North Kingdom was able to complete the changes to the model in time, and filmed all the footage of it in just one day. Then all the elements were brought together in the production of the site. In total, from the first briefing from GS&P to the finished website, the project took approximately five months for North Kingdom to complete. By combining old-fashioned qualities such as modelmaking and a classic board game structure with dollops of digital whiz and interactivity, GS&P and North Kingdom created a hugely popular website. The Get The Glass game received more than four million unique visitors, who spent an average of nine minutes each on the site – ample time for the California Milk Processor Board to get their message across.

07-08 Images from the Get The Glass website reveal how the model island was incorporated into the digital campaign. The interactive board game proved a fun way of entertaining viewers while subtly teaching them about the benefits of drinking milk.

07/

Canal+
The March of the Emperor

BETC Euro RSCG

Created for French pay-for-view television channel Canal+ in 2006 by BETC Euro RSCG in Paris, this commercial forms part of a series of ads that aims to emphasize the channel's cinematic credentials. The spot portrays a situation familiar to everyone: the confusion that reigns when a story is lost in translation. The scene opens on two friends in a café, discussing a movie that one has seen on Canal+ the night before. The film is La Marche de l'Empereur/The March of the Emperor (the French title for March of the Penguins), a nature documentary that tells of the annual journey of the emperor penguins of Antarctica. Not knowing the film though, the girl imagines it is a film about Napoleon.

As her friend's description continues, telling tales of hundreds of emperors marching for days, sliding on their bellies and being attacked by seals, she envisions the scenes with multiple versions of the French leader. Her shock and confusion reaches a climax as her friend tells of the penguins' mating behaviour, before the ad's tagline then appears, stating 'Movies are made to be watched. Canal+ The Cinema Channel'.

'The brief was that if you don't have Canal+, you don't have culture, you are nothing,' says Stéphane Xiberras, president and executive creative director at BETC. 'So when you have a discussion with your friends, if you don't have culture, you're dumb. But if you have Canal+, you're so brilliant you can talk about the latest films.' Xiberras knew from the start that for the ad to work, it needed to be centred on a real film, so that the audience watching would recognize what was going on as it unfolded, and thus be in on the joke. Choosing the right film proved problematic – it had to be something that would appeal to a French audience (so therefore not an American film), yet also be relevant internationally, so the ad could have a life outside France on the internet. The March of the Emperor was a French-made documentary that had recently been released in France and been a huge success, so the agency took a bet on it also being popular overseas.

The ad was shot in Iceland by Australian directing collective The Glue Society. 'The script that came in from BETC was more or less as per the finished ad,' says Glue Society director Gary Freedman.

01

01–03 Photographs from the shoot for the March of the Emperor ad, which featured a large number of actors dressed as Napoleon. The crew experienced widely varying weather conditions in Iceland, which hampered filming.

'I like the element of chance when you do things for real – you end up with something different than if you devised it completely.'

02-03

'It was immediately likeable – just a very funny scenario. I did a treatment that was based around the idea of uncertainty. She is uncertain of the film that she imagines and the Napoleons in the film are uncertain of what they are doing. They don't quite know why they're doing the things they do. It's as if they are responding to the changes in the narrative right at that moment – they behave as if on "automatic", as if they have lost their own free will. But they have a perspective on what they are doing – they have doubts. I wanted to render them vulnerable, like pawns in a big game. We know that whatever she imagines from the description has to happen in this film – but the Napoleons are also aware of this! They are resigned to their fate, so at the end of the ad, when the narrative says that "they were all having sex together for hours", they only need to give each other a bashful look and it says it all.'

The weather gods were not on The Glue Society's side during the shoot. 'The first shoot day we travelled up to the glacier in the snow-cat, which is like a tank – you can't see out of it unless you're the driver,' says Freedman. 'We were all excited about the amazing vista of mountains and landscapes we were about to see. And when we got to the top and all jumped out we saw nothing! Just white. White snow and zero visibility. You could not see further than a few feet in any direction. It was in fact dangerous, as if you walked ten feet in any direction you could get lost from the group and just be wandering about in "white". So no shoot. Then we had too much snowfall so we couldn't get up the mountain. Then we had extremely warm weather, so the snow melted in some of our locations. It was a nightmare. But these things have a way of working themselves out.'

The patchy snow was resolved in post-production, alongside other inconsistencies caused by the bad weather conditions. Otherwise, surprisingly little post-production was required on the ad. 'The seal was shot in camera,' says Freedman, 'and it was as rudimentary as tossing fish at the seal for it to catch in its mouth. Then we replaced the fish with a Napoleon who we shot hanging from a wire. I like the element of chance when you do things for real – you end up with something different than if you devised it completely.'

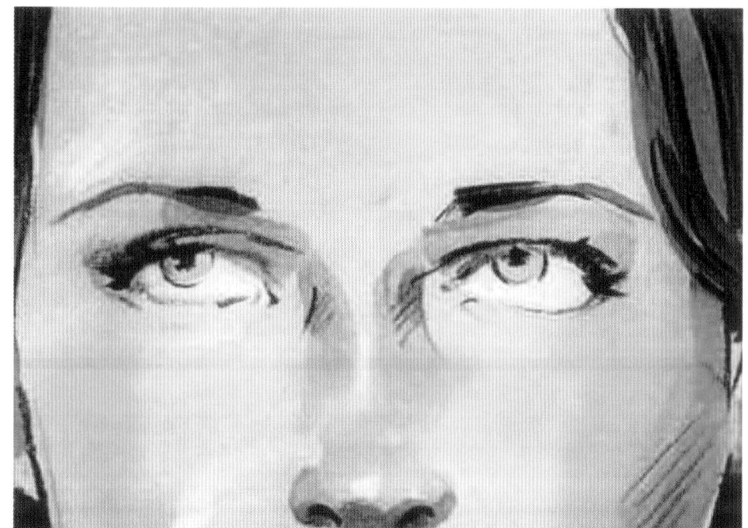

04

04 An early storyboard for the ad, by the advertising agency, BETC Euro RSCG.

'When I love the script, I don't want to go to the shoot. If you go to the shoot, it's impossible to do the edit.'

Unusually, Xiberras didn't attend the shoot, preferring to maintain the distance required to see the film through fresh eyes when it was delivered. 'I decided not to go, because when I love the script, I don't want to go to the shoot,' he says. 'If you go to the shoot, it's impossible to do the edit. It's very difficult to judge and just see the images and the edit. Personally I need space and distance, otherwise you're too close to it.' The tactic paid off, and Xiberras spent considerable time working on the edit of the film, ensuring that the relatively complex story was clearly conveyed in 60 seconds.

The finished ad proved immensely popular with the target French audience, and was also hugely successful around the world, despite suffering its own 'lost in translation' moment, when the film's international title was changed from The March of the Emperor to March of the Penguins, somewhat undermining the ad's central joke. The wit and humour of the commercial rose above such details, however. 'The response to the ad was amazing,' says Freedman. 'You never quite know how things are going to turn out – there is always an unknown. Sometimes things come together and have "magic" and sometimes not. I think this ad just had something about it that clicked with people. It's undoubtedly a very good script, but I think it's one of those ads that stays with people for all sorts of reasons that are hard to pin down.'

05

06-09

'Sometimes things come together and have "magic" and sometimes not. I think this ad just had something about it that clicked with people. It's undoubtedly a very good script, but I think it's one of those ads that stays with people for all sorts of reasons that are hard to pin down.'

05 The film crew at work during the shoot in Iceland, with spectacular natural scenery as their backdrop.

06-09 Stills from the completed ad. The Napoleons, as imagined by the female protagonist in the spot, experience a number of challenges, including being attacked by a giant seal.

08/

Carlton Draught Big Ad

George Patterson Partners

01

The epic television commercial has been a central feature of advertising for decades. Its defining characteristics are a dramatic setting, a huge cast, significant dollops of post-production, and a rather po-faced disposition. All of which makes it ripe for satire. In 2005, Melbourne-based advertising agency George Patterson Partners decided to spoof it. The Big Ad spot, for Carlton Draught beer, was the third ad in the Made From Beer campaign, which parodied traditional advertising notions. The first, Horses, mocked the earnest tone of many beer ads, while Canoe sent up clichéd ideas about masculinity. The third ad took the idea to a new level, however.

'It's a big ad! Expensive ad! This ad better sell some bloooooooody beer!'

'Carlton Draught's theme is "a good honest beer",' explain the creatives on the ad, writer Ant Keogh and art director Grant Rutherford. 'So we were searching around for things we thought were a bit bogus, that we could take the piss out of, and we hit upon the idea of sending up "the epic". It seems brands, especially airline or sports companies, tend to reach a point where they use "big" as their idea. It's almost a given that you make a big ad. Obviously, epic ads like British Airways and Qantas came to mind. Also, Hollywood seems to be throwing a lot of money into big historical films, some better than others. We've seen epic scenes with gladiators and armies and Orcs, but we really felt the beer drinker was unrepresented. We wanted to redress that balance.'

The commercial's soundtrack sets its tone – the creatives reworked Carl Orff's triumphant cantata Carmina Burana by accompanying the familiar music with unexpected lyrics. As the ad gets underway, scores of men are shown striding through an epic landscape dressed in multi-coloured gowns. While they walk, they chant 'It's a big ad, very big ad, it's a big ad we're in', with the words also provided as subtitles. As the camera pulls back to a series of wide shots, we're shown the people forming various shapes en masse, including a face and what appears to be a glass of beer. Meanwhile, the music intensifies: 'It's a big ad! For Carlton Draught! It's just so freak...ing HUGE!' We then reach the ad's climax, where a giant hand is shown lifting the Carlton beer towards the face.

03

02

01-02 The cast perform for the cameras during the shoot for Big Ad, which saw hundreds of actors come together to simulate a giant man drinking a glass of beer, in a send-up of epic television commercials.

03 Still from the finished commercial.

04

The yellow-clad actors playing the beer then dance delightedly into the mouth of the face, while the last lines make the joke clear: 'It's a big ad! Expensive ad! This ad better sell some bloooooooooody beer!'

The clients at Carlton Draught liked the irreverent idea from the start, and grew to love it as the creative team made it more expansive. 'Big Ad started as a specific parody of an epic Australian airline ad, but going back to the client we realized we would need to be broader about it, which led us to something much better,' says Keogh. 'The notion and the words "big ad" were in the original version, but when we locked onto that idea, rather than sending up an airline, it became a larger thought. It really started to work when we sent up the whole thought of "epic" or "big" by repeating the line "it's a big ad" in a focused and relentless way.... When we went back, the client actually said the words "this is the ad I've been waiting for", so it's one of the best presentations I've done. It's actually a difficult script to present because of the musical aspect, but I made a little video that substituted the ridiculous new words against the original Latin version of the song.'

Despite the commercial being a parody, it would only have worked if it was convincing, which meant that the shoot required the same commitments – financially and creatively – as any other epic ad. It was shot in Queenstown in New Zealand by director Paul Middleditch, who had previously made the Canoe ad in the Made From Beer series. Middleditch brought in Andrew Lesnie, who had worked on the 'Lord of the Rings' series as cinematographer, to bring an epic touch to the photography of the ad.

'The client didn't get uptight about anything and that filtered on down the line.... Everyone from the client to the extras seemed to be on the same page.'

'For the idea to work, we obviously needed something spectacular,' say Keogh and Rutherford. 'We had around 500 extras, and had the music playing over huge loudspeakers in the middle of an enormous valley. We shot the sequence in sections, so gradually over a few days the extras got to hear the words of the song and started laughing. We thought that was a good sign. Very soon the extras were in on the act, dancing around like lunatics, just like the main cast. It was a great feeling on set.'

'Despite being a huge shoot, it was very relaxed. It was one of the most enjoyable shoots we'd been on,' they continue. 'The client didn't get uptight about anything and that filtered on down the line. We just let Paul get on with it. I think we hardly asked for any changes. We knew he was on exactly the same page. Everyone from the client to the extras seemed to be on the same page.' In fact, the only hitch that Keogh can recall from the shoot was bad weather on the first day. 'It cost about $100,000,' he says. 'That meant some scary phone calls for the account service guys and the client.'

The post-production on the ad was a three-month job by Animal Logic, who created many of the wide shots in CGI, using original plates shot from a helicopter. Composer Cezary Skubiszewski rescored

'Carmina Burana', and the new version was played by the Melbourne Philharmonic Orchestra and sung by a choir of 200 people. 'It was quite funny seeing them all sing those ludicrous words,' say the creatives. 'At one point early on, we had the lyric "big like Jon Bon Jovi's hair", but thought maybe it was a bit distracting. Still, it would have been fun to hear the choir sing it.'

Rather than immediately put the ad on television, the client and agency decided to try a 'soft' launch, via the internet. This is now standard practice when releasing ads, but back in 2005, when Big Ad came out, it was still fairly experimental. It became a huge viral hit, receiving millions of views within days, and quickly spread outside Australia to the rest of the world. The commercial has now entered the popular culture annals of Australia: 'At the football, the crowd sang the song along with the ad,' says Keogh. 'In Australia it was voted ad of the decade, and in the top 50 Aussie ads of all time by the public.'

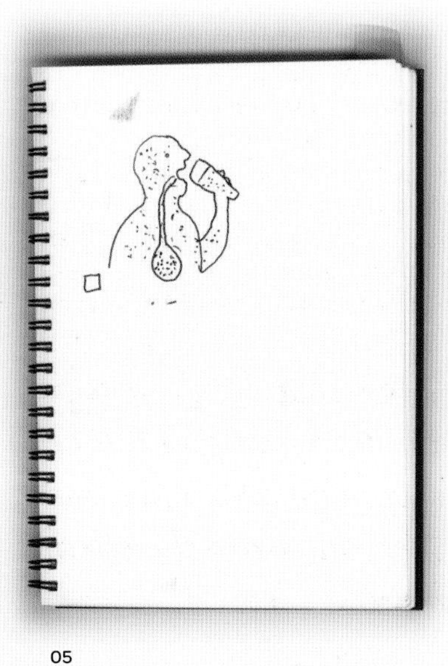

05

'We were searching around for things we thought were a bit bogus, that we could take the piss out of, and we hit upon the idea of sending up "the epic".'

04 Storyboards for the commercial show how each shot in the ad was carefully planned.

05 An early sketch by creative Ant Keogh shows the giant face consuming the beer.

06

07-08

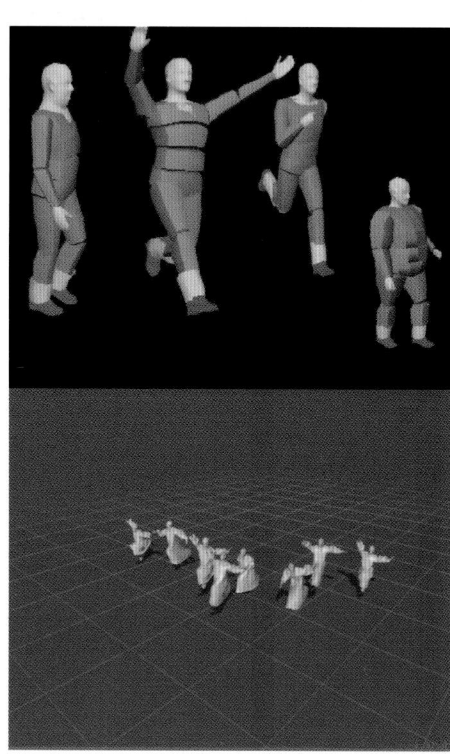

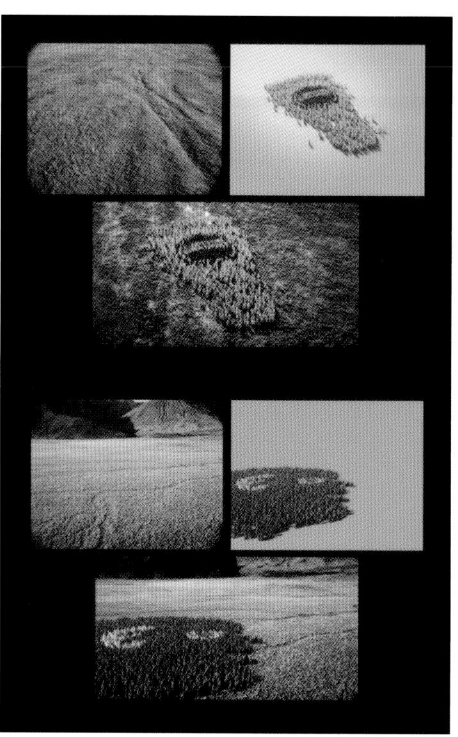

09-10

06 Photograph taken during a post-production shoot for the ad.

07-08 Part of the crowd was created in CGI, with these figures later placed within the ad. The development of the CGI people is shown here.

09-10 These images reveal how the crowds of figures and the landscape were shot separately, and then placed together in post-production.

11 Stills from the final ad show the giant guzzling down the glass of Carlton Draught. The subtitles reveal some of the amusing lyrics written to accompany the soundtrack, which was set to the familiar tune of Carmina Burana by Carl Orff.

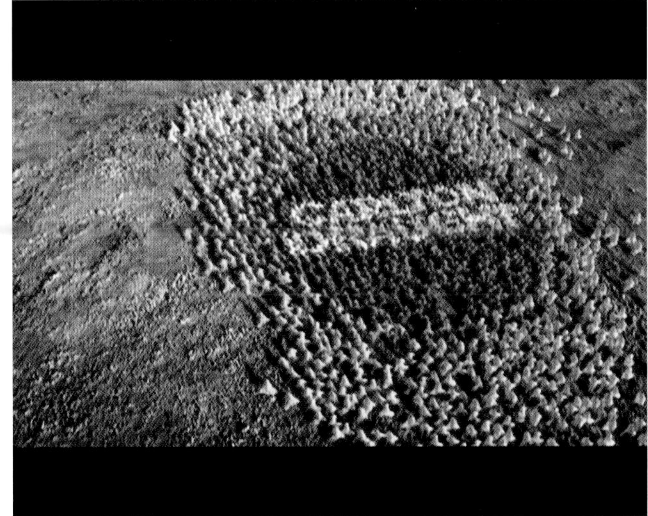

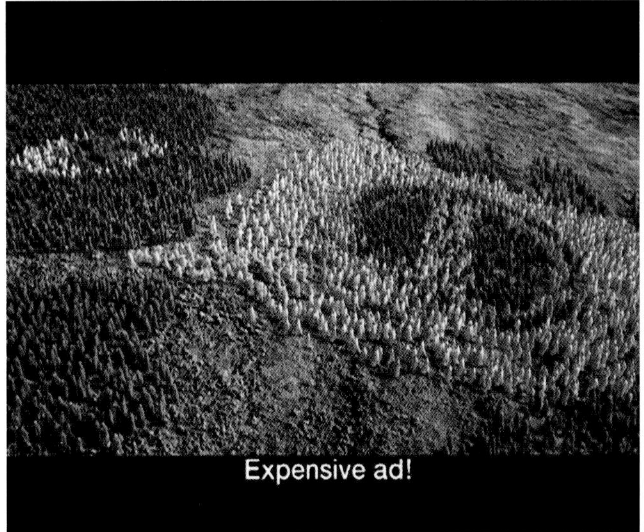

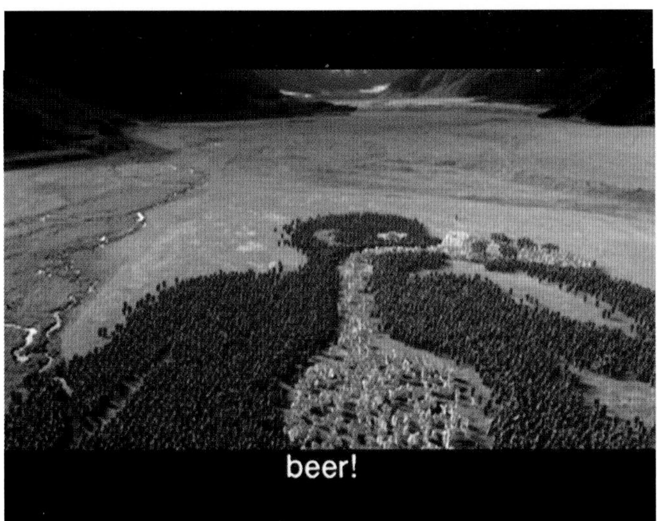

11

'For the idea to work, we obviously needed something spectacular. We had around 500 extras, and had the music playing over huge loudspeakers in the middle of an enormous valley.'

09/

Coca-Cola Happiness Factory

Wieden + Kennedy Amsterdam

Coke's Happiness Factory ad introduces viewers to a marvellous, magical world, all housed within a humble drinks vending machine. The spot begins with a man putting a coin into the slot of the machine, before the action switches to inside, where a lavish animated world awaits. We see various characters producing the bottle of Coke: filling it, sealing it with a cap, chilling it and then sending it out into the world via a triumphant, carnival-esque launch party. Created by Wieden + Kennedy Amsterdam and directed by Psyop in New York, Happiness Factory was Coke's first global brand campaign for over ten years. The brief that the brand gave the agency was simple: 'Happiness in a bottle'.

Wieden + Kennedy began thinking of ways to articulate this, and remembered a previous piece of work by Psyop that sparked the idea for the ad. 'We had been collaborating with a number of animation companies to create short films we called "bottle films",' remember Rick Condos and Hunter Hindman, creative directors on the spot. 'One of those companies was Psyop. They had sent through a treatment for a simple cut-paper animation that represented the inside of a Coke machine. While it was wildly different from the spot we ended up making together, we loved the base concept.... We wanted to create an entire world inside of the machine – to write a new mythology for Coca-Cola that would reawaken the love we all shared for the brand at one time.'

'Coke is one of the few brands that almost everyone in the world has experienced,' they continue. 'So we needed a simple story with archetypal characters that demonstrated the happiness that is delivered with every bottle. We looked at Pixar films, epic films like Lord of the Rings and Star Wars, and the art of Hieronymus Bosch. We wanted to create a world that felt big and cinematic, but still human and emotional. More than anything, we wanted to try and create something unexpected and unique for a brand that had a long history of great commercials.'

The creatives explored other options before settling on using animation. Initially they considered a live-action spot, but felt that an animated world would ultimately appeal to a wider audience. Various

02

01-03 The Coke Happiness Factory commercial took viewers into the animated world within a Coca-Cola vending machine. The spot showed a fresh bottle of the fizzy brown stuff lovingly prepared for its purchaser by a range of unusual but lovable characters.

04-05 Drawings of two of the characters: the Mortar Man (04), who has the task of looking after all the other creatures in the Happiness Factory (and is later catapulted in a stream of fire during the Launch Parade at the end of the spot), and one of the Love Puppies (05), who kiss each and every bottle before it is sent out into the world.

01

04

03

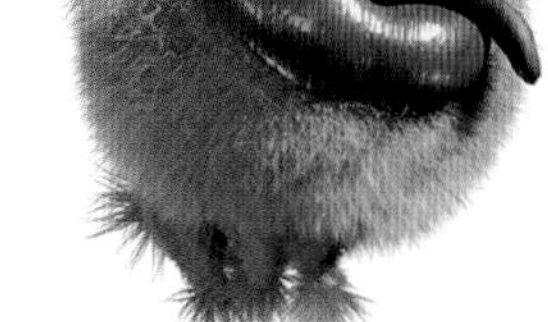

05

06

'We wanted to create an entire world inside of the machine – to write a new mythology for Coca-Cola that would reawaken the love we all shared for the brand at one time.'

07

production partners were looked at for the job, but it was decided that Psyop was 'the obvious choice'. For Psyop, the pitching process was indeed surprisingly straightforward: 'This is probably the spot we are most recognized for and one of the shortest pitches we ever did,' say directors Todd Mueller and Kylie Matulick. 'It was around four days, from getting the brief to flying to Amsterdam for the kick-off meeting! This happened at a time when Coke really wanted to push their brand and were prepared to take the risk, and had a lot of faith in us to come up with something great. The creative process went extremely smoothly.'

Psyop worked closely with Wieden + Kennedy to devise the script. 'We would spend hours coming up with characters,' say Condos and Hindman. 'Breaking down the story. Crumpling up paper and starting all over again. It was unlike any other project we had worked on. Finally, we broke the story down to its guts. Deliver the bottle. Fill the bottle. Love the bottle. Chill the bottle. Celebrate the bottle. From that framework, we built a world. We commissioned artists to create matte paintings for our backgrounds. We sweated the details of every frame.'

Coke has a history of animated characters in its advertising, with its polar bear ads particularly well-loved by audiences. For Happiness Factory, a quirkier set of characters was created, which exist entirely in a world of the imagination. Each of the figures has a specific role in the ad: Chinoinks (pig Chinook helicopters) transport the bottle, while the Capper catapults onto to it, placing the lid on top. The bottle is sealed with a kiss by the Love Puppies and then chilled by the Penguins using pulverized snowmen.

'The main approach for all the characters was to make sure there was a little salt with the sweet,' say Mueller and Matulick. 'We wanted to keep them quirky and edgy but lovable. We really wanted to raise eyebrows with our character design, and make people take a closer look, and be surprised by all the unexpected details. They also needed to be relatable and inspire happiness within people.'

'We did a couple of characters that were deemed unnecessary for the spots,' they continue. 'There was one who was polishing the Coke bottle like it was in a disco car wash; a Rembrandt painter who would paint the labels on; and we had a couple of fun ideas for the "loving the bottle" scene that were a little too risqué. We designed hundreds of characters, including all the ones we just experimented with on paper, that didn't make it.'

Happiness Factory was six months in the making. While certainly a challenging ad to make, it is surprising to discover that neither Wieden + Kennedy or Psyop remember any major headaches in its creation. In fact, for the agency, finding the music was perhaps the hardest part of the process. 'I think we put over 200 tracks, many of them composed, against the pictures throughout production,' say Condos and Hindman. 'In the end, Human in New York created the music, which can still be found on many Coke spots.'

The spot launched in 2006 and was an immediate success. The campaign has since aired in more than 100 countries worldwide, and has spawned a number of sequels, including a longer piece that takes the viewer on an epic journey deep into the animated world of the ad.

06 Drawing featuring a Majorette character. The Majorettes lead the Launch Parade that takes place at the end of the Happiness Factory commercial.

07-10 Detailed storyboards by the directors at Psyop reveal how each shot of the Coke Happiness Factory commercial was carefully planned.

11 Early ideas for the style of the commercial, shown alongside images of the industrial buildings that inspired part of the ad's look.

12 A drawing of one of the proposed backdrops for the animation.

13 An early drawing showing the coin first entering the animated world of Happiness Factory.

14 Early sketch revealing the development of the characters, including some that didn't make it into the final ad.

08-10

'We broke the story down to its guts. Deliver the bottle. Fill the bottle. Love the bottle. Chill the bottle. Celebrate the bottle. From that framework, we built a world.'

11

12

13

14

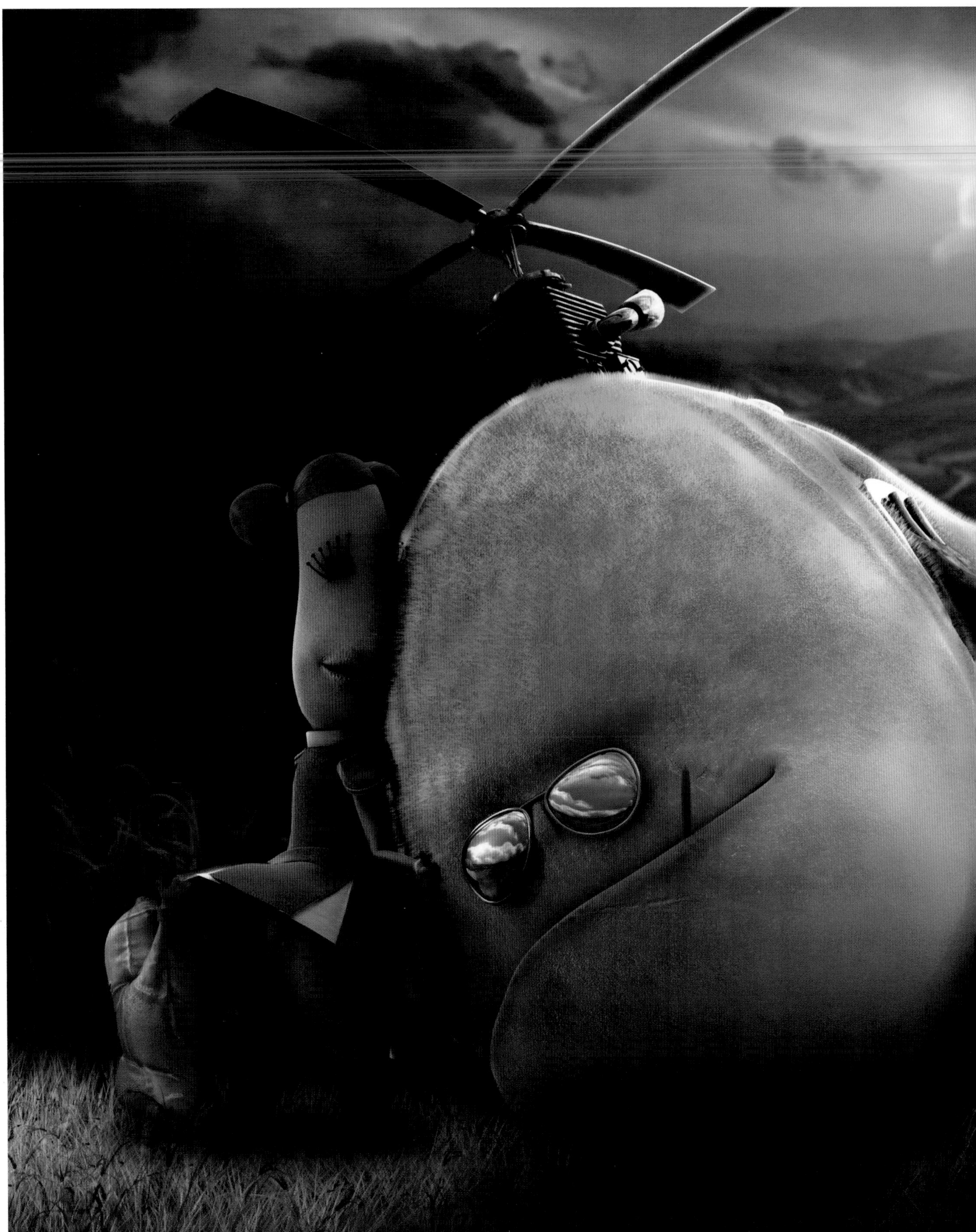

Meet the characters

Happiness Factory's cast of characters, as described by Wieden + Kennedy

Chinoinks
Chinoinks are giant flying pig-borgs who airlift Coke bottles through the Happiness Factory with dedication and the tightly knit subculture of hardened long-distance truckers. Their CB radio-style chatter is nearly incomprehensible to outsiders.

Love Puppies
Love Puppies are hyperactive critters who are by far the hardest to tame and manage in the Happiness Factory. Their three purposes in life appear to be to eat, emote and reproduce, all of which they perform extremely well. Instead of generating waste, a Love Puppy gives birth to another Love Puppy.

Workers
The Workers are the most populous species in the Happiness Factory, coming in all shapes, sizes and specializations. Originally from a far-off, forgotten place in the Hinterlands, the Workers display an uncanny affinity for sensing Cola, the sacred element around which their entire tribal culture revolved.

Cappers
A rare blend of steely nerves and corrosive cockiness, the charismatic Capper is a Top Gun who loves to live dangerously. He thrives on the acclaim he receives for performing his ballistic ballets, catapulting himself at nearly impossible trajectories and in fearless defiance of gravity to land caps on the Coke bottles with perfectly applied force. Statistically speaking, his success rate is pretty good.

Penguins
Primarily responsible for cooling Coke to a perfect icy crispness, they also tinker with their subzero calculation systems, have nerdy arguments over trivia, gloat over their temperature-controlled vintage Coke cellars, and tell each other terrible maths jokes.

Mortar Men
Every morning, Mortar Men zip themselves into their shiny suits and prepare to do what they were trained to do from childhood: ensure the safety of everyone in the Happiness Factory, to be catapulted in a stream of fire during Launch Parades, and to put the wellbeing of others ahead of their own.

Poppers
Exhibiting a tendency to get overexcited at the slightest provocation, Poppers will gladly end their own lives by exploding with enthusiasm. Literally. When they pop in a runaway chain reaction, thousands of tiny bits of glittery Popper bubbles settle like glowing snow and infuse the people of the factory with seminal moments of joy.

Aviators (Flying Machine Guys)
Itinerant, roaming mechanics who can fix anything up and make it nearly good as new, zipping about in their agile, home-rigged and half-baked Flying Machines, Aviators are the nomadic 'junkmen' of Happiness Factory.

Majorettes
The Launch Parade is the most crucial step in the preparation of a Coke bottle. This is when the entire community of the Happiness Factory is drawn together to celebrate and infuse the bottle with their collective enthusiasm as they send it on its way to the Outside. Majorettes are the de facto conductors of this major event.

Bandroids
Bandroids are the resident mariachi masterminds of the Happiness Factory, who pipe the musical soul into each bottle of Coca-Cola. The many species of Instrumentalists include the Nostril-In Player (Nose Flute), Pounders (Drums), and Tubalators (Tuba). Each naturally talented species has evolved to form a symbiotic relationship with their instrument and with one another. Bandroids tend to worship Majorettes.

15

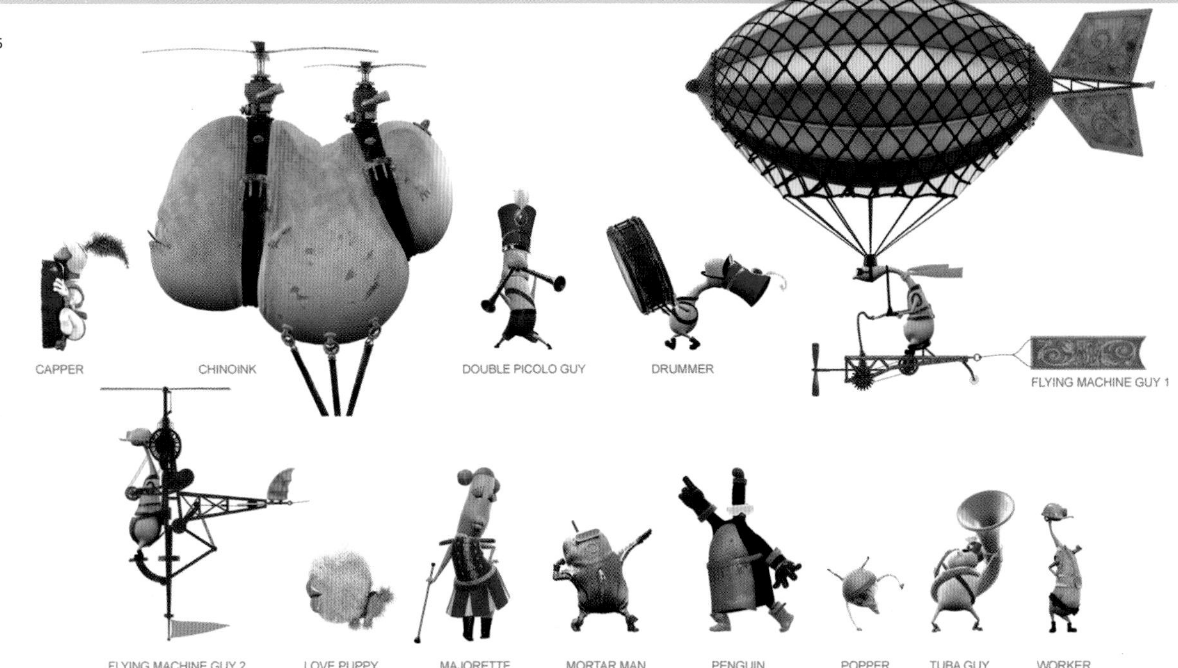

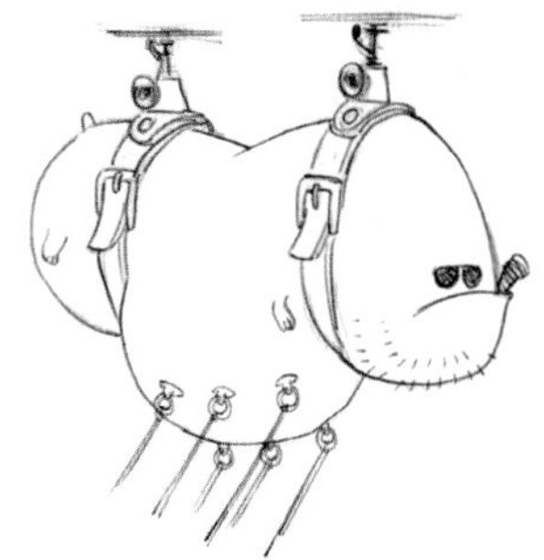

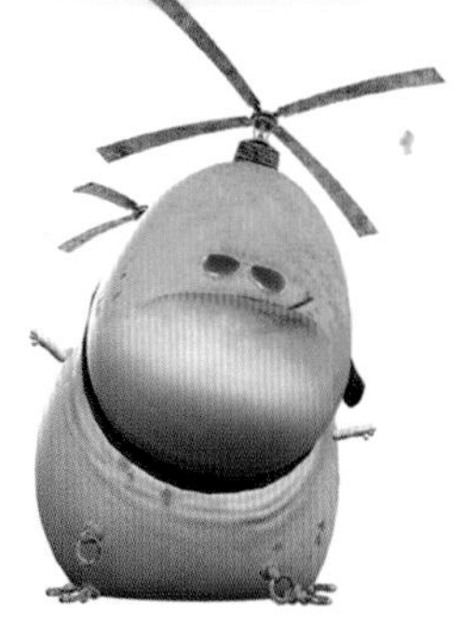

16

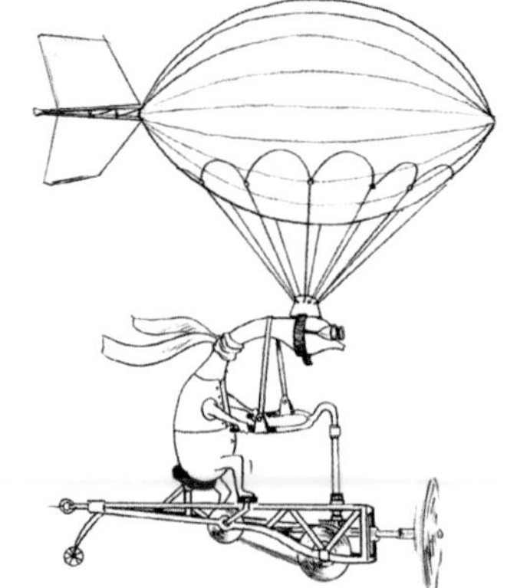

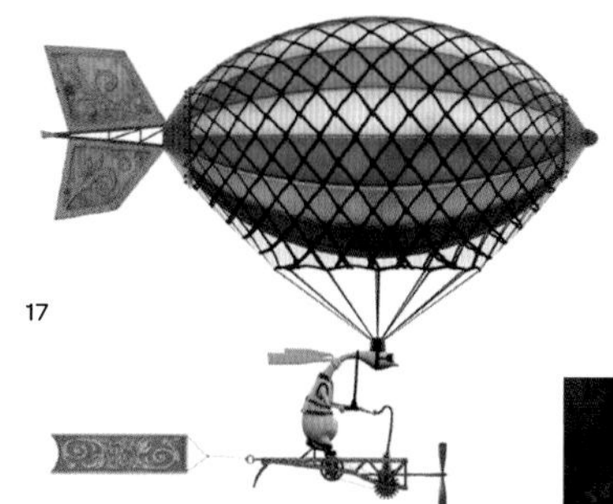

17

'The main approach for all the characters was to make sure there was a little salt with the sweet. We wanted to keep them quirky and edgy but lovable.'

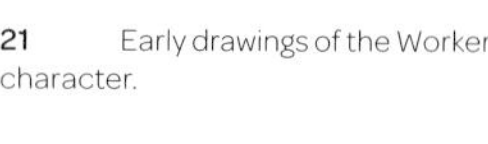

15-18 Characters in the Coke Happiness Factory spot.

19-20 Stills from the final commercial show the characters at work in the Coke Happiness Factory.

21 Early drawings of the Worker character.

18

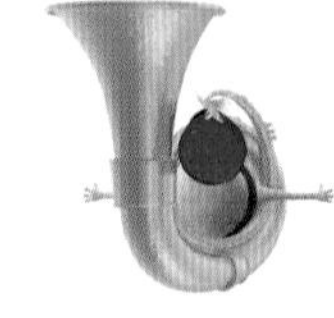

20

19

21

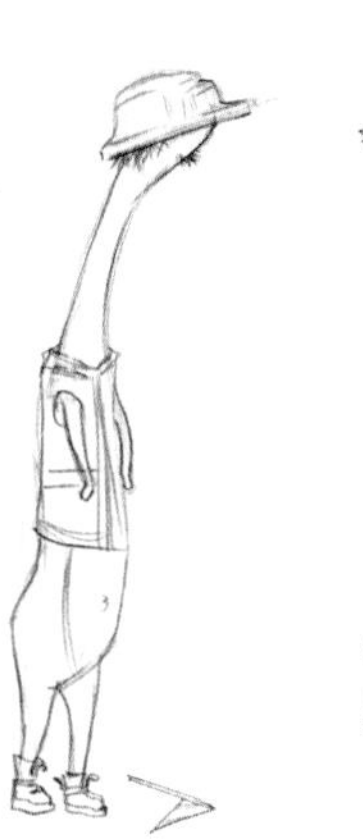

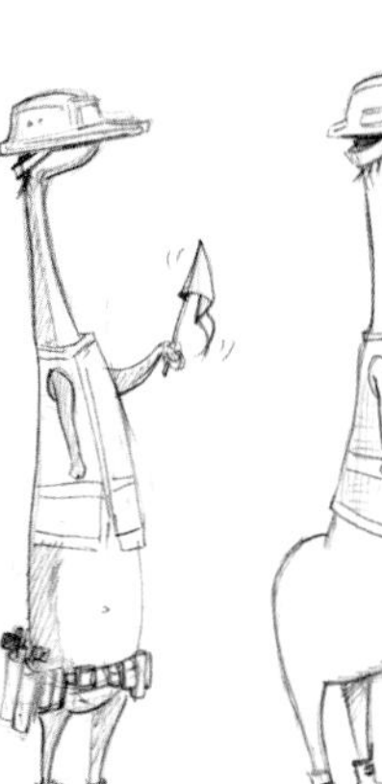

10/

Coca-Cola
Yeah Yeah Yeah La La La

Mother

'The brief was that Coke was looking for a big campaign for the summer. A campaign to launch summer for teenagers.' According to Thierry Albert, a creative at Mother ad agency in London, this is how Coke's unusual ad, Yeah Yeah Yeah La La La, began. The 2009 ad started with the tagline, which came from the mind of another Mother creative, Rob Doubal, who worked on the campaign alongside Albert and Damien Bellon. 'We were all working on a Coke summer campaign when our friend Rob Doubal came up with this weird sentence,' explains Albert. 'From there, Damien and I thought that an instrument and some weird creatures would be the best way to spread those beautiful but weird words into the world.'

'The brief was that Coke was looking for a big campaign for the summer. A campaign to launch summer for teenagers.'

01-06 The Yeah Yeah Yeah La La La campaign for Coke featured a brightly coloured organ (shown centre) that contained a band of unusual-looking but highly tuneful creatures. Shown here are photographs from the making of the creatures and from the shoot for the ad, which took place in New Zealand.

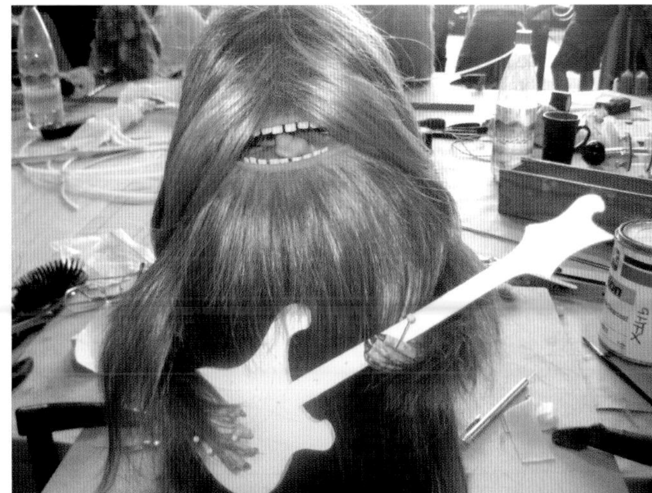

01-02

03

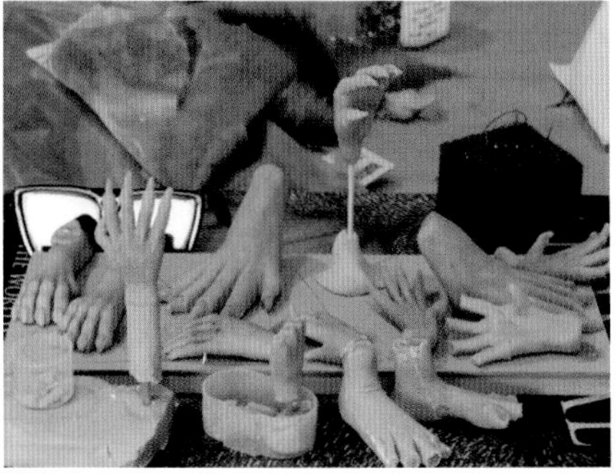

04-06

07

08

'We wrote this story about an organ player who has built a strange instrument with bits of a Hammond organ and bobs of computers,' continues Albert, 'and who uses it to feed creatures with Coke so they can sing.' Albert and Bellon turned to director Dougal Wilson to help them design the set and the creatures for the bizarre spot. 'We always wanted to work with Dougal as we have always admired his work,' says Albert. 'We were waiting for the right project and this one seemed to be perfect, because it's close to a music video – Dougal is one of the best promo directors around – and it has crazy creatures in it, and some animation as well. It also needed a great attention to detail and crafting and Dougal is a perfectionist.'

Mother approached Wilson with an illustration to help explain the strange idea for the ad, which featured an ancient 'kitten-organ', a musical instrument containing real cats, who would yowl when different keys were played. 'They'd found this illustration,' explains Wilson, 'an old, old picture that is on Wikipedia. Apparently there was a physician in a royal court – I'm not sure which century it was – where the king was suffering from some sort of mental malaise, so he devised this kitten-organ, which he thought would rouse him from this catatonic state, because there's no way you could ignore that.'

Work on devising the creatures and the organ that they would be placed within began, with no avenue left unexplored in the search for exactly the right look for the ad. 'Damien, the art director, was pretty full on with the amount of reference material for the organ that he gave me,' says Wilson. 'I love old synths and organs, so that was one side of the research, finding all that, and then the other side was looking at the creatures. We looked at all sorts of things like cats and monkeys, but the one that seemed most relevant was a sloth, a baby sloth.' Initially Wilson felt that all the creatures should be the same. 'I wanted to approach it super-logically and make all these creatures identical, but in different sizes, to represent different notes, like pipes on an organ,' he says. 'So a fat one would make a low note, and a little one would make a high note. They were adamant that they should all be random and different sizes – they wanted it to be less logical, more creative. They were right, because it would have been pretty boring if they were all the same.'

'We were specific in the storyboard, but a story like this is quite a complicated thing to communicate.... I don't think I've ever done anything in so much detail, but at the same time it still felt quite chaotic while we were shooting it.'

Wilson did introduce a second group of creatures to the spot, however – a band that is revealed halfway through. 'I thought it would be good to have a different chapter halfway through the ad,' he says, 'which also reveals where the music is coming from. So down below there's a second tier of doors, which open up revealing these dudes. And it gives you another gag.'

The music was a central element to the ad, with part of the brief from Coke being an ambitious request to create an 'anthem of the summer' via the spot. The team commissioned a number of demos from musicians, all of whom devised a song around the words of the ad, 'Yeah Yeah Yeah La La La'. Calvin Harris's version was eventually chosen, and a 12-inch single of his track was released as the ad launched.

While this song was being prepared, the creatives were occupied in constructing individual personalities for each of the creatures, to help define how they would behave. Among the singers are Nufsaid, described by Albert as 'the one who never says anything. He likes to watch the clouds and chew on cherry stones'; Samson: 'He doesn't like his nickname, but with curly eyebrows like that, what else was he expecting?'; Crétin: 'He used to be called Stupid but didn't like it so the others changed it to Crétin – stupid in French – and now he's very happy with it'; and Lick, who 'has the biggest tongue you have ever seen, which gives him an unbelievable sense of rhythm. He could make a herd of cows tap dance.'

Casting for an actor to play the organist in the spot was similarly rigorous: 'He had to feel like he had a big story behind him, he had to feel a bit dubious and like he'd been to a lot of places,' says Wilson of the figure they wanted to present.

'He wasn't the smartest character in terms of his appearance, but he looked quite wise – a bit of a vagabond I suppose, a travelling salesman type, wheeling his organ from town to town. Slightly Pied Piper-esque – a bit of a mythic character who just pops up in places and hands out

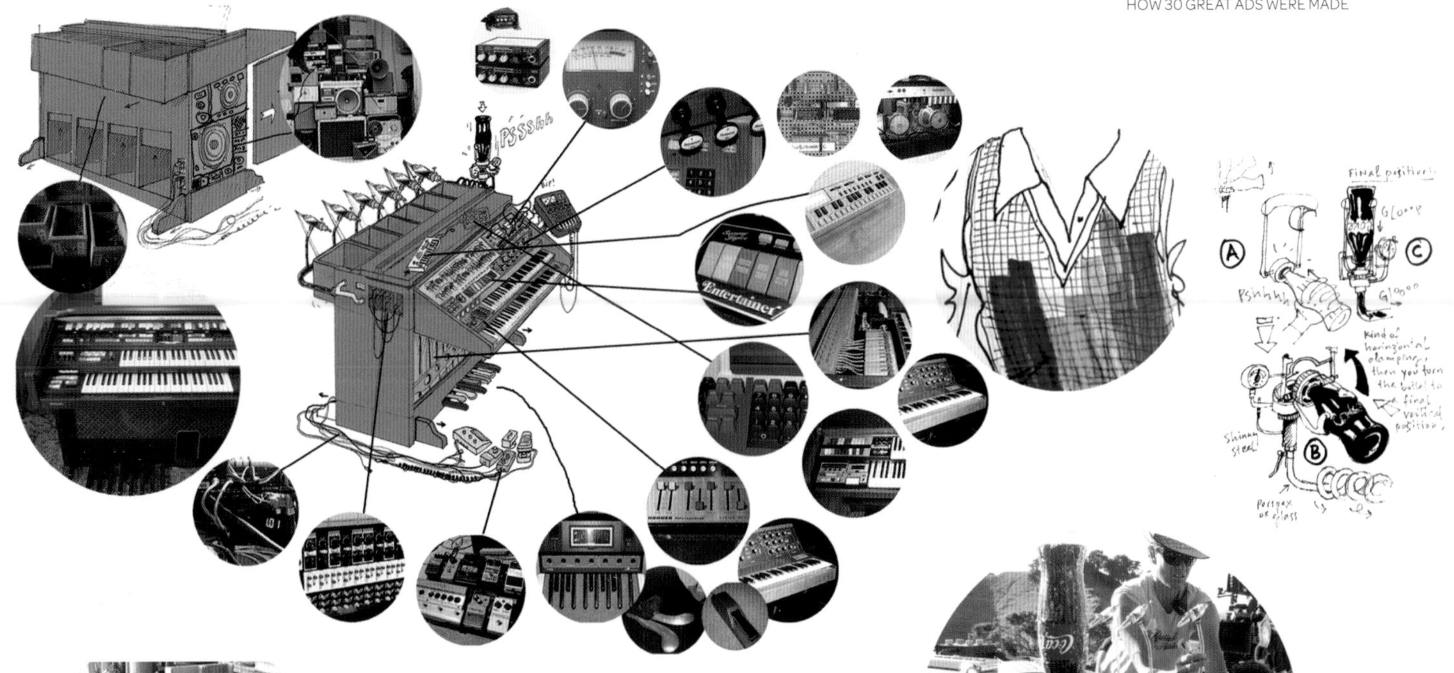

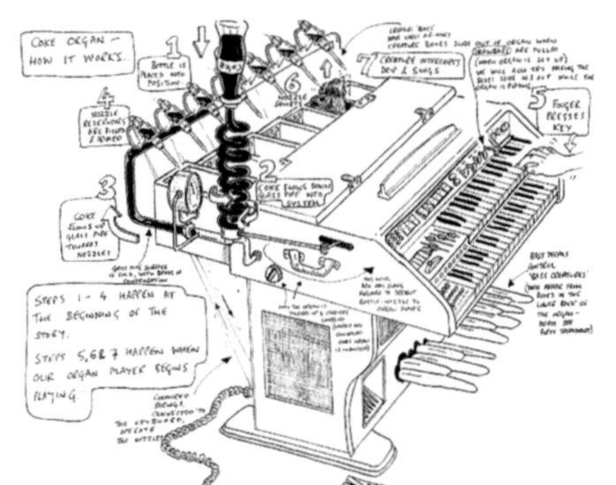

09

10

07 Mother creative Thierry Albert pictured alongside one of the Coke creatures.

08-09 Early drawings and designs for the creatures and the organ. The organ features a bottle that distributes Coke to the creatures, encouraging them to sing.

10 Pages from director Dougal Wilson's sketchbook that was filled with ideas and imagery during the development of the ad.

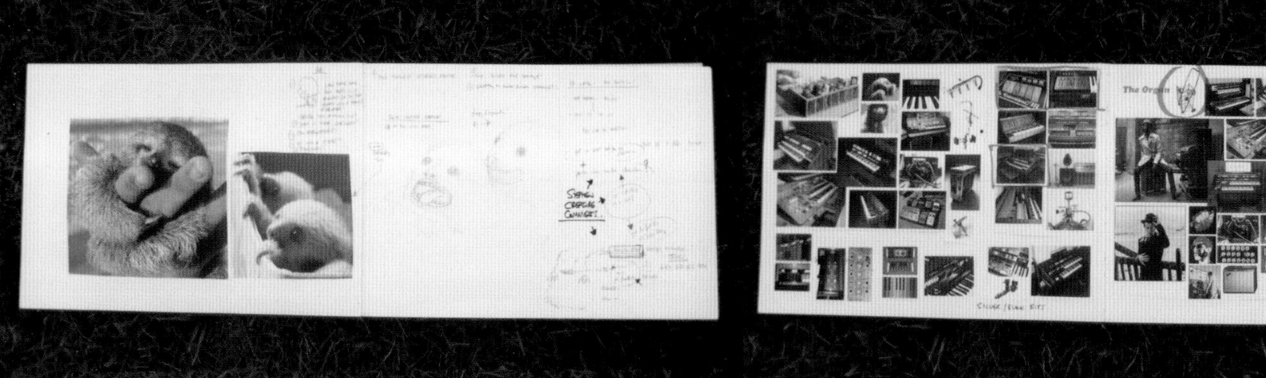

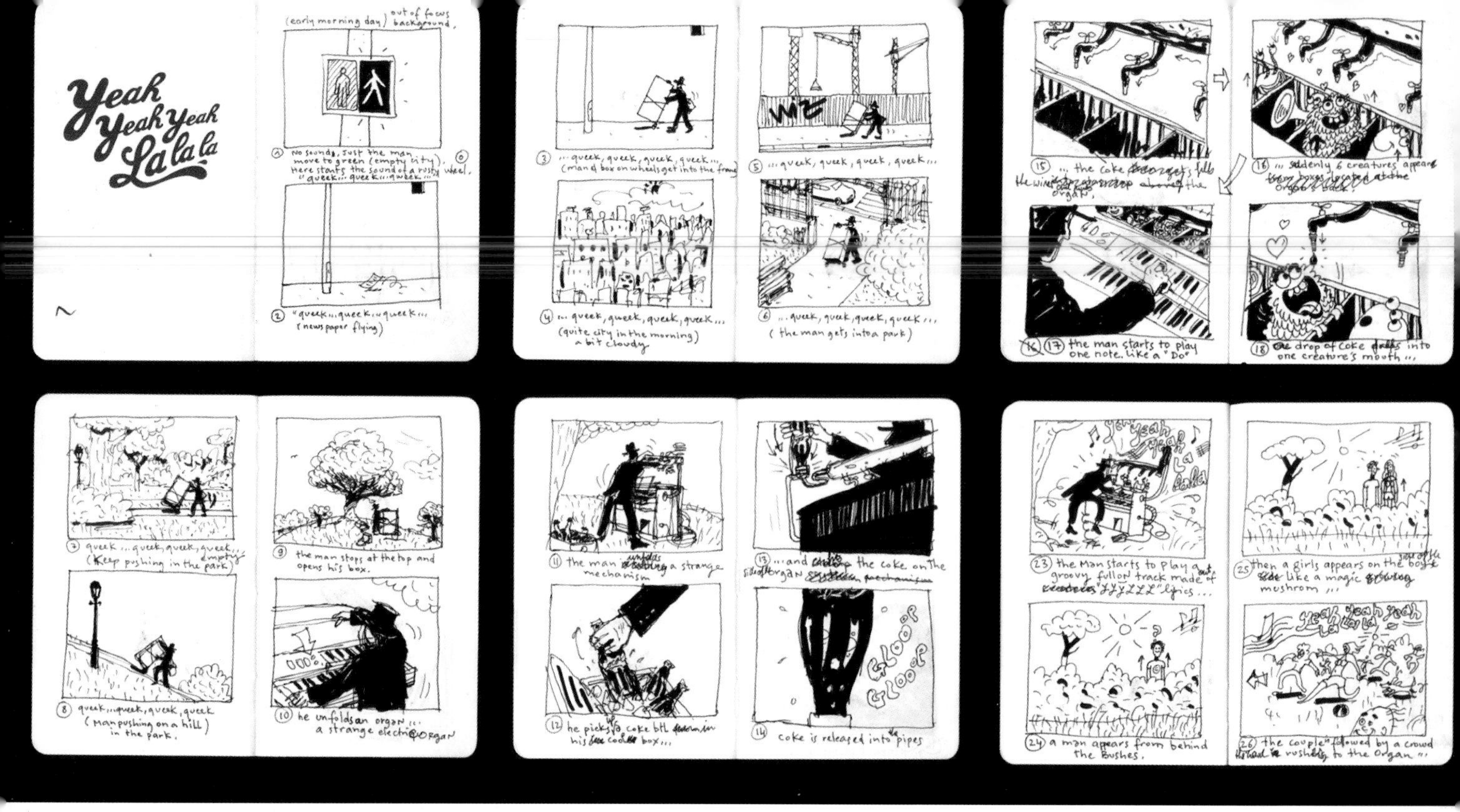

Yeah Yeah Yeah La la la

(early morning day) out of focus background
1. No sounds, just the man move to green (empty city). Here starts the sound of a rosty wheel. "queek...queek...queek..."
2. "queek...queek...queek..." (newspaper flying)

3. ...queek, queek, queek, queek... (man & box on wheels get into the frame)
4. ...queek, queek, queek, queek... (quite city in the morning) a bit cloudy

5. ...queek, queek, queek, queek...
6. ...queek, queek, queek, queek... (the man gets into a park)

15. ... the coke falls ... the organ.
17. the man starts to play one note, like a "Do"

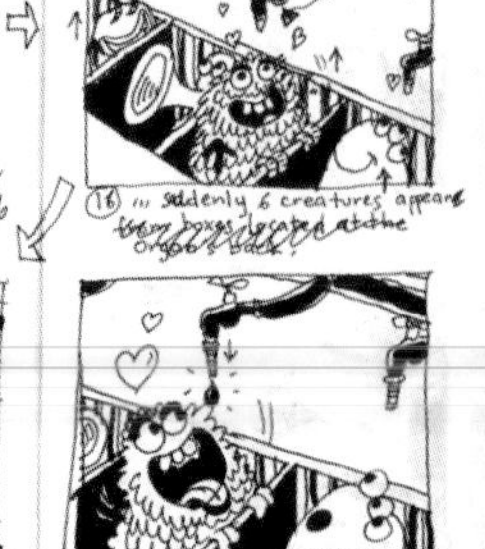
16. ... suddenly 6 creatures appear
18. One drop of coke falls into one creature's mouth...

7. queek... queek, queek, queek... (Keep pushing in the empty park)
8. queek...queek, queek, queek (Man pushing on a hill in the park.)

9. the man stops at the top and opens his box.
10. he unfolds an organ... a strange electric ORGAN

11. the man unfolds a strange mechanism
12. he picks up a coke btl. from his box...

13. ...and drop the coke on the ORGAN
GLOOP GLOOP
14. coke is released into the pipes

Yeah yeah La la la
23. the Man starts to play a groovy fullon track made of "YYYYYYY" lyrics...
24. a man appears from behind the bushes.
25. then a girls appears on the top of the like a magic mushrom...
Yeah yeah yeah La la la
26. the couple followed by a crowd rushing to the Organ...

11

12

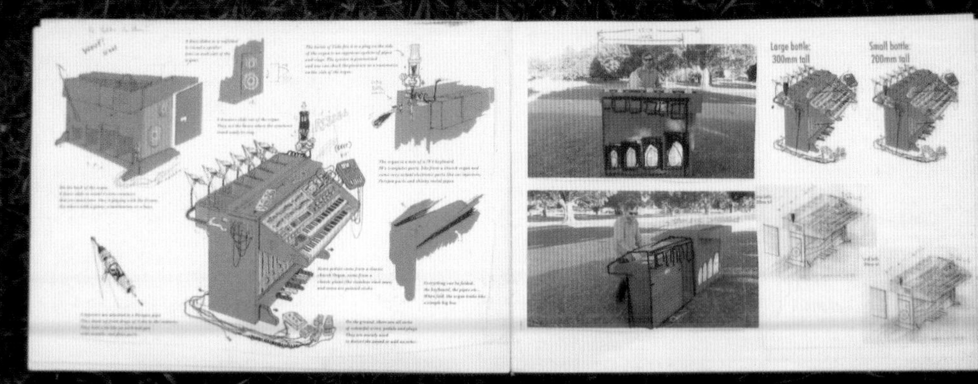

14

Coke! If he were too clean-shaven and good-looking and nice, it would end up looking very, very cheesy. We were desperate to try and keep him looking a bit rough and swarthy.'

Despite this meticulous preparation, the shoot itself was not without its difficulties. The combination of detailed puppeteering with wider shots showing people dancing to the music proved especially tricky. 'It's dealing with things that are very, very small and fiddly,' Wilson says, 'but then also shots that are very wide and have a lot of scale to them. So it was an exhausting shoot.' The film was shot over eight days in New Zealand, on a piece of Maori land featuring a large hill, which in itself created problems, due to strong winds. 'Often we took the organ down to the bottom of the hill and just shot close-up stuff there, because you wouldn't be able to tell where it was,' continues Wilson. 'It was quite gruelling because somehow we were always short on time – we often are on my shoots because I try to get a lot of shots in so I have the option in the edit. We were specific in the storyboard, but a story like this is quite a complicated thing to communicate.... I don't think I've ever done anything in so much detail, but at the same time it still felt quite chaotic while we were shooting it.'

Other, far more unexpected moments, also occurred. 'A funny/scary moment was when a cow broke its leg on the hill close to where we were shooting,' says Albert. 'It was wandering around, it had nothing to do with us... but two officials came around, shot it and decided to carve it up in front of everybody, just before lunch.'

In spite of these complications, with Yeah Yeah Yeah La La La, Mother and Wilson created one of the most surreal and imaginative ads ever made for Coke. There are references to previous ads for the brand within it – the iconic 1970s spot where teenagers assemble on a sun-drenched hilltop in Italy comes to mind – but the film emits a quirky, individual style that ultimately feels more akin to a music video than a commercial. The spot didn't quite achieve the hit record with the music that Coke had hoped for, but their decision to work with Calvin Harris proved wise; the musician achieved a series of hits that summer, offering the Coke ad an added sense of coolness by association.

11 Dougal Wilson's hand-drawn storyboards for the spot reveal a detailed plan for the variety of shots he needed to complete during the shoot in New Zealand.

12 Still images taken from the completed ad.

13 A limited edition 12" record of Calvin Harris's soundtrack for the ad, which was released to coincide with the launch of the campaign. One of the creatures from the ad stars on the picture disc.

14 Further pages from Wilson's sketchbook, showing the detailed development of the organ that was featured in the spot.

13

11/

Guinness noitulovE

Abbott Mead Vickers BBDO

Guinness has a considerable advertising heritage. The brand has built a reputation for pithy taglines and equally striking imagery, stretching back to its earliest advertising slogans. So when Matt Doman and Ian Heartfield, creatives at Abbott Mead Vickers BBDO in London, were looking for inspiration for a new brief for the brand in 2005, they decided to look back to the company's history. 'We'd always liked Good Things Come To Those Who Wait,' says Doman. 'We thought it was the best campaign you could ever do for Guinness. So we asked whether there was a possibility of it coming back on the table.'

'Good Things...' was first introduced as a tagline by AMV BBDO about ten years previously, and referred to the notorious settling time that a pint of Guinness requires when bought in a pub. It had been attached to some of the brand's most successful ads, including the 1999 Surfer ad, directed by Jonathan Glazer, which features the distinctive image of a group of white horses to demonstrate the power of the waves. 'Good Things...' had been dropped as a campaign when Guinness's advertising went global, as the rest of the world uses a fast-flow system to pour the drink, making the sentence irrelevant. But as this new campaign was for the UK only, it was reasonable for Doman and Heartfield to suggest its return. 'The idea was born out of the ultimate wait,' continues Doman. 'Weirdly, the ad came out pretty fully formed from what I remember.'

A clue to the ad's theme is in its name, noitulovE, which is 'Evolution' spelt backwards. The spot opens on a group of three young men at a bar. As they take their first sip of Guinness, they are shown reversing out of the pub, down the street, and through history. We see them rapidly de-evolve, become Neanderthals, chimpanzees, then birds, fish, small dinosaurs and finally mudskippers, before the tagline arrives triumphantly on the screen. The ad may not be an accurate demonstration of reverse evolution, but it is certainly a striking one.

What appears a simple idea proved hugely complex to make. The first hurdle for the creatives was getting the ad past the research groups, a selection of people who are asked to react to a rough version of the spot. These opinions can determine whether an idea will even get out of the

01-07 Stills from the finished Guinness commercial. The spot told a backwards story of evolution, beginning with three friends in a bar drinking Guinness, who are then shown zipping back through history, becoming chimpanzees, then birds, fish and finally mudskippers.

01-07

'It was a slightly unusual Guinness ad because it had a sense of humour to it, it was a vaguely witty ad. Guinness hadn't done that before – everything had been very straight and serious.'

'Every shot had a different technique. There was no one way of doing it from beginning to end; it's almost as if every shot was treated like its own commercial in its own right.'

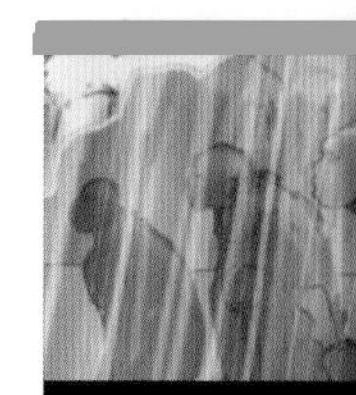
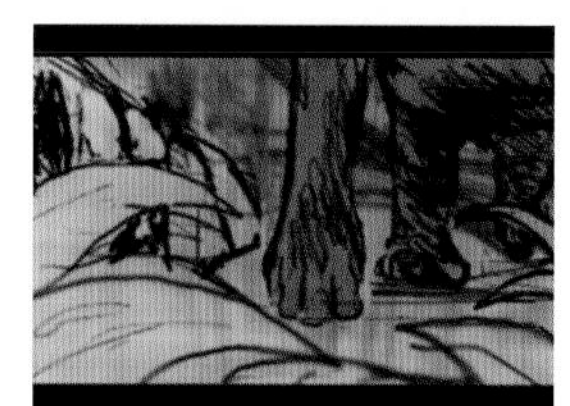
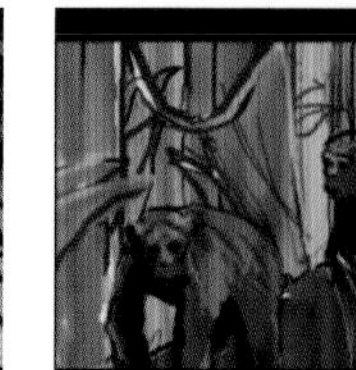

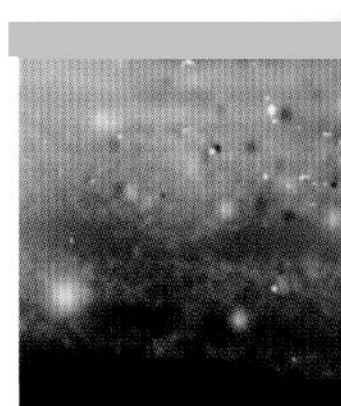

08

starting blocks. 'To get stuff through research, it's got to be up, feel-good,' explains Heartfield. 'Anything dark or edgy or weird makes people nervous, so it doesn't ever get past that first group of people in a room. You have to play a slightly different game.'

'You have to do animatics [a rough mock-up of the ad with moving images] and storyboards, and carefully choose the music,' continues Doman. 'It's almost like you don't research the ad that you really want to make; you make an ad that's good for research, and then you change it afterwards.'

The ad eventually went through four rounds of research as it was developed. By the second stage, Doman and Heartfield had chosen a director for the spot, who helped prepare the storyboards. From the get-go they knew they had an unexpected ad for the brand, requiring a particular type of director. 'It was a slightly unusual Guinness ad because it had a sense of humour to it, it was a vaguely witty ad,' they say. 'Guinness hadn't done that before – everything had been very straight and serious. We thought we couldn't do better than Surfer – achingly cool, black and white, an amazing piece of cinematography – and we just thought no-one's really done a light-hearted Guinness ad.'

The team also knew that the ad would require a director with vast skills in post-production, in order to achieve the rapid evolutionary changes required by the narrative. This mixture of humour and post led them to Daniel Kleinman, who was known for his witty campaigns for brands including John West Salmon and Xbox (see page 128). 'What you've got to be careful of with an idea like that is, if you haven't got the money or the time behind it, it can really fall flat on its face,' says Heartfield. 'But knowing that you had someone of Kleinman's calibre, who really wanted to do it, and do it well... once he was on board, you could relax to a certain extent.'

'It was a really simple script,' says Kleinman of first reading the idea. 'You think it is so complicated, incorporating millions of years of history, but you can write it in three or four sentences. I think that's the best sort of script. The moment I saw it, I thought "this could be great, this could be really interesting". It threw up lots of visual stuff that I could get my teeth into.'

'The challenge was to work out what the story was going to be,' he continues. 'From humans to Neanderthals was fairly easy... then they become chimps and then go up in the air.... From then on we were just pulling ideas out of our heads, what would be funny. It's not meant to be a history lesson; it's not correct in a sense of Darwinian science – we probably weren't ever fish or ostriches or whatever. I just wanted to try and get in many different types of environment, so you go in the trees, under the water, in the air, running over land, digging under the ground – to make it constantly surprising and interesting as you go along, and then it's kind of funny as well.

'It was great fun to work out and storyboard. But then comes the big major challenge, which is, "how the hell do we do it...?" Every single shot had lots and lots of different elements in it. I think one of the most interesting things about it, and innovative things, was there were more techniques than I've ever used before. Every shot had a different technique. There was no one way of doing it from beginning to end; it's almost as if every shot was treated like its own commercial in its own right. Some of it is animation, some of it is in-camera stuff, some of it is make-up, some of it is time-lapse, some of it is composite stills – it was all sorts of different things all mashed together. In the end that gave it a kind of mad energy that seemed to work.'

Kleinman worked with William Bartlett at post-production house Framestore to create the many special effects within the ad. Some of the shots were created fairly conventionally – the team filmed time-lapse imagery in Iceland to get the background landscape shots, and the three men in the ad wore prosthetic costumes to become Neanderthals – but after that things became a little weirder.

08 Early storyboards for the noitulovE commercial by director Daniel Kleinman show how the ad was planned visually.

09-11

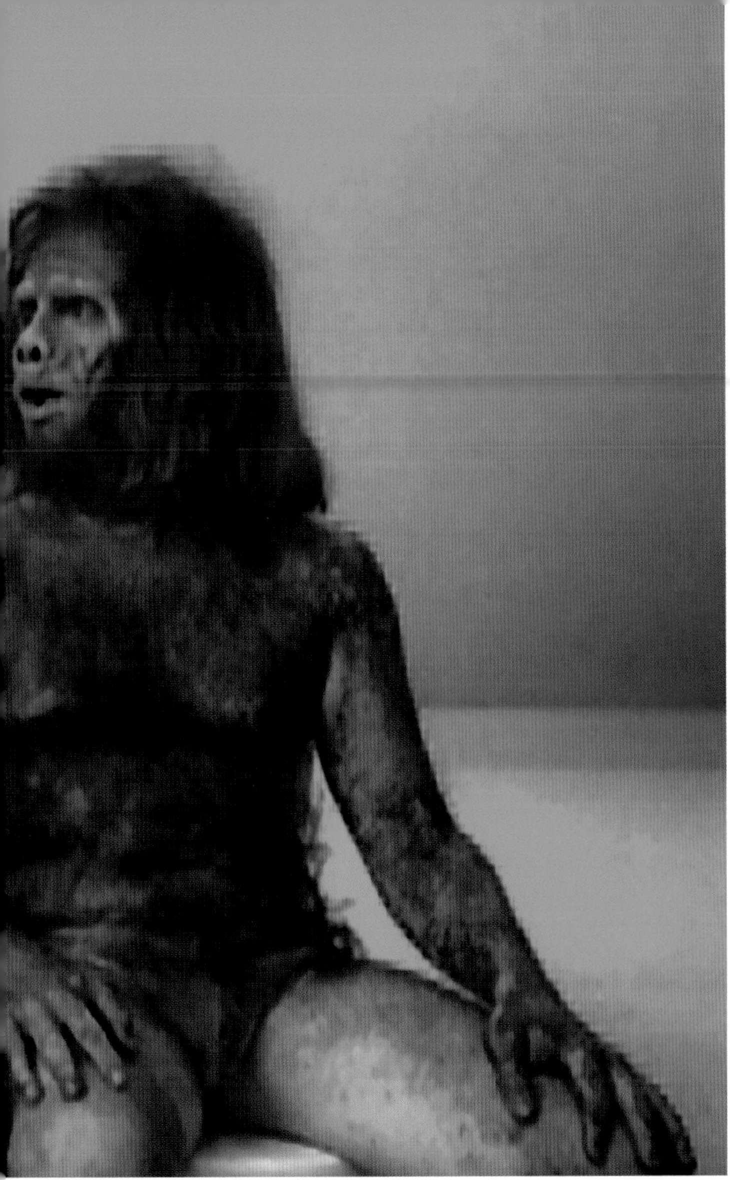

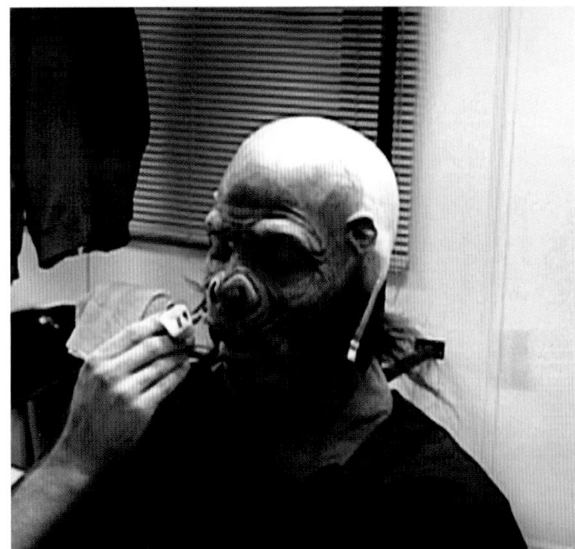

12-13

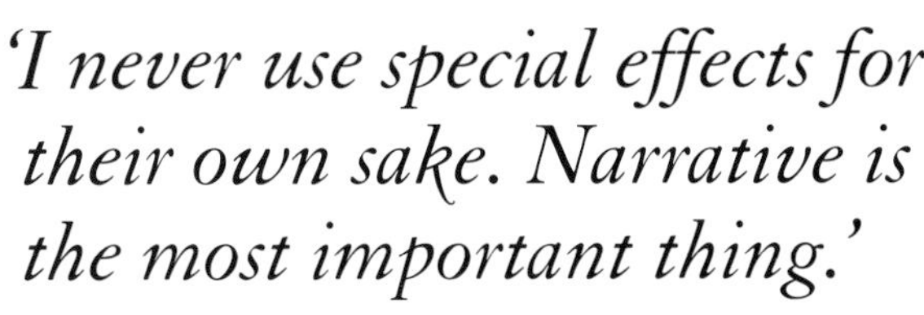

'I never use special effects for their own sake. Narrative is the most important thing.'

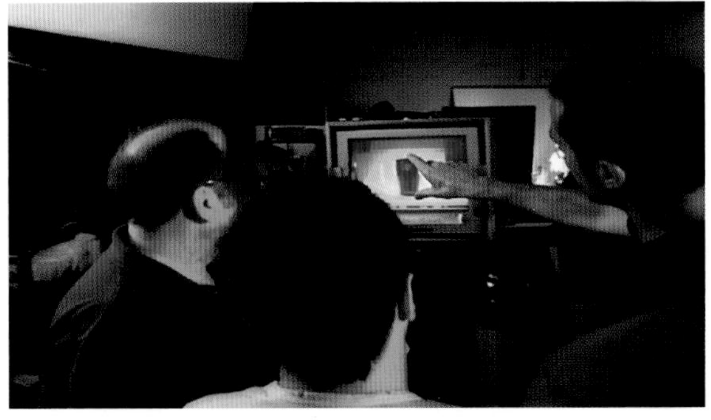

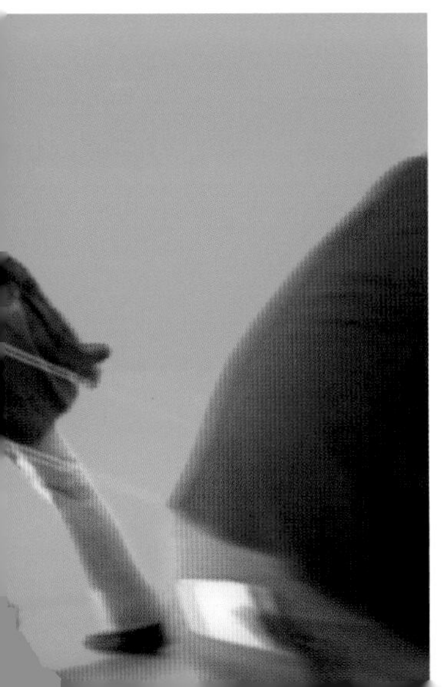

09-13 The three main actors on set, shown in full Neanderthal make-up, with director Daniel Kleinman (12) and also performing for the camera. In order to get the correct look for the backwards walk in the film, Kleinman actually had the actors walk forward dragging heavy weights, and then ran the resulting film backwards.

14-15 The team discusses different shots for the commercial.

14-15

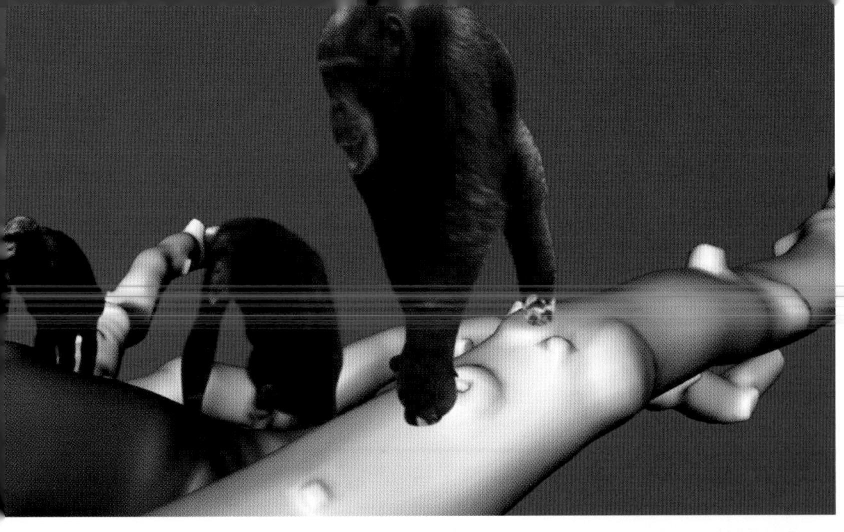

16-18

19-22

'Some of the rock erosion and volcanoes were created with a mixture of flour, yeast and mud all mixed up on a hot plate.'

16-18 The chimpanzees are added to the scene in post-production; the three main actors shown on set filming the opening scene; early image showing the design for the bar.

19-22 The noitulovE spot incorporated some unusual special effects, including using a blow-torch to heat the leaves of a plant in order to make them gently sway, as if in a breeze, and filming a baked mixture of yeast, flour and mud for the volcano scenes.

'The edit isn't just putting things in the right order – you're still creatively making the narrative, in a literal sense.'

'To create some of the plants moving, I experimented with using stop-frame animation and moving the plants by slightly heating up the leaves between each frame with a cook's blow torch,' says Bartlett. 'This was fairly effective at giving an interesting movement. I also used scissors for variation.'

'Some of the rock erosion and volcanoes were created with a mixture of flour, yeast and mud all mixed up on a hot plate and filmed stop frame against the back of my blue sofa at home,' he continues. 'The moving rocks in the background of the shot where the fish jumps backwards out of the pool onto dry land are a mixture of Special K cereal and Grape Nuts! I don't want to make it sound as if the whole ad was created in this rather homemade way. Most of it was done with very sophisticated, cutting-edge technology on very expensive computers. I think it is the mix of styles and techniques that gives the ad its charm.'

One of the major aspects that Kleinman brought to the ad was an attention to detail, and a constant sense of experimentation, which led to other odd moments during the shoot. 'There were subtle effects that worked quite well that you probably wouldn't even notice,' he says. 'I wanted the cavemen and the people who were half-Neanderthal, half-monkey men to walk in a different way, so we got in a movement trainer who studies monkeys and chimps and trained the guys to move.'

The backwards momentum of the ad also threw up some unique problems, particularly as Kleinman was keen to avoid it looking simply as if the men were walking backwards at the start. 'I wanted it to feel like there was almost a magnet behind them, pulling them backwards,' he explains. 'In order to do that, because I was running the film backwards, I had to get them to lean forwards and walk at a more extreme angle than you can physically walk, so I tied heavy weights behind them and got them to walk forward dragging these heavy weights, and then in post I took the weights away.'

Throughout the complex creation of the ad, Kleinman and the creatives had to show its development to the client, which was an uneasy procedure for all involved. 'The edit process was several months,' says Kleinman, 'and it required a lot of hand-holding because you were looking at a shot and there's nothing there. There'd be a time-lapse still of an Icelandic landscape with a grey square flying through it to represent what might happen, and you're showing this to people. The client was quite nervous, and they wanted to see it in all the stages as it progressed. They were seeing it in early stages, which normally you wouldn't show people. In that sense they were very good, because they did trust us.'

'The post was terrifying,' agrees Ian Heartfield. 'It builds in layers; it's not like a live-action shoot where you'll know whether you've got a good ad almost immediately. If it's that amount of post, you don't see how good it's going to be until it's really late.'

'The way I explained it was that you do the shoot, but actually the shoot isn't finished yet,' says Kleinman, 'because the edit and the special effects are still part of the shoot. You're still creating the images, you're still creating the characters and making them move and do all sorts of stuff that you would do on the shoot. The edit isn't just putting things in the right order – you're still creatively making the narrative, in a literal sense. But it was something I'd never done before, and perhaps no other commercial had had so many different techniques involved all at the same time before. It's moving into new territory, which was exciting.'

Towards the end stages of making the ad, a major change was instigated. From the very beginning, the ad had been set to a particular piece of music, a track by Groove Armada. The piece had proved popular with everyone, from the research groups to the director, yet the team brought in musician Peter Raeburn to see if he might suggest any alternatives. He quizzed the team in depth about the ad and eventually returned with the Sammy Davis, Jr recording of Rhythm of Life, from the musical Sweet Charity. The track had a seismic effect. 'It sounds like an exaggeration, but it remains for me the single best moment I've had in advertising, when he played this bit of music to that film, because it just changed it completely,' says Heartfield. 'I never would have got to that myself. It just changed everything, it really did.'

When talking about making noitulovE, the creatives talk about the 'moons aligning'. Through having a great idea, for a prestigious client, they were able to get access to some of the most talented people working in advertising. But what is perhaps most interesting about noitulovE is that, despite it being such an effects-laden ad, which took so many hours in post-production to create, it is the humour that stands out most. Perhaps unsurprisingly, this was Kleinman's intention all along. 'I never use special effects for their own sake,' he says. 'Narrative is the most important thing. So all the effects are a means to an end, which is to make it a flowing, easy-to-watch, amusing thing.'

23 The final shot in the ad shows the famous tagline, which was resurrected for this commercial after being dropped from the brand's advertising for some time.

12/

HBO
True Blood

Digital Kitchen

The brief that HBO sent out for the launch of its second series of vampire show True Blood was simple but deadly: 'create buzz'. It is surprising, then, to discover that Chicago-based agency Digital Kitchen's solution was to use one of the oldest, and arguably least 'buzzy' mediums of advertising: the poster. While still central to many ad campaigns, the poster or billboard seems rather staid in these digital, interactive times, with innovation in the medium thin on the ground. Yet this is just what Digital Kitchen achieved.

The campaign drew on the central tenet of True Blood, which is that vampires live among us and are part of reality. For the launch of the first series, New York ad agency Campfire had created a complex prequel campaign to introduce the show's themes and increase anticipation around the start of the series. This included sending out to fans vials that supposedly contained the synthetic blood from the show, which allows vampires to live openly among humans. When Digital Kitchen began working on the account, it decided to take this blurring of reality and fiction even further.

'We said, if vampires are among us, how would they be marketed to?' explains executive producer Todd Brandes. The agency came up with the idea of doing a co-branded poster campaign, where famous clothing, car and lifestyle brands would advertise their products to a fictional vampire audience in a tie-in with HBO.

'We approached brands and said that our idea is that the True Blood vampires are part of society, they're part of culture, and they're just as deserving to be marketed to as any human would be,' continues Brandes. 'We said, it's going to be playful and fun, and it's going to be an ad for your brand; we're going to be completely respectful of your mark and your tone.' Digital Kitchen needed permission to use the brands in the campaign, but otherwise proposed to create the ads entirely themselves. 'Ultimately, that was the challenge,' says Brandes. 'The challenge was convincing

'We said, if vampires are among us, how would they be marketed to?'

01 One of the finished posters for the HBO True Blood campaign, shown in situ. The ad markets an Ecko perfume 'exclusively to vampires'.

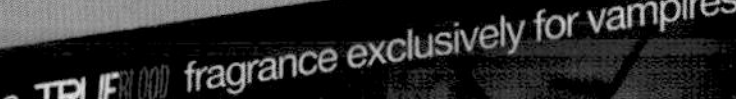
a TRUEBLOOD fragrance exclusively for vampires

*ECKŌ
BY
MARC ECKŌ
truebloodfragrance.com
ATTRACT A HUMAN.

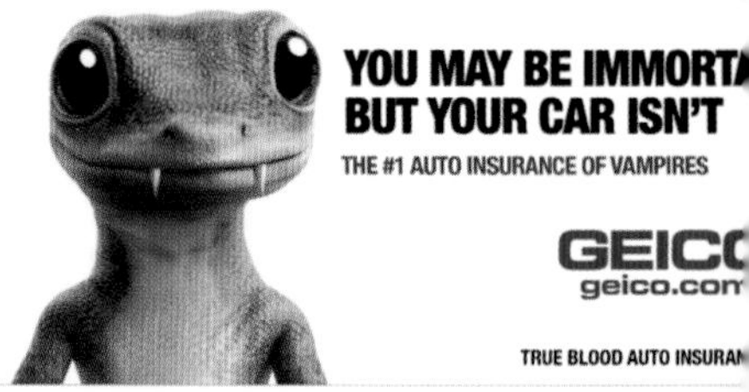

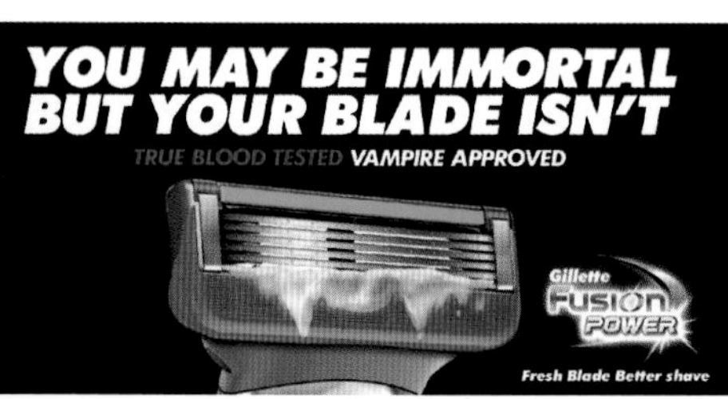

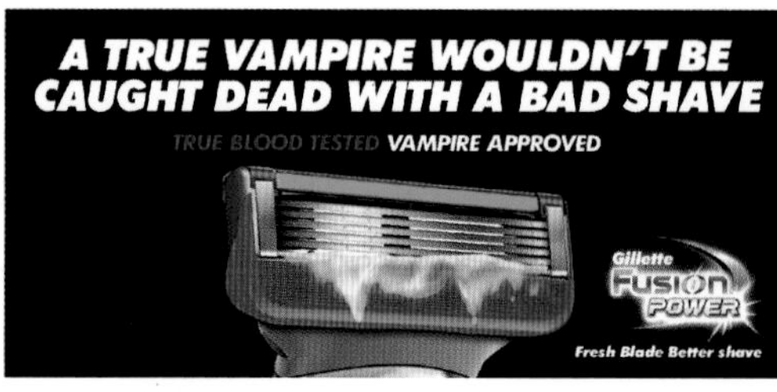

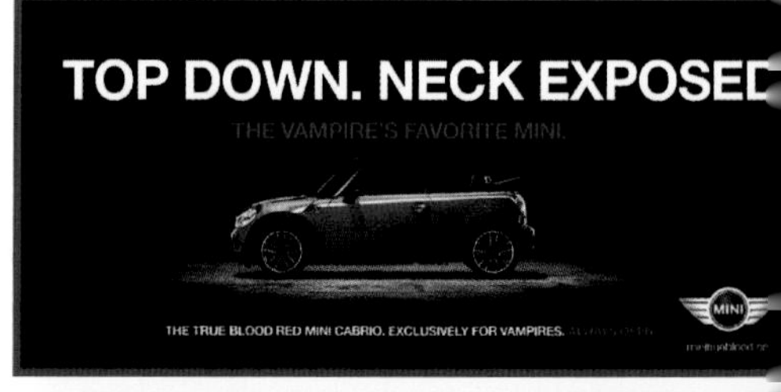

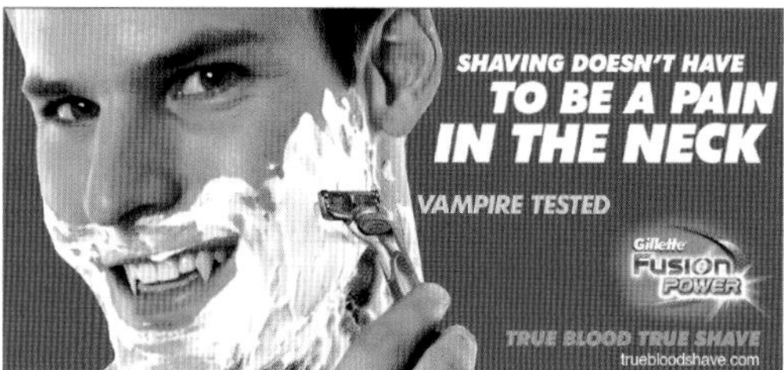

02-06

'It's one thing for an agency of record who've worked with Gillette or Monster for 10 or 15 years… we're coming in on day two and all of a sudden we have to design an ad that feels spot-on for these brands. We turned around ads in a matter of 24 or 48 hours.'

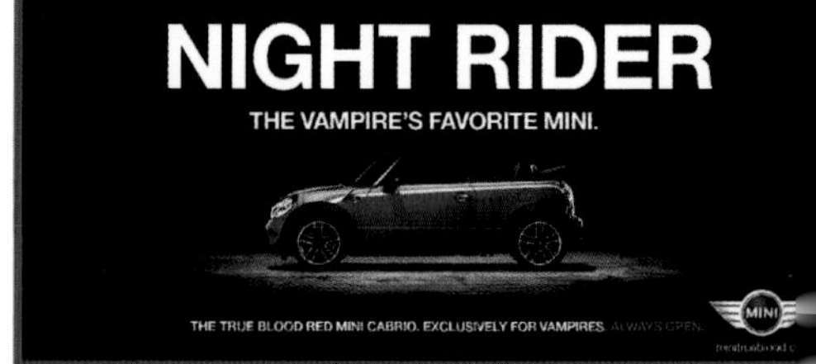

'Everybody's looking for a way to stand out in the glut of communication, and this just happened to be an idea that everybody thought "that's new, that's different, that's fresh, that's cool".'

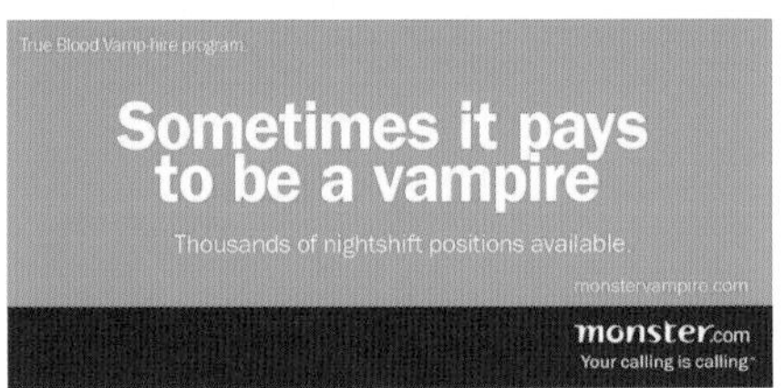

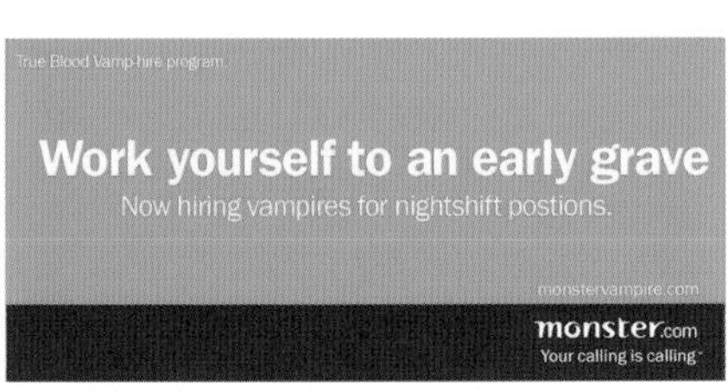

07

02–07 Digital Kitchen worked with six brands to create advertising for vampires in the HBO True Blood campaign. Shown here are a number of the different ideas for posters that were proposed to the brands. The whole campaign was completed in just eight weeks, during which time the team created the equivalent of seven different ad campaigns: an overarching one for HBO, and then individual poster campaigns for the six other clients involved in the project.

them that you were going to be able to capture the tone of their advertising, the tone of their brand and their mark, and be completely respectful of it and true to it.'

Brandes was surprised by how many companies were keen to be involved. 'Obviously I believed in the idea,' he comments, 'but having worked on the client side you just know approvals and layers and what it takes to get stuff done, and we just had so little time.' But the brands jumped to be a part of the project. 'Everybody's looking for a way to stand out in the glut of communication, and this just happened to be an idea that everybody thought "that's new, that's different, that's fresh, that's cool". There were several that turned us down, though I have to say nobody turned us down for any other reason than that the R-rated content of the show was not something they could go along with. We went to some brands that were more wholesome, and they said, "it's a great idea, guys, but I can't sell that through". We even had brands we turned down! We reached out to a lot of people simultaneously – obviously we had to – so we had a real juggling act to see who would come on. We had a first-come, first-served basis.'

Among the clients that took part in the final campaign are Mini, Harley-Davidson, Gillette, Monster, Ecko Unlimited and Geico. The in-house team at Digital Kitchen designed the co-branded ads for True Blood in just eight weeks. 'The thing I'm most proud of is that we ultimately had seven clients in the span of eight weeks,' says Brandes. 'We had HBO and we had six others. We were dealing with their agencies, we were dealing with their marketing departments and we're not a big company, we're just a few people. It's one thing for an agency of record who've worked with Gillette or Monster for 10 or 15 years... we're coming in on day two and all of a sudden we have to design an ad that feels spot-on for these brands. We turned around ads in a matter of 24 or 48 hours.... The initial ads we gave to people, we were probably spot-on 50 or 60 per cent of the time straight out of the box. In terms of the creative, it was entirely left up to us; we had a lot of say. Everybody was great – that was the other genius part, it would never have happened without their commitment, their commitment to our time line and turnaround. It just speaks volumes of what people can actually do if it's a good idea.'

Alongside the 2009 print campaign, which ran on billboards and in the press, Digital Kitchen created a series of internet films that also bent reality, and included vampires appearing on news reports. But it was the simplicity of the poster campaign that caused the most impact, and demonstrated that, when used with flair and imagination, the billboard can still be a creative force in advertising. 'The whole idea of the campaign is to try and get this WTF moment,' says Brandes. 'You're walking down the street and you go, "wait, did I just see that?" It's completely disruptive and that was totally the goal.'

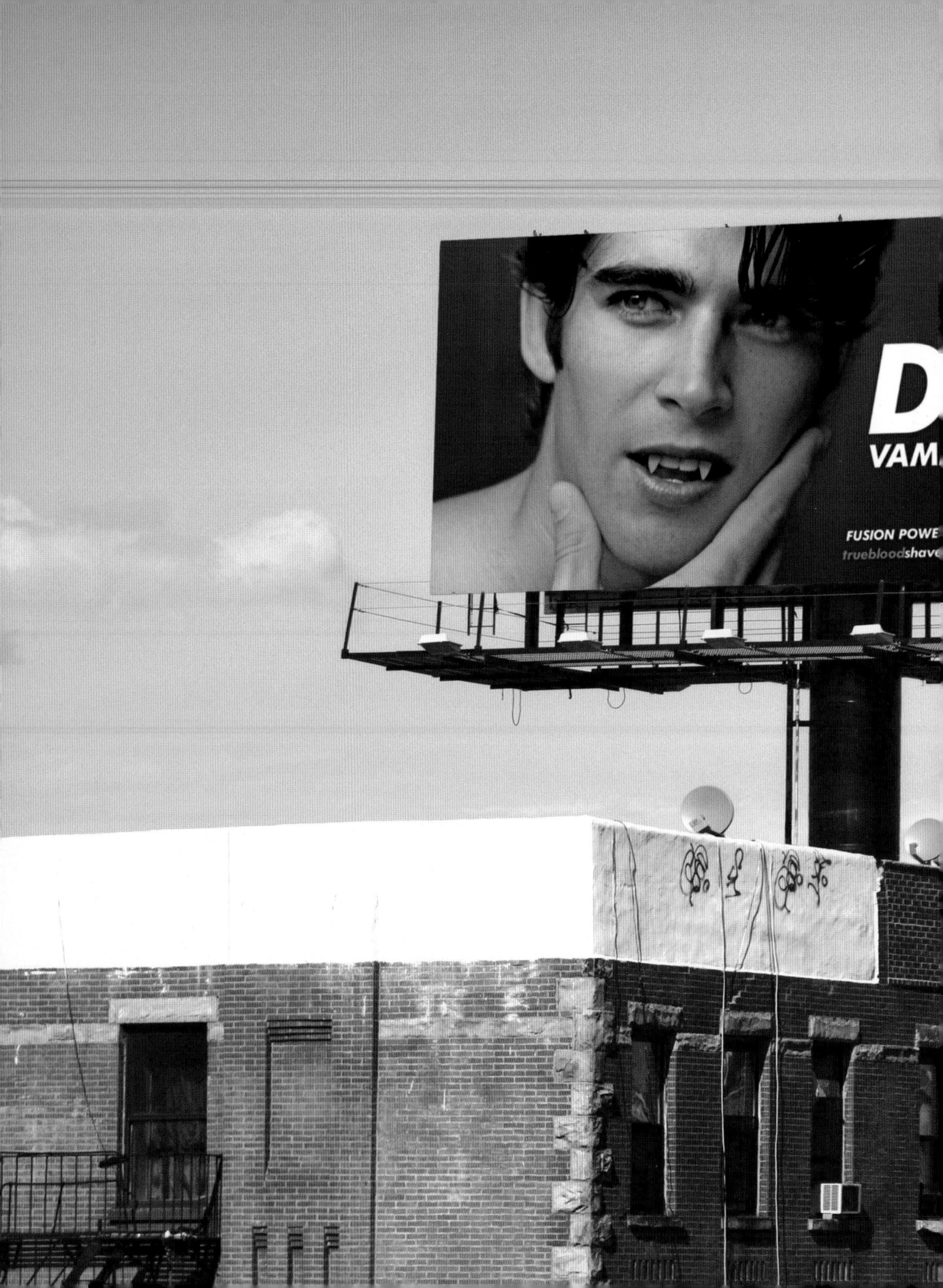
D
VAM
FUSION POWE
truebloodshave

EADSEXY
RES PREFER THE FUSION SHAVE
TRUEBLOOD SPECIAL EDITION.
Gillette
The Best a Man Can Get™

01

13/

HBO Voyeur

BBDO New York

HBO Voyeur began with an event held in New York, before becoming a global phenomenon via a dynamic and interactive website. The aim of the campaign was to articulate the U.S. television channel's skill for creating great stories. As storytelling in the modern age happens across all media, from television to the internet to conversations in the street, both HBO and its agency, BBDO New York, knew that a simple TV ad stating this wouldn't be enough. Instead, they created a complex and absorbing narrative that played out across a multitude of media, and invited HBO's audience to join in.

'The first brief was to say that HBO were the pre-eminent storytellers,' explains Greg Hahn, executive creative director on the project alongside Mike Smith. 'The big shift we did on that brief was rather than to tell it, we decided to show it. That changed the way we looked at it. Rather than just going out and doing ads that said "HBO do great stuff", we went out and created great content that was HBO-quality.'

The creatives came up with the theme of 'voyeur' based on their own experiences of living in New York City. 'If you look across the street in New York there are 10,000 stories going on all the time,' continues Hahn. 'That is our story device, but we made it HBO-quality stories that are going on. It's a simple thread that connects everything together, this idea of voyeurism.'

'All of us moved to New York at exactly the same time,' continues Smith. 'We came from LA, from Minnesota... other places

02

01 At the centre of the HBO Voyeur campaign is a film featuring a four-storey apartment block with the fourth wall removed, allowing the public to peer inside. The four-minute-long film, which reveals the various dramas that happen to the characters in the block over the course of an evening, was projected life-size onto a wall in downtown New York.

02-04 Production photographs taken during the shoot for the HBO film.

03

04

'Rather than just going out and doing ads that said "HBO do great stuff", we went out and created great content that was HBO-quality.'

05

where we weren't in such close proximity to other people. I remember staring out my bedroom window in New York and watching all these people live their separate lives. I think all of us had that same sort of epiphany that these stories are all around us.'

From this, the creatives came up with the idea to create a four-minute film that allowed viewers to see into a set of apartments within a building and observe the narratives that connect all those dwelling inside. It was decided that the film should initially be projected onto a wall in the city, so that the apartments and people were shown life-size. Such an idea would also link the campaign in people's minds to the classic movies Rear Window and Cinema Paradiso. 'We had the notion of voyeurism and storytelling, and we felt the smartest way to [express this] was to project a cross-section onto the side of a building and show compelling stories there,' says Smith. 'We'd never really seen it done before and knew it was going to be tricky to pull off.'

The first obstacle was finding a space. The team began by looking at media spaces, but found none were suitable, so they handed the job to a location scout instead. 'We were trying to find a place where people could really enjoy it, and stand or sit in front of the building,' explains Brian DiLorenzo, director of integrated production at BBDO. The perfect building was found in the Lower East Side, in an area that, appropriately enough, DiLorenzo describes as 'the Rear Window neighbourhood'. As it wasn't within an area where advertising typically appeared, however, the team had to approach six different city departments to get permission to show advertising in the space.

Then there was the issue of whether the projection would be strong enough for the whole campaign to work. 'We took two feature-film-quality cinema projectors – there were some that existed for outdoor projection – and we doubled them up because we wanted to be a lot brighter than the surrounding light pollution that comes from cities,' says DiLorenzo. 'It was a matter of making sure that we could line up all the pixels in a way that didn't detract in terms of resolution and gave a "pop". The pop is what really helped at the event – it made it seem as if there were a dimension to the building, that it was inside the walls instead of just being projected on the wall.'

BBDO commissioned director Jake Scott to create the film. 'He's a great visual storyteller,' says Smith of the decision, 'and he's incredibly collaborative.' The creatives worked with Scott to devise the various stories that would play out across the building, which contained eight apartments that were all joined by a central stairwell. The key was to create narratives that could be easily understood without sound, so the writers used big physical gestures and created archetypal scenes of comedy and tragedy. 'At the bottom left you had a husband and wife who were arguing, and you realize that the argument is about him leaving because he's having an affair with the woman in the top part of the building,' says Smith. 'Across the hall you have a woman who has a heart attack and dies. On the upper left, you had a couple who were about to give birth. You have a serial killer in one, and you have a couple who are renovating their apartment.'

The film had to be choreographed almost like a dance, and incorporated certain gestures or 'beats' that could be used as cues for the actors. 'There are four of those within each story,' says DiLorenzo, 'if you watch for them you can see them. It's organic, but there are gestures where all of a sudden in each apartment, everyone for a different reason is pointing. Stuff like that was all done to allow the actors to have performances but know that they had some sort of beat so they could work out the timing.'

This timing was vital as Scott shot the film floor by floor, building it up like a layer cake. Two cameras shot the action simultaneously, one filming the left apartment and stairwell, the other the right apartment and stairwell, and then the two

06

05-06 Director Jake Scott gives instructions to the actors on the set for the HBO film.

07

08

07-08 Sketches and storyboards by the advertising agency show how the ideas for the film were developed.

'The thing that was probably most surprising to me was that we put all this content out and we kept writing and making more stories and taking stuff deeper and deeper.... There was a point between all of us when we thought, "is anybody really going to go this deep?"'

films were synched. For the finished film, all four floors were joined together and the ceilings were painted and added in digitally.

While the film was being created, BBDO was working with digital agency Big Spaceship to design the website for the ad campaign, which would carry on the narrative begun in the projection online. Big Spaceship brought the original film into the site, but added the chance for viewers to zoom in and interact with it. They then extended the city, so that users could explore a vast cityscape, where new stories could be discovered. As well as interacting with the site's navigation, users were also offered the chance to choose a soundtrack for the experience online. 'We gave six composers the opportunity to do a soundtrack. They ranged from Clint Mansell, who did the music for Requiem for a Dream, to people from the pop music industry, to traditional feature film composers,' says DiLorenzo. 'Big Spaceship made it so you could literally switch on the fly and hear one of these different compositions.'

The site went live at the same time the projection launched in 2007. The agency gave out invitations to the first screening to help build excitement around it, but once it aired it quickly attracted the attention of the wider media. The projection was a huge success, playing for two long weekends and attracting repeat viewers. 'We could have been shut down for many reasons but they didn't get one complaint from any of the neighbours,' says DiLorenzo. 'We would go back every couple of nights just to check on it ourselves and you'd see people who'd packed sandwiches to bring down to watch it.

09 A dramatic moment during the filming of the HBO Voyeur film.

LEARN MORE
HBO FORUMS
HBO
TERMS OF USE
THESTORYGETSDEEPER.COM

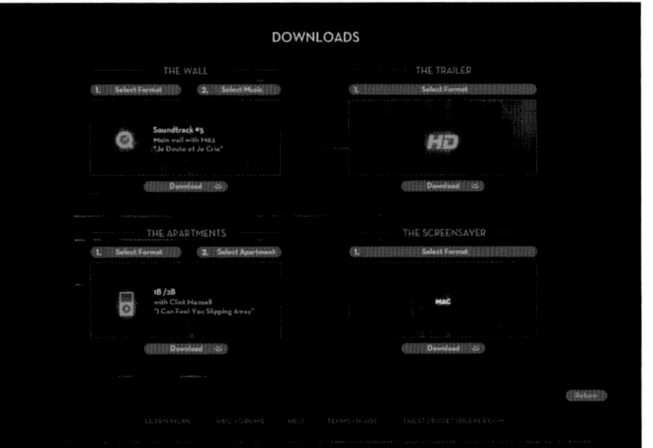
DOWNLOADS
THE WALL
Select Format
Select Music
Soundtrack #5
Download
THE TRAILER
HD
THE APARTMENTS
Select Apartment
THE SCREENSAVER
MAC
Return

Myreson
FUNERAL HOME

10

LEARN MORE
HBO FORUMS
HBO
TERMS OF USE
THESTORYGETSDEEPER.COM

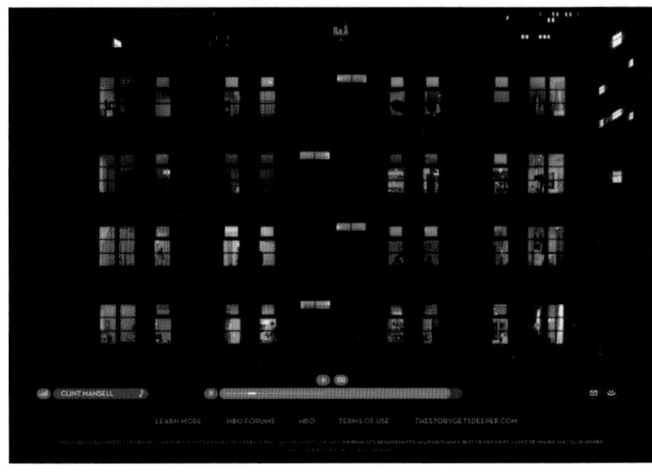
CLINT MANSELL
LEARN MORE
HBO FORUMS
HBO
TERMS OF USE
THESTORYGETSDEEPER.COM

CLINT MANSELL
LEARN MORE
HBO FORUMS
HBO
TERMS OF USE
THESTORYGETSDEEPER.COM

'It was gratifying seeing people talk to each other and figure it out as a group,' he continues. 'It was meant to have this communal thing, and it's too much to see in one sitting. That was another reason we wanted to have the different music as well. We were able to play the soundtracks so every time it would loop there would be one of the other composer's tracks going against it. You'd hear different music and it would highlight different emotions, so you'd pick up things you didn't see in the first round.'

A promo for the project also aired on TV and in cinemas to draw viewers from outside New York to the website. Once there, viewers interacted with the content more quickly than even BBDO expected. 'The thing that was probably most surprising to me was that we put all this content out and we kept writing and making more stories and taking stuff deeper and deeper,' says Smith. 'There was a point between all of us when we thought, "is anybody really going to go this deep?"'

They quickly discovered that people would. Among the new offerings was another film, The Watcher, which viewers could download from HBO On Demand. Clips could also be downloaded to iPods and PSPs, and tips and clues to the stories were sent out to mobile phones. A new character, a fictional blogger, then extended the story via his site, The Story Gets Deeper, which added new twists and turns to the plot. In the end, the team felt forced to announce an end point to the project, and they awarded those who followed it until its final moments with a document announcing that it was over.

While only a small group of dedicated fans completed all of its elements, HBO Voyeur was designed so that it would be comprehensible with only a small amount of contact, and enriching with more. In the end, millions of voyeurs joined in with the different aspects of the campaign, proving that if audiences are offered ad content that is intelligent and absorbing enough, they will eagerly become involved.

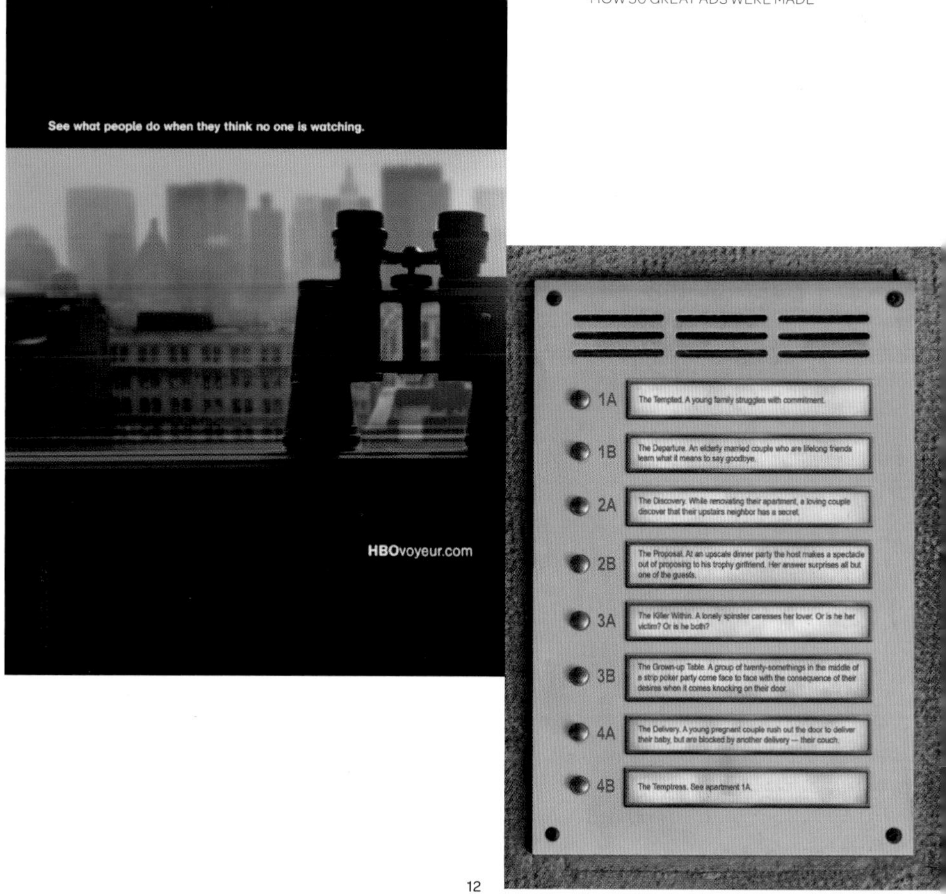

'We wanted to have the different music as well. We were able to play the soundtracks so every time it would loop again there would be one of the other composer's tracks going against it. You'd hear different music and it would highlight different emotions, so you'd pick up things you didn't see in the first round.'

10 At the same time the film aired on the streets of New York, a website was launched, inviting those outside the city the chance to enter into the campaign. The site, designed by digital agency Big Spaceship, showed the film but also gave viewers the chance to engage further with the narrative.

11-12 This programme was given out at the HBO Voyeur live event in New York. It gave brief information about the people living in the different apartments featured in the film, but also led viewers onto the website, where they could discover more treats connected to the campaign.

14/

Honda Cog

Wieden + Kennedy London

When Wieden + Kennedy in London launched its Honda Cog commercial in 2003, it caused surprise, delight and controversy in equal measure. Running at two minutes in length, the film is elegant and seemingly simple, showing an epic chain reaction constructed from parts of the Honda Accord car. Despite being intrinsically linked to the Accord, the spot was in fact originally written in response to a brief for the Honda Civic. 'We wrote this for the Civic because the Civic absolutely felt like the beauty of function,' says Ben Walker, who created the ad alongside Matt Gooden. 'The Civic is Honda's real baby; they're more proud of that car than they are of their racing cars.... For them, the Civic is the embodiment of what makes Honda so brilliant.'

'We thought, what's the best way of showing the beauty of function? We remembered a film by Fischli & Weiss [Der Lauf der Dinge/The Way Things Go], which is an amazing film. We thought, surely we can make something using the car that would have the same beautiful function and show the engineering,' Walker continues. 'Honda loved the idea, but only had six weeks to make the ad, so ended up making something else.' When the Honda Accord brief came along at a later date, though, the client suggested that the team revisit their idea, and work on Honda Cog began. 'I think with all these things there's a series of lucky events that make it fall into place,' says Walker. 'The lucky thing about Cog was that Honda was desperate to turn the Accord into a sector D car, which is more expensive, so they really wanted to tell an engineering and a beauty story. They wanted to raise the level of this car, and they saw that car parts and showing this absolute finesse was a way of doing that. So they bought into it.'

Walker and Gooden began work on the spot by exploring different chain reaction ideas with the car parts, to see whether the idea would even be feasible. The intention was to create a spot that had an evident human touch, which would stand out among the slick CGI styling that was ubiquitous in car ads at the time. From the very start, Walker and Gooden were keen that the chain reaction should be real, and

01-04

'It's an amazing editing job that everyone thinks is one shot.'

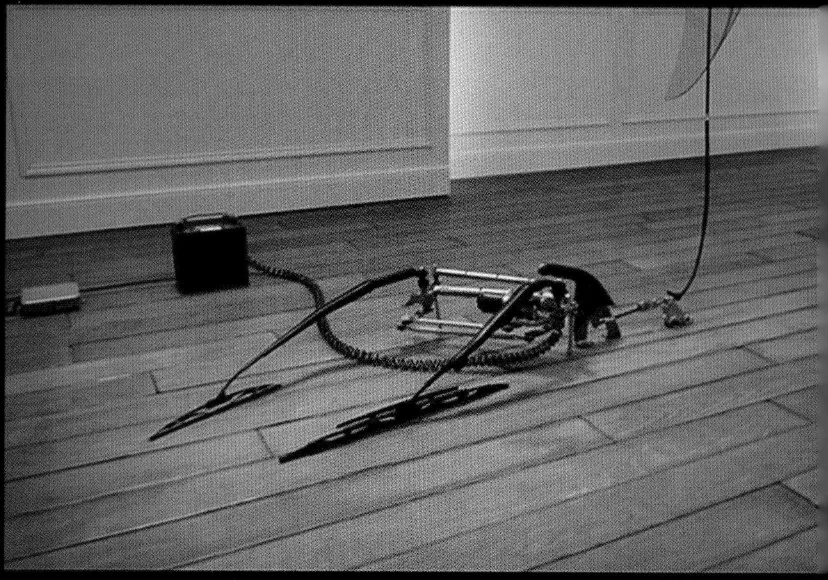

01-04 Stills from the finished Honda Cog commercial. Running at two minutes in length, the ad featured an epic chain reaction made from different parts of the Honda Accord car, including the windscreen wipers and the exhaust pipe.

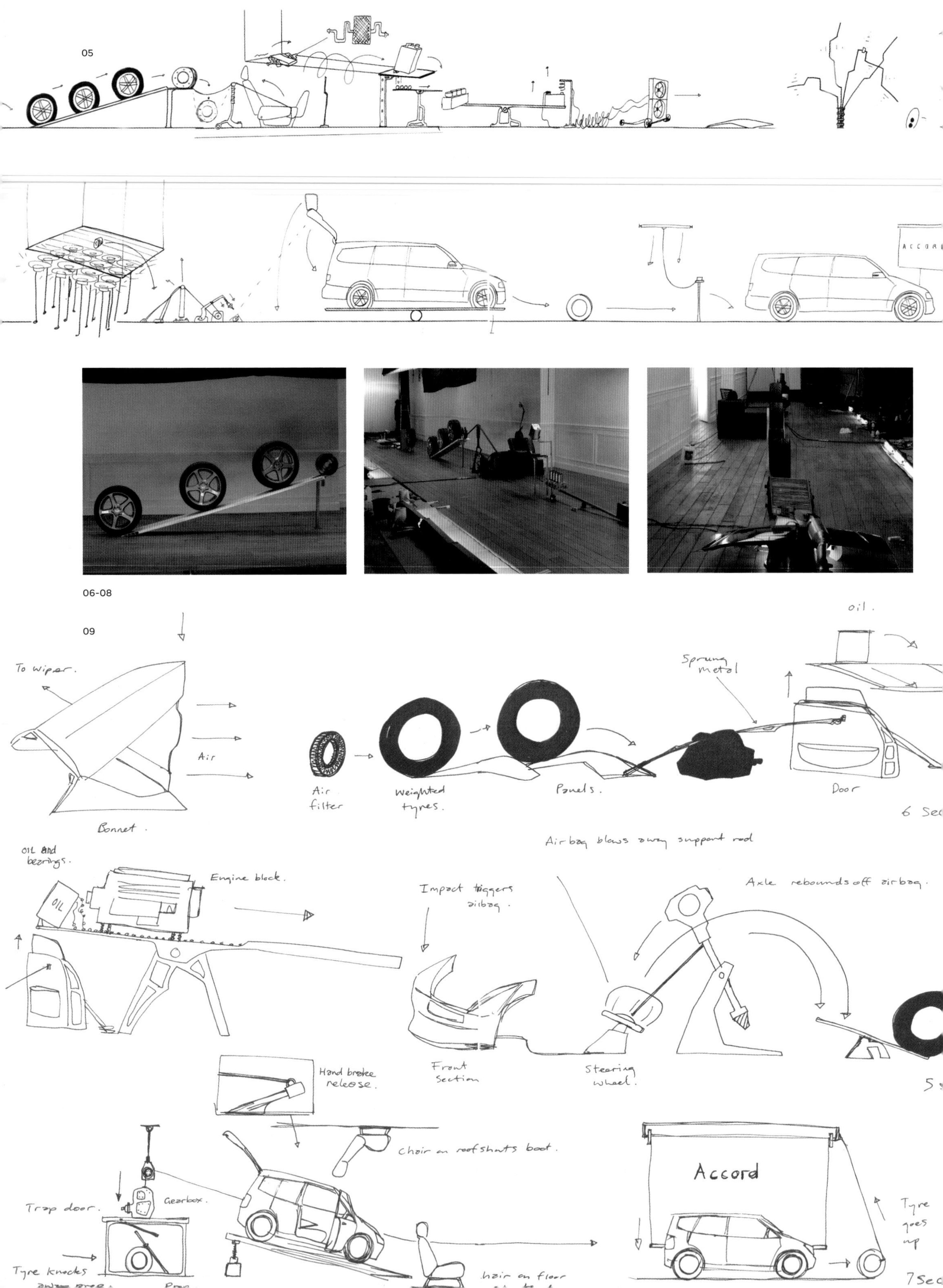
ACCORD
To wiper.
Air
Bonnet.
Air filter
Weighted tyres.
Panels.
Sprung metal
oil.
Door
Airbag blows away support rod
OIL and bearings.
Engine block.
OIL
Impact triggers airbag.
Axle rebounds off airbag.
Front Section
Steering wheel.
Hand brake release.
Chair on roof shuts boot.
Trap door.
Gearbox.
Tyre knocks
Accord
Tyre goes up

05

06-08

09

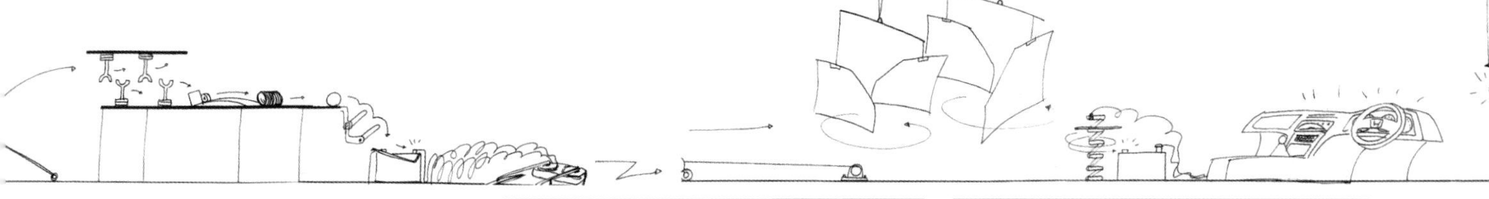

05, 09 Sketches for the Honda Cog ad show the planning for many of the effects that appeared in the final chain reaction.

06-08, 10-12 The team created the set for the shoot in a warehouse in Paris. The set took three months to build.

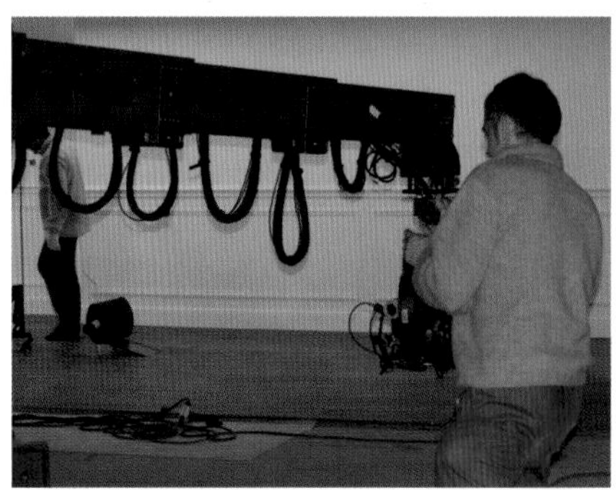

10-12

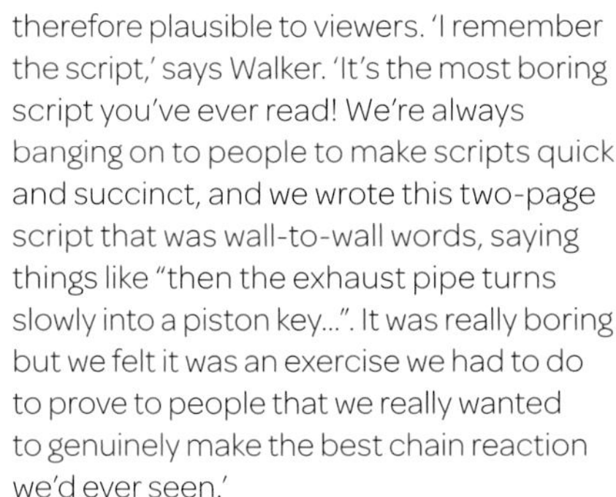

therefore plausible to viewers. 'I remember the script,' says Walker. 'It's the most boring script you've ever read! We're always banging on to people to make scripts quick and succinct, and we wrote this two-page script that was wall-to-wall words, saying things like "then the exhaust pipe turns slowly into a piston key...". It was really boring but we felt it was an exercise we had to do to prove to people that we really wanted to genuinely make the best chain reaction we'd ever seen.'

'What we found in the end, though, is that we wrote this incredibly precise script, but we were totally guessing at everything,' he continues. 'We had ball bearings dropping down into half a tyre and then rolling up and out, and we didn't even know whether a ball bearing could do that. It got to a stage where you had to start testing things.'

At this point, Walker and Gooden commissioned French director Antoine Bardou-Jacquet to work on the project, in part because of a complex animated music video he had directed for musician Alex Gopher, which featured whole cities constructed out of type. 'From his animation stuff, you just knew that he had a detailed mind, and that's what made us choose him,' Walker explains. 'Well, that's what interested us in him. What made us choose him above all the other people we spoke to was because his treatment was not so much about what he was going to film, but the team of people he was going to get together to help build it. He was concentrating totally on the right part of it. He got this amazing team together and said, "if we're going to crack this, we need to have all these people on board". That's why he won the job.'

The team spent a month testing whether the chain reaction would work. Having discovered it would, a further three months were then set aside to build the actual chain. The construction took place in a warehouse space on the outskirts of Paris. 'We used every single minute of the three months,' says Walker. 'In fact, we could have gone on. There are still bits when I see it now... there's a bit just after halfway that I don't think is very good and I think we ran out of time on that. We had this spinning cylinder thing, which span beautifully and knocked something else, and it worked all the way through testing, and then come the shoot it just didn't work and everyone was baffled as to why. So we had to quickly think of something else, and it's not very good what we thought of.'

Despite Walker's concerns, the film is full of amazing moments, all timed to perfection. Tyres roll uphill, windscreen wipers dance. At one point, a tiny rod spins delicately before hitting a connection that starts up the car's engine, and in turn its stereo. The music that pumps out is The Sugarhill Gang's Rapper's Delight, which was chosen over What You Give Is What You Get by The Jam. 'It was quite a big old decision,' says Walker of the music, 'I wanted The Jam, because I thought it was more boy racer, but I think Rapper's Delight is more classic.' The spot then ends with a shot of the finished car and a final comment from Garrison Keillor, the U.S. writer and broadcaster and the 'voice' of Honda, who proclaims, 'Isn't it nice when things just... work'.

The ad only aired on TV a few times, largely because of its length. Much of the momentum around its launch was achieved via the internet, despite it being the early days of viral marketing. Within 24 hours of the ad's launch, the Honda website received a deluge of visitors, many of whom requested a DVD version of the film, in response to an offer made online.

Alongside the accolades, Cog quickly began to also receive criticism. This centred around accusations of plagiarism,

'The lucky thing about Cog was that Honda was desperate to turn the Accord into a sector D car, which is more expensive, so they really wanted to tell an engineering and a beauty story. They wanted to raise the level of this car, and they saw that car parts and showing this absolute finesse was a way of doing that.'

13-15

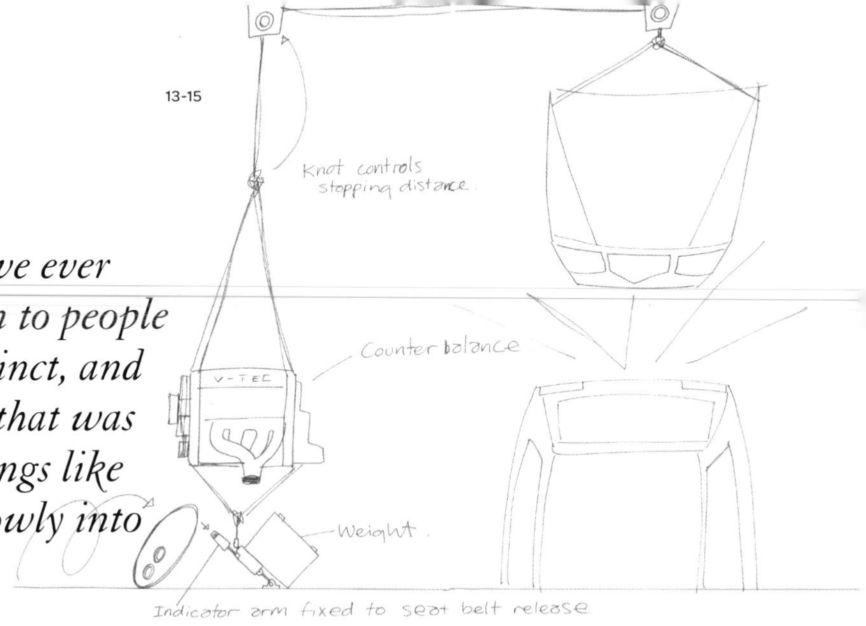

'It's the most boring script you've ever read! We're always banging on to people to make scripts quick and succinct, and we wrote this two-page script that was wall-to-wall words, saying things like "then the exhaust pipe turns slowly into a piston key…."'

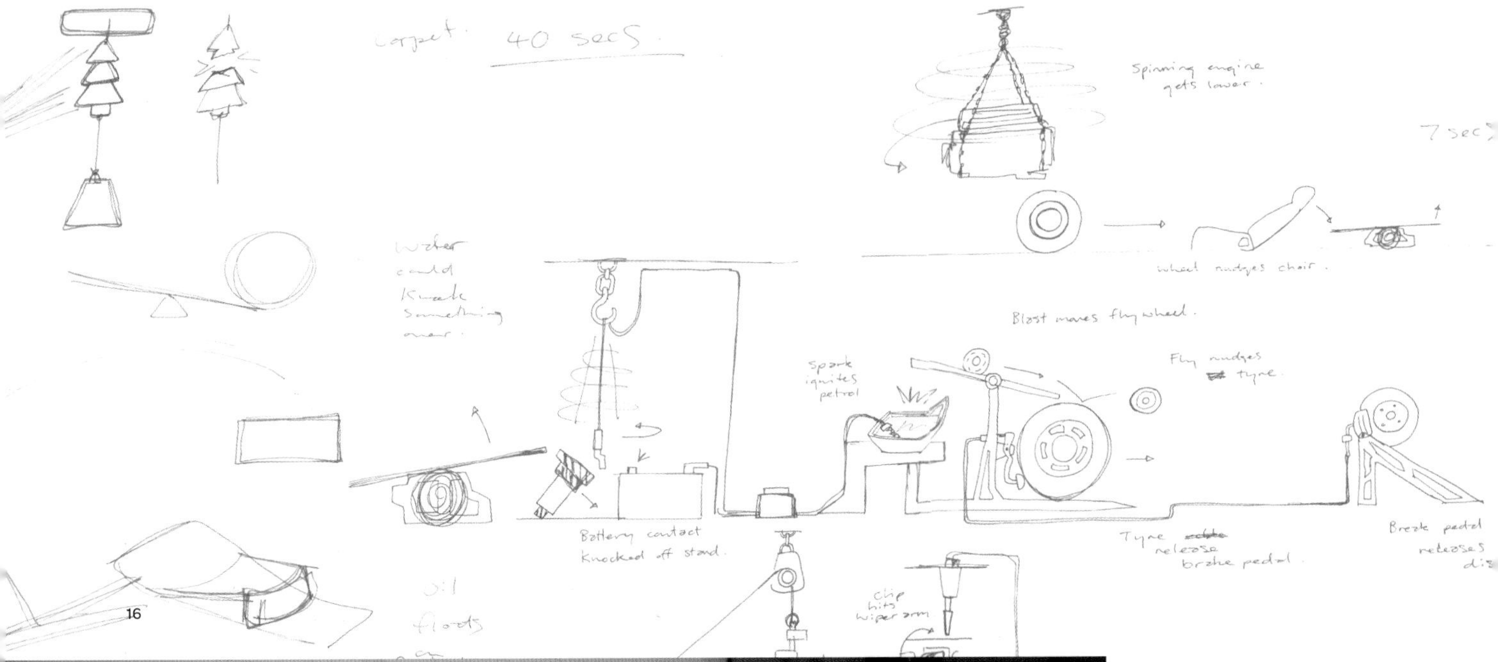

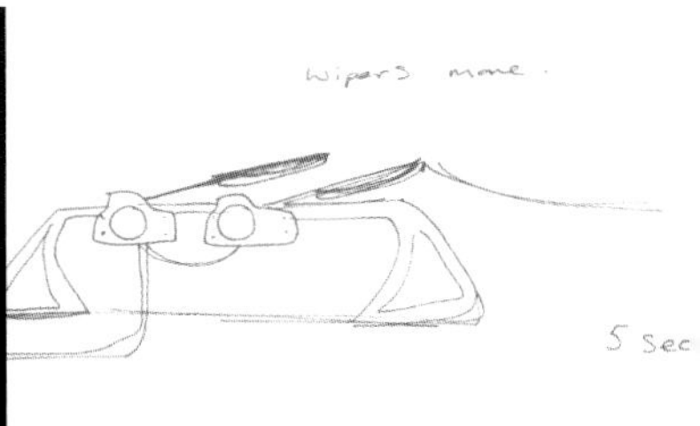

16

13-15 More drawings showing various ideas for how the Honda Accord car parts might be used in the chain reaction. The notes on the sketches are written by the advertising agency creatives, Ben Walker and Matt Gooden.

16-21 Production photographs taken during the construction of the set for the Honda Cog ad, as well as on the shoot itself.

17-21

22-23

24

22-25 Photographs taken on the set for Honda Cog. When the finished film was released, it was rumoured that it had taken over 600 takes to complete, although the creatives now say it was probably around 100. Due to its length, the ad only aired on TV a few times, though was covered in the media across the world and quickly became an advertising sensation.

specifically from the artists Fischli & Weiss, who felt it was too similar to the art film that had informed Walker and Gooden's early ideas for the spot. The art duo threatened to sue, though in the end no lawsuit was brought.

Looking back at the controversy now, Walker and Gooden are adamant that Cog remains distinct from The Way Things Go. 'We got a tape together of hundreds of chain reactions,' says Walker. 'From the beginning of [BBC television series] The Great Egg Race, the chain reaction in The Goonies, Heath Robinson... we had a lot of Heath Robinson stuff in. We had this wonderful tape, which Fischli & Weiss's film was bang in the middle of. Of course, if you're going to attempt a chain reaction, if you haven't looked at what they've done, you'd be an idiot. We never denied that, but we wanted to do something different. People still argue about it, but we genuinely set out to do something different. The film from start to finish took six months, and if we'd just been ripping off what they'd done, we could have done it in six weeks.'

Regardless of these critical rumblings, Cog went on to be hugely influential, especially on other ads. As testament to its success, a number of spoof versions were created for other brands, and the ad arguably began a trend for using authentic stunts in ads (instead of CGI) that lasted for years, spawning spots such as Skoda's The Baking Of (see page 164) and Sony's Balls (see page 172).

A surprising amount of mythology grew up around the ad too, much of which turns out to have been exaggerated. It was rumoured that the spot had taken more than 600 takes to complete, though in fact it was probably around 100, according to Walker and Gooden. They also dispel the enduring myth that it was filmed in one complete run. 'The only reason we didn't do that in the end was because we couldn't find a studio that was literally long enough,' says Walker. 'So Antoine's idea was to split the ad in half and sew the two halves together.' To counter this element of fakery, the team made sure that if the space were large enough, the chain reaction as it stands would indeed have worked. In the end though, there were several different joins in the final spot. 'That's the amazing thing about that film – there are actually three or four edit points in there,' says Walker. 'Because the flow of it was slightly better on one take than on another, not because you couldn't do it. And you can't see those bloody joins, which is incredible.'

'A lot of it's to do with timing as well,' Walker continues. 'Because each time you did the chain reaction, it lasted a different amount of time. Obviously if we're doing something in exactly two minutes, you couldn't have that – so we had to speed bits up, slow bits down, chop new bits in. It was very complicated, and in fact as an editing job, it was quite amazing. It's an amazing editing job that everyone thinks is one shot.'

25

15/

Honda Grrr

Wieden + Kennedy London

The Honda Grrr ad started with a song. The 90-second-long television and cinema spot, by Wieden + Kennedy in London, forms part of The Power of Dreams series of commercials for the Japanese car brand, a set of ads that are notable for wildly varying in style. Grrr followed Cog, a hugely successful ad for the Honda Accord that featured an elegant chain reaction of car parts (see previous ad). By contrast to the restrained sophistication of Cog, Grrr is brash and exciting, incorporating psychedelic animated visuals and a jaunty tune. The aim of the ad was to promote Honda's new i-CTDi diesel engines.

01-10 Stills from the finished commercial reveal the bright colours and general exuberance of the Honda Grrr ad. The ad was 90 seconds in length and set to a song performed by Garrison Keillor.

Despite the fact that Honda designer Kenichi Nagahiro had designed the new engine from scratch, Wieden + Kennedy were pitching to a tough audience, who at the time were deeply suspicious of diesel. Rather than ignore this resistance, the creatives addressed it directly, and introduced the notion of 'positive hate' in an attempt to get audiences to rethink their views. 'With each ad you want to see a different aspect of the Power of Dreams,' explains Grrr writer Michael Russoff, 'so that gives you licence to do something different each time – you're meeting the power of dreams from a slightly different viewpoint. So the power of dreams in this case could be about positive hate – doing something, making something, ripping something apart, changing it. Whereas in Cog the power of dreams was a fine, beautifully constructed, well-made power of dreams.'

'With each ad you want to see a different aspect of the Power of Dreams, so that gives you licence to do something different each time – you're meeting the power of dreams from a slightly different viewpoint.'

01-10

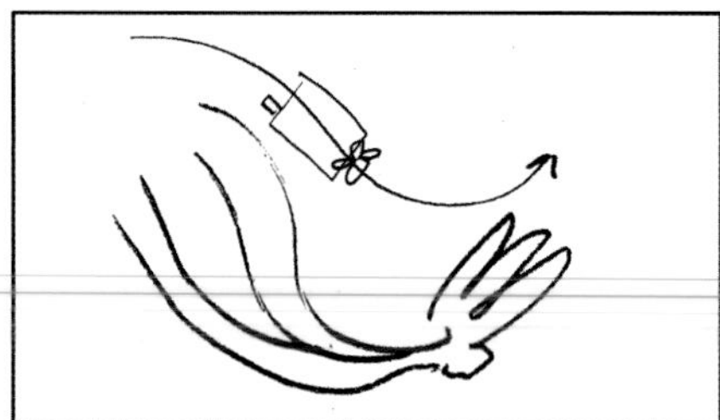

11

11-12 Images by Honda Grrr's directors, Smith & Foulkes, show how the animation for the ad was slowly developed.

13 Sketch from a very early storyboard for the ad, by creatives at the ad agency Wieden + Kennedy London.

14-15 Images sent by the directors to the ad agency as part of their pitch to work on the ad. Included in their early suggestions was an idea to have boy statues pissing on the engines, though this was dropped from the final spot.

13

Grrr features bunnies, seals and rainbows changing a set of old, smoky diesel engines into the shiny new Honda version, all set to a deeply catchy soundtrack. 'It was always going to be musical,' continues Russoff. 'We were thinking, "how do we make people excited about something like a diesel engine? We could do a song.... We could do the greatest jingle that's ever been done, we could take people with us." The musical thing felt like a good way of doing it. We didn't want it to be aggressive hate. We thought music could take the edge off.'

The song in the ad is written by Russoff, and invites us to 'hate something, change something, make something better'. Although in this instance the sentiment applies to the diesel engine, part of the song's charm is that its expression could refer to any number of situations. In talking about the writing process, Russoff makes it seem simple. 'I remember trying out some songs I'd written already, and in one of them, which had completely different lyrics, "hate something, change something" just fitted.... The atmosphere felt folksy, warm and charming. Then we just wrote a couple more verses and Bob's your uncle!'

'We took a guitar into the meeting with the client,' Russoff continues, 'I don't think they'd had that before. We performed it. I think you have to go for it – make them feel what you feel about it. They loved it – it's the only time I've been in where they've said "we want it to be like that, that feeling that you just had there, just make that".'

Unusually, the creative team recorded the song before approaching any directors to work on the animation. A consistent element to the Power of Dreams ads is a voiceover by U.S. writer and broadcaster Garrison Keillor. Usually each ad involves Keillor performing a speaking part, but here the creatives were keen that he be the one to sing the song. 'He took a bit of convincing to sing,' recalls Russoff. 'I remember being very nervous about asking him; we sort of worked up to it. I knew he could sing because I'd heard him sing on other stuff. Also with the Honda ads, you always want to find something else to do with Garrison, so we thought, "let's have him sing!"'

'We took a guitar into the meeting with the client. I don't think they'd had that before. We performed it. I think you have to go for it – make them feel what you feel about it. They loved it.'

'He wasn't sure in the beginning, and it was touch and go whether or not he'd do it. But he did it very naturally. Sean [Thompson, a creative on the ad] is whistling on it – he had a wonderfully pathetic whistle. Then we're all backing singers. Usually with Garrison you just get a couple of takes and that's that. You take what you're given with him. Often that's a good thing, because he's got his own way of doing it. That's not what you heard in your head... but it's right. I think we did a few takes and that was it.'

The song opens with a spoken introduction, in which Keillor invites the audience into the story by saying 'here's a little song for anyone who's ever hated, in the key of grrr'. Charming and simple, the

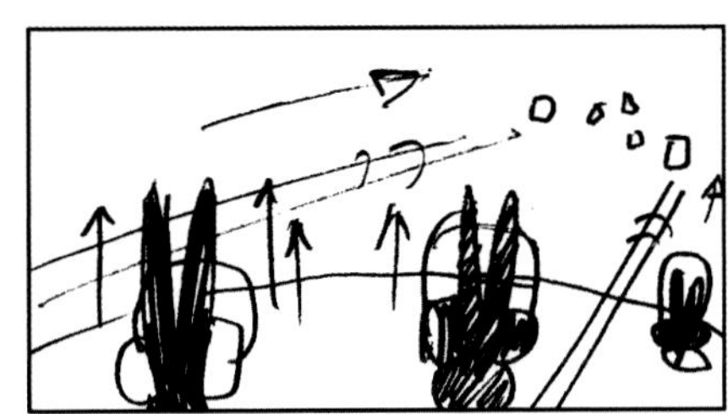

12

intro in fact required quite a lot of protection by the creatives to make it in. 'Even that little introduction felt like we were doing something a bit different,' explains Russoff. 'An ad has to start straight away because you only have a short amount of time... and suddenly here was this different tone to begin with. I remember really protecting that first ten seconds throughout the whole process, to keep that magical slow beginning that people aren't expecting.'

With the song complete, the creatives began looking for an animation director to create the visuals for the ad. At this stage the storyboards by the creatives were minimal, although the notion of old engines flying through the space was in place. Such a loose visual brief, coupled with a strong soundtrack, proved popular with the directors that Wieden + Kennedy approached, and a buzz began to form around the script even at this early stage.

A number of excellent pitches were submitted, though directing team Smith & Foulkes' ideas stood out. 'I think we described their visual style at the time as if Liberace had designed a golf course or something,' says Russoff. 'It was gloriously camp and over the top, yet really charming. For their pitch they'd done some frames of hate world, and there were peeing statues [these were dropped from the final film], the engine flying through and it just looked amazing. You just looked at it and knew you hadn't seen it before – it was a bit of a no-brainer really.'

'Anything just silly, but really quite ornate,' is how Smith & Foulkes describe the type of imagery they wanted to create for the ad. They cite visual references such as Chinese propaganda art, Bollywood, and,

14-15

16

'The web five years ago really felt five years ago and the limitations were enormous, but funnily enough that made everyone a little more creative.'

17-18

16, 19-21 Work-in-progress images for the design of the Honda Grrr game by Unit9. The game was free to play online and released at the same time as the ad.

17-18 Screenshots of the finished game. The game continued the message of the ad, with players encouraged to turn bad things into good things to collect points.

22 A sketch by Unit9 shows how the game's detailed structure was planned.

as Russoff guessed, Liberace. The directors introduced the idea of using positive imagery to turn the squadron of old diesel engines into the new Honda one. 'It was key for us that it wasn't just beautiful images, it was also comedy, there was humour and wit to it, and a narrative flow that you could actually follow,' they say. The flow of the ad was in fact the only point of tension between the creatives and the directors on the job, with the creatives wanting a left-to-right, platform game-style progression, while the directors wanted to create a more expansive world. The end result contains aspects of both.

'I've never worked with directors I've trusted so much,' says Russoff. 'Maybe because it was animation. But there was so much they were doing that was right – I remember the first time I saw the rabbits with the earmuffs and thinking "that's crazy, but great".' Wieden + Kennedy endeavoured to give Smith & Foulkes space to work, without breathing down their necks too much. 'Let them be brilliant at what they're brilliant at, give them that freedom,' says Russoff. 'I think if I was directing that's what I'd want from a client. I think sometimes creatives feel a bit threatened by that. It's just crazy – if you're going to spend a long, hard time thinking who's the best person to direct it, when you give them the job, give them the job. Don't get in the way of it.'

Smith & Foulkes met regularly with the creatives to show them the development of the ad over the four-month animation process. The trust that Russoff speaks of is vital in the making of an animated work, as it is often only near the end that the full complexity of the piece will be seen. Up until then, there are only gestures of what's to come, yet the early decisions that are made about the timing and the direction of the piece are vital, and usually final. 'We work slightly differently from live action in a lot of ways,' say Smith & Foulkes, 'because we almost edit up front. Before we start on the job, the editing is from the storyboard and you make an animatic, so you get the flow. Especially when we already had the song, you could almost understand the flow of what's happening from thumbnail sketches. And that's what you make – as opposed to live action, where you shoot reels of stuff and then shape it into a story at the end.'

That's not to say that animation is entirely without spontaneity. 'Animators are like actors,' the directors continue. 'We have to direct them into a performance. They do stuff sometimes that's amazing that you don't expect, and that really works better than anything we could come up with.... Or they do it really badly and have to do it over and over again until they've got it right.'

Released in 2004, the commercial that resulted from this excellent working relationship wowed audiences, picking up applause from the both within the ad industry and outside. It also set a new benchmark for the use of animation in ads. 'I think it's interesting since Grrr came out to see how things have changed for animation in commercials generally,' reflect Smith & Foulkes. 'It's tougher to make a statement like that, and for audiences to go "wow, look at that, that's new and different". I think it's become tougher for animation generally to stand out and be surprising.'

19

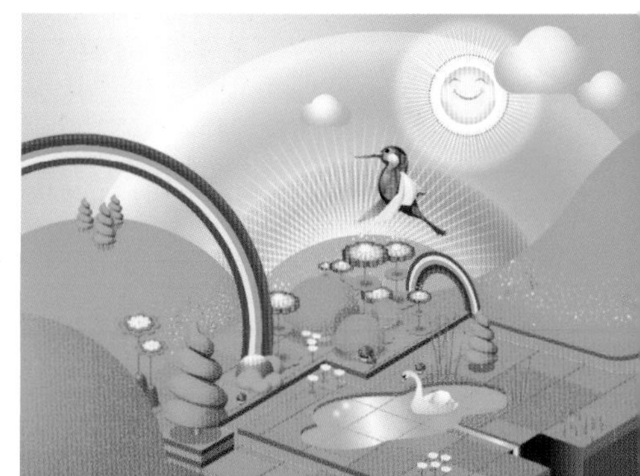

20

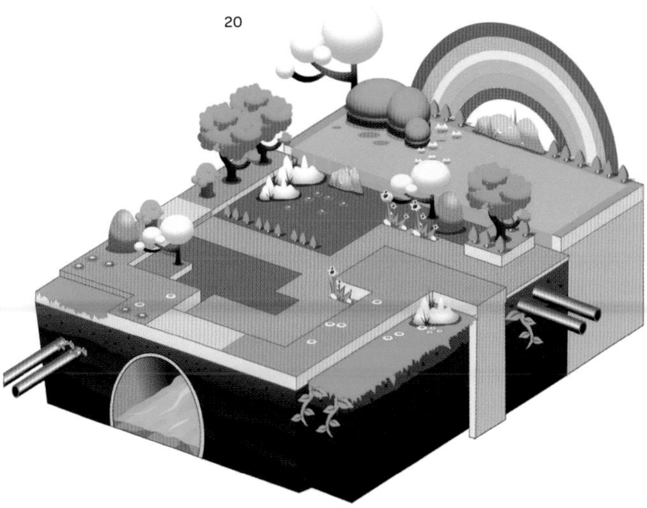

21

22

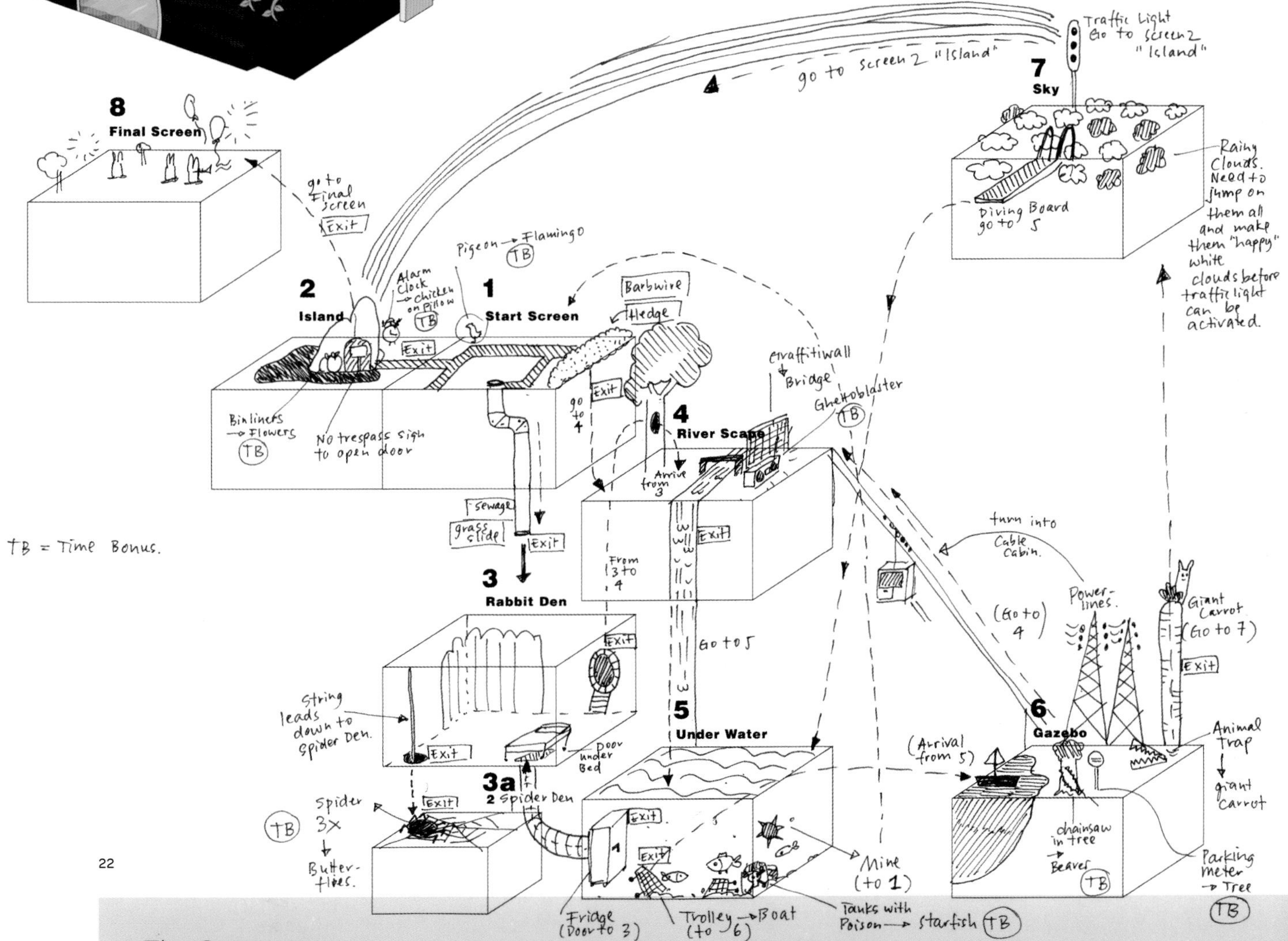

The Grrrgame

honda.co.uk/grrrgame

In addition to the film, the Grrr campaign included print and radio commercials as well as an online presence, in particular a web game that was designed by Unit9 digital production company. The game features characters from the ads that can be manipulated around a board game-style layout. 'The web five years ago really felt five years ago and the limitations were enormous,' says Piero Frescobaldi, creative partner at Unit9, of working on the project. 'But funnily enough that made everyone a little bit more creative. We decided that rather than taking the narrative, we would take the tone of voice and sense of happiness from the ad and turn it into a game where you go around changing things into other things. It was a lot harder to make than it looks – none of the work that was done for the TV commercial could actually be used in the game, because at the time resolutions were very different. We had to recreate an illustrative style that was in line with the ad, without actually being the same. That worked very well, because no one actually feels that there is too much of a difference.' Unit9 animated the game entirely in-house, in just two weeks.

16/

Johnnie Walker
The Man Who Walked Around The World

BBH London

The Man Who Walked Around The World is a six-minute-long film for whisky brand Johnnie Walker, starring actor Robert Carlyle. The 2009 film opens with the ultimate Scottish cliché – a lone bagpiper playing a poignant tune as the mist rolls in across the Highlands. This conventional mood is shattered by Carlyle's opening lines however, as he bellows 'Hey, piper! Shut it!' The actor then takes the viewer on a journey into Johnnie Walker's past, explaining the humble beginnings of the young John – 'just a local farm boy' – and how his father's death when he was 14 years old sparked off a walk that took him from owning a grocer's shop in Kilmarnock to running one of the first major whisky distilleries in Scotland.

As Carlyle strides through the Scottish landscape, passing yaks, barrels and other props for the story along the way, he tells how the Johnnie Walker brand grew under John's son Alexander, and spread across the world. He explains the development of the brand's distinctive square bottle, designed so there would be fewer breakages when being shipped, before turning to John's grandsons, George and Alexander II, who commissioned the brand's iconic logo of the striding Edwardian dandy.

If all this sounds unusually in-depth for an advert, it's because The Man Who Walked Around The World in fact began as an internal brand education film, and was never intended to reach the wider public. 'That's how it started – "do us a brand film",' says Justin Moore of BBH ad agency in London, who wrote the script for the film. 'I quite liked the idea of writing something a bit longer than a minute – I like working with Johnnie Walker, I know the brand and it felt like an interesting technical exercise, to do the research and write a long piece of speech that's cooler than your average brand film.'

From the start, Moore wrote the piece to be shot in one take, a suggestion that was wholeheartedly embraced by the director, Jamie Rafn. 'At the very first meeting, Justin and I discussed how brilliant this would be as a real single take,' says Rafn.

'Mick Mahoney, who was creative director on the project, was also convinced by this somewhat ambitious approach and managed to convince the client that we could pull this off. Needless to say this

01

02

01–02 Actor Robert Carlyle stars in this film for Johnnie Walker. The ad began as an internal film for staff, but proved so popular when leaked online it was eventually released as a short film.

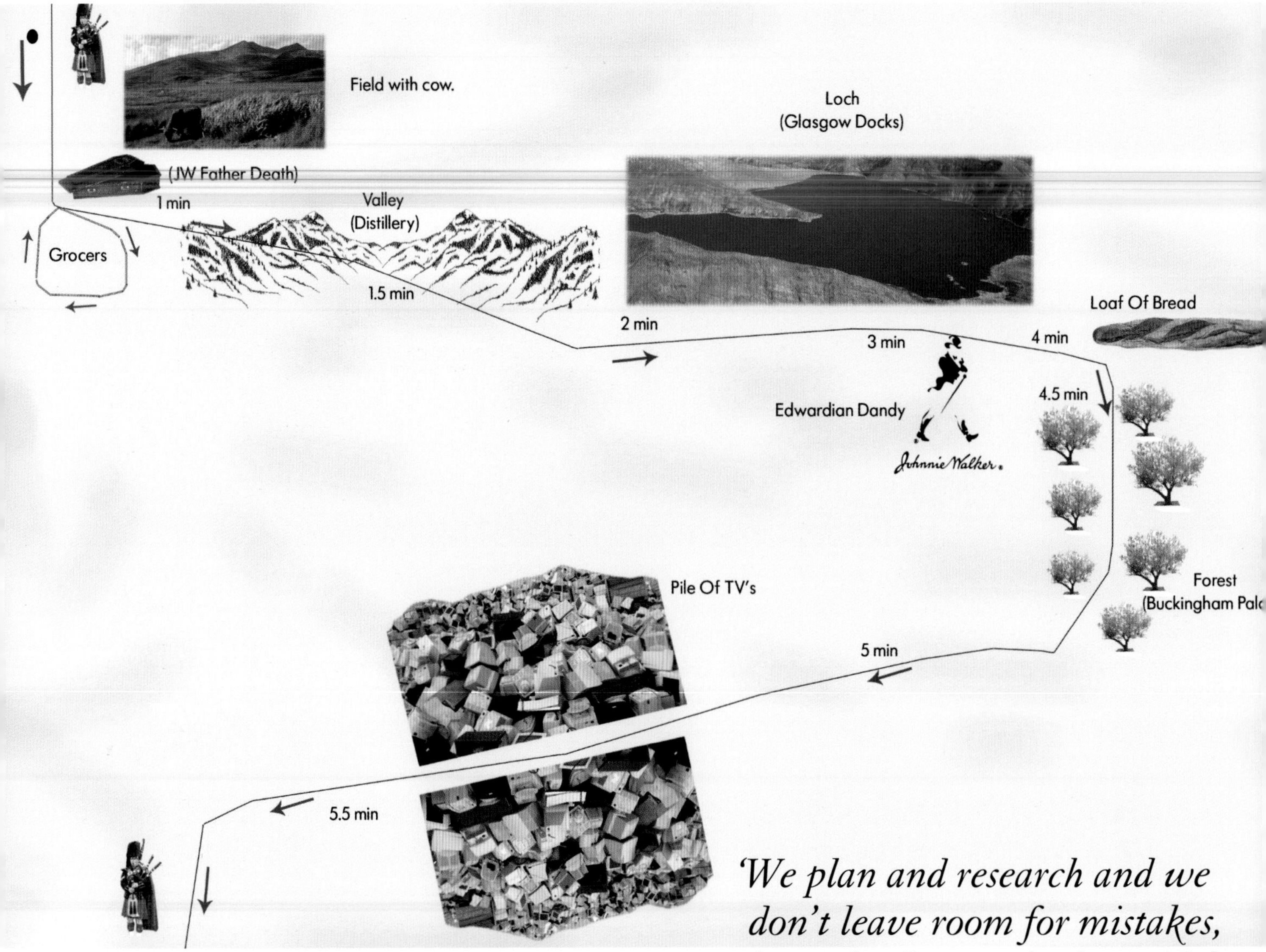

Field with cow.
(JW Father Death)
1 min
Grocers
Valley
(Distillery)
1.5 min
Loch
(Glasgow Docks)
2 min
3 min
4 min
Loaf Of Bread
Edwardian Dandy
Johnnie Walker.
4.5 min
Forest
(Buckingham Pal
Pile Of TV's
5 min
5.5 min

03

04

05

'We plan and research and we don't leave room for mistakes, but mistakes can be beautiful. Mistakes are where you get to new places. We don't often put ourselves in a place where it might go wrong.'

03 BBH copywriter Justin Moore's early plan of some of the objects that would appear during the course of Robert Carlyle's walk.

04-05 Images showing the recording of The Man Who Walked Around The World film.

06-07 Photographs taken during the shoot for the film, showing the 'rickshaw' that held the camera, and various parts of the set that Robert Carlyle had to pass at specific points during the filming.

06

07

08

09

10

08-10 Stills from the finished film. Carlyle completed his performance in just one take, meaning that little post-production was required on the film. The take that was finally used occurred at the end of the last day of filming, as the sun set, giving the film its steely grey look.

'People love beautifully crafted stuff. They love to look at something where they know that the people who made it sweated blood to make it as brilliant as it could be.'

caused us all a certain amount of anxiety.' Such risks are unusual in advertising these days. 'We're rather risk-averse,' admits Moore. 'We plan and research and we don't leave room for mistakes, but mistakes can be beautiful. Mistakes are where you get to new places. We don't often put ourselves in a place where it might go wrong.'

The team knew they needed an excellent actor to carry off such a wordy script in one take. The performance also required perfect timing, to ensure that certain props would be passed on the walk when relevant words in the script were spoken. Carlyle was their number-one choice. 'I was on edge for weeks and weeks, saying, "if he doesn't do it, it's going to be shit, it's got to be him",' remembers Moore. Carlyle's agreement to be part of the project was therefore a great relief, and also confirmed to the creative team that they had written something special. At this stage, however, the original plan for the film to be just an internal film for Johnnie Walker staff remained in place.

The film was shot in three days in Scotland, near Loch Doine. The first day was for rehearsal, with two days reserved for shooting. 'The biggest challenges were technical,' says Rafn. 'My producer, Steve Plesniak, and I did loads of prep. The moment we got the brief we went off to Hyde Park in London with an HDV camera and started walking it through. Steve would read and drop index cards with things like "cow" written on them while I staggered backwards with the camera. By doing this again and again we could work out the spacing between the props and areas where we might need more or less. We then transferred that process up to Scotland on the recce, so that by the time we were ready to shoot we were very well prepared and knew exactly what all the potential problems were from a technical point of view. In spite of all our preparation though, the things we couldn't account for were things like midges. The whole crew had their jumpers pulled over their heads. This was okay for all of us behind camera, but it wasn't really going to work for Robert, who somehow managed to deliver his lines, hit his marks and give an amazing performance while ignoring the multitude of midges swarming around his head.'

Other things went wrong on the shoot, including the rickshaw that was pulling the camera falling over, but the major obstacle the team faced was the one they had set for themselves – the need for the ad to be completed in one take. The first day of shooting resulted in no usable film, and the pressure remained throughout the second, and final, day. 'We had nothing really until the last take on the last day, with light falling,' says Moore. 'We had one take that was alright, and another half a take, and we were wondering if we could trick it together. Post is good enough now... maybe there's something we could do to stitch it together. It was the last take on the last day, with the light going from the sky – that's why it looks so cool and steely, it went dark immediately afterwards – and he nailed it and everyone roared, literally cheered and roared and kissed each other, it was amazing. Then we went home.' The film was polished in post-production, including Carlyle post-synching the vocals, but the team strived to keep the authenticity of the one take. 'We wanted it to be authentic, to be honest,' says Moore. 'But it should look really lovely as well, it should be beautiful, it should be a joy to watch.'

The film reached the wider world by accident. Initially leaked online, it began to gain attention but was rapidly removed by the team. Eventually though, it was decided that it should have a broader life on the internet. 'I think everyone realized that that's the world now, that stuff cannot be put in a box and expected to stay there,' says Moore. 'It's just how it goes; if people like stuff, they tell other people about it. We talk digitally, we have a whole existence in another place.... I'm really pleased, because you did feel a little sad that it was only ever going to be seen at sales conferences and by people who had the right log-in for the Johnnie Walker intranet.'

'I was surprised by its popularity online,' Moore continues, 'because I thought it was a bit weighty and a bit wordy to live in that world. But I think that was why it was interesting as well, and it made me think that we need to think more smartly about what people want to watch. People love stories – that's eternal and unchanging – and people love great performances. And actually, people love beautifully crafted stuff. They love to look at something where they know that the people who made it sweated blood to make it as brilliant as it could be.'

17/

Microsoft Xbox Halo 3

TAG/McCann Worldgroup San Francisco

When Microsoft released its third game in the Xbox Halo series in 2007, it wanted its marketing to do more than simply sell the product. 'Halo 3 aimed to be the biggest entertainment debut in history,' says Taylor Smith, global communications director at Microsoft. 'We wanted to make an entertainment statement – this is gaming, gaming has arrived as an entertainment medium, think about it in the same vein that you think about blockbuster movies.' This was no small ambition. While video games have achieved a huge cultural impact, influencing everything from cinema to advertising, there is still often a perceived computer games 'type'. This is particularly true when it comes to the genre of science fiction war games, the territory that Halo is in.

'Halo 3 aimed to be the biggest entertainment debut in history. We wanted to make an entertainment statement – this is gaming, gaming has arrived as an entertainment medium, think about it in the same vein that you think about blockbuster movies.'

01-02 At the heart of the complex Halo 3 campaign is a film depicting an epic battle. Rather than filming with actors, the war scenes were hand-crafted using tiny figures on a giant diorama; these images are stills from the final film.

01-02

'We came up with this idea of honouring a hero, the way that humanity has always honoured heroes. Which is something that we figured everybody could relate to.'

03

The Halo games are centred on Master Chief, a cybernetically enhanced human soldier who is engaged in a battle against an alliance of alien races called the Covenant. The first two games in the series proved hugely successful, but with the third Microsoft wanted to reach a wider audience than simply the fans of the previous episodes. 'It really has mass appeal,' says Smith. 'The product was built to do that – it was the first Halo game on Xbox 360, so the graphics and the game play and all that sort of stuff were meant to really dazzle people and appeal to a wider audience. But we knew we had a lot of work to do from a marketing standpoint to take it out to a broader set of consumers.'

The ad agency, TAG (now known as agencytwofifteen) in San Francisco identified three different target audiences that the marketing had to speak to. 'We needed to talk to people that were within the Halo core; we needed to talk to entertainment enthusiasts who had never even bought a video game, much less owned an Xbox; and then there were people who were fence-sitters, between the two,' say Scott Duchon and John Patroulis, creative directors on the project. 'So when we briefed our teams on it they all laughed at us a little bit, that we were embarking on such a huge undertaking.'

They did come up with an idea, however, which was to step away from the specifics of the Halo story and focus the advertising on a more general notion of soldiers and warfare. 'We came up with this idea of honouring a hero, the way that humanity has always honoured heroes,' Duchon and Patroulis continue. 'Which is something that we figured everybody could relate to. If you were inside the Halo core, you'd take that on and go "that's cool, that's what I've always liked about him", and anybody outside of that would go "the fact that I missed [the first two games] is okay, because there's something really compelling and emotionally resonating for me".'

The creatives drew on classic heroic tales such as Beowulf and the legends of King Arthur as inspiration for building their own mythology around Master Chief. They proposed building a 'virtual museum', centred on a giant diorama that would depict battle scenes and war stories in a format that people could understand from having experienced similar historical exhibits in real museums. The diorama would be used across all the marketing for the Halo 3 game. The intention was to create a sophisticated film, set to classical music and featuring no game footage – all techniques far removed from typical computer games marketing.

TAG commissioned director Rupert Sanders to work on the project. 'My treatment really focused on how to create the diorama and the story to be told within,' he says. 'My first decision was that it should be a real object, that could be exhibited in a museum. A handcrafted piece that used no digital effects and abided by the rules of a diorama, i.e. anything we saw in motion had to be held there as if viewed in a museum. We looked at a lot of modelmaking, mainly depicting World War II scenes and mostly from hobbyists. We also looked at museum dioramas and Jake & Dinos Chapman's Hell. The challenge was to create emotional scenes and movement with frozen figures.'

'I wrote a war story that told of a battle that had turned against the marines, and tried to capture the fear and horror of war,' Sanders continues. 'It started with a group of soldiers trapped in a bunker, moved out through streets where marines were being decimated, and then moved out across a polluted river where marines were caught in the mud while being fired upon by banshees from above. It then moved up to a heavily defended bridge and then to a mountain swarming with hundreds of enemies. The story finally climbed up this hill where a Christ-like Master Chief was held aloft by Chieftans – the battle looks lost, but then we see the primed grenade in his hand and he looks up to the camera as if to say "the battle is not lost, yet".'

Xbox loved the idea and work began on the diorama, which grew beyond anybody's initial expectations. 'We had envisioned something that was the size of a room, then kept getting reports back from the teams building it, who were just pouring their hearts and souls into making this thing much bigger, and much grander, than frankly we were paying for,' says Taylor Smith. 'It was one of those things where you take a brand like Halo, which people are already interested in, and you put a really nice idea around it, get good people involved and it just keeps going and going to a bigger and more exciting place than you could even imagine. It wound up being the size of a giant warehouse – it was massive in scale. All the characters were handcrafted. Really amazing.'

Creating each individual soldier was a complex process, as Rupert Sanders recalls. 'We decided to make 3D scans of actors and ourselves in various emotional states (I am a crying soldier, hiding behind his rifle). These were then outputted and painted and attached to bodies in pre-determined

04

06

05

07

03-04 The team spent weeks carefully creating the giant diorama, before then shooting the Believe film and other films for the campaign within it.

05 The diorama grew beyond everyone's initial expectations: the final set was the size of a giant warehouse, and sections had to be built outside.

06 To give personality to the characters, the team made 3D scans of people's faces in various emotional states, which were then painted onto the figures.

07 Each figure was individually designed and painted before being placed within the diorama.

08

08-09 Storyboards were used to map out the dramatic scenes that would appear in the final film.

10-14 The film saw the Halo games' hero, Master Chief, and his soldiers pitched against an alliance of alien races called the Covenant. Every scene was carefully built by hand.

10

09

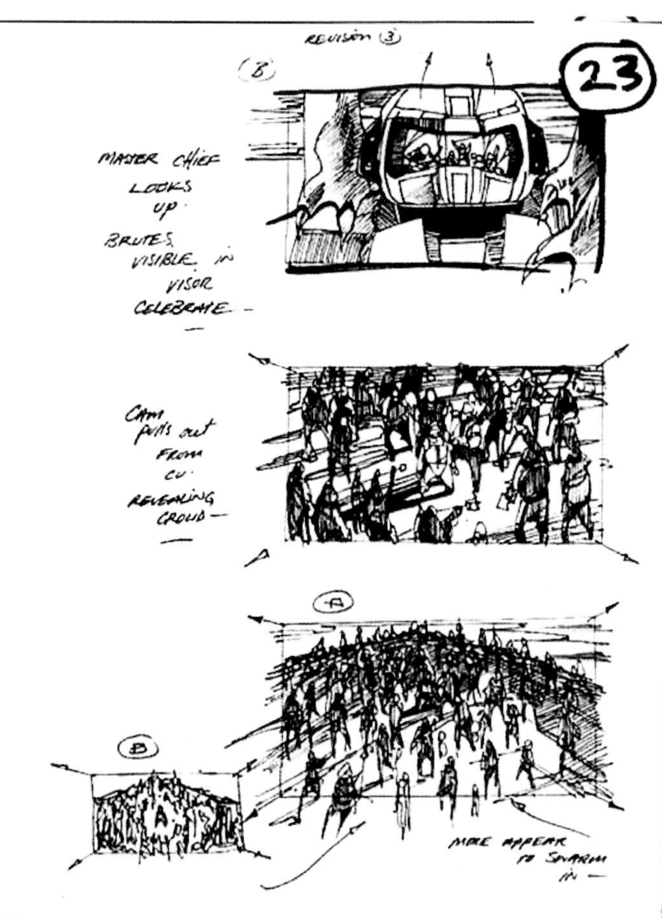

11

12

13

14

'It was one of those things where you take a brand like Halo, which people are already interested in, and you put a really nice idea around it, get good people involved and it just keeps going and going to a bigger and more exciting place than you could even imagine.'

15

16

postures that were required for each scene. This was done by Alan Scott at Stan Winston Studios (now Legacy Effects), who created all the handpainted heads, as well as 500 marines and 1,500 enemy brutes and Chieftans.'

Sanders worked with New Deal Studios to create the sets for the action sequences. The diorama featured trenches and explosions, destruction and despair. In fact, the violence depicted was so great as to cause some concern among the creatives that the film would be banned. 'Everyone had thrown themselves in and built this big, beautiful diorama, and we're shooting it, and as the days are going by, it just became more and more apparent that we really had created this incredibly violent piece,' say Duchon and Patroulis. 'Which is what we all got excited about, but we had to make sure that this thing could air.' In the end, the ad benefited by being a model, as using figurines allowed the team to show imagery that would have been banned in an ad that used real actors. There was also concern not to offend anyone, which was a particular worry regarding some extra web films made as part of the campaign, where veterans looked back on their days on the battlefield. 'Microsoft as a client didn't want to get anyone upset at them, and we certainly didn't want to create a bad PR story for Xbox or Halo,' say Duchon and Patroulis. 'But we showed a lot of care and sensitivity. We were all amazed by the response from veterans, and from people who are serving in the military overseas. There were lots of comments on YouTube saying things like "this makes me feel proud of serving". But we could have made this whole thing and someone could have said "nope, the way Iraq is right now, we're not going to run this".'

The finished campaign broke in a number of different stages. Before the main diorama film was released on TV and in cinemas, a number of web films were seeded online. A website was then launched when the main film aired, offering a flythrough of the diorama and more detail of the idea. In addition, the team made a making-of film, which rather than showing the making-of an ad campaign, remained within the fiction TAG and Xbox had created and showed the making-of a monument to war, as if the events shown in all the films were real. Initially there were plans to exhibit the diorama in various venues, but this proved prohibitively expensive. Sections were taken from it and displayed in retail spaces, however, and an exhibition of still photographs taken in the diorama were shown at the IMAX cinema in London as part of the campaign.

Xbox's approach to advertising Halo 3 was risky, but the elegant films struck a chord with audiences, leading to Halo 3 becoming the fastest pre-selling game in history. The campaign also achieved the ambitions laid out by Microsoft at the start: the game made a cool $170 million in sales on the first day of its release, making it the biggest launch in entertainment history.

15-18 The film showed scenes that were filled with violence and despair, but due to being created using models, rather than actors, it escaped censorship.

17

18

BELIEVE

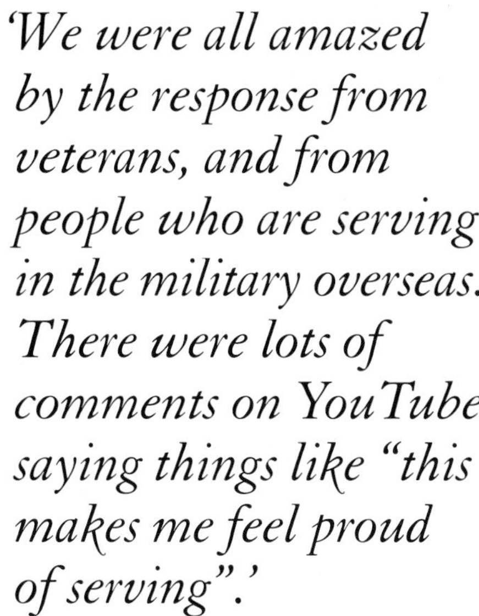

'We were all amazed by the response from veterans, and from people who are serving in the military overseas. There were lots of comments on YouTube saying things like "this makes me feel proud of serving".'

19-25 Stills from the final Believe film.

18/

Microsoft Xbox
Mosquito; Champagne
BBH London

'When we did the Xbox launch [in 2002], Sony PlayStation was leading the market. They were leading the market to a point where they were defining all the codes of the video games category. Video games were equal to Sony PlayStation.' When Microsoft decided to release the Xbox, its first ever games console, it hired BBH advertising agency in London to create its European launch campaign. But as Fred Raillard, the creative on the project (alongside his partner Farid Mokart), explains, the team faced a major problem: the dominance of the Xbox's key competitor, Sony. Not only was the PlayStation console itself hugely popular, but so was its marketing, which was cool and different, and influential.

The Xbox launch needed to present an alternative. 'We had to change the centre of gravity of this market,' Raillard continues. 'We had to shake up the rules in order to just be seen.' Xbox faced other problems too. 'We knew that our console was not better than Sony in terms of quality,' admits Raillard. 'It was way weaker in terms of the number of games. We only had eight games at the launch, and Sony had 3,000, so it was a really hard launch.... We had to change the way people thought about this market. We had this idea that the most interesting thing when you're playing video games doesn't happen inside the screen, but happens inside the room. That's the starting point – Sony was talking only about the experience inside the game, and we decided to talk about the effect of that video game on people in real life. Which is now the basis of the communication for the Wii, for instance, but at that time it was very new.'

Fred & Farid (working for BBH at the time though they later started their own agency) focused the campaign on the idea of play. 'We decided to change the perception of video games by talking about fundamentally what playing means,' says Raillard. 'Kids play, but by getting older, we play less and less. We have rules – we have to win the game. We thought this was something that was very essential and central – playing – and we thought that maybe the best way to launch Xbox was not to talk about video games, but to talk about playing. We would attach the launch to a bigger idea, which is the place of playing in our lives.'

After writing 'about 100 pages of ideas', the team isolated two, both of which emphasized the importance of play, though in totally different ways. When presenting the ideas to Xbox, Fred & Farid focused on just one, and introduced it with a certain degree of showmanship. 'They were waiting for the idea for three months,' remembers Raillard. 'We came in with a big white board, and said "the launch is behind this". We turned the big board, and there was one tiny mosquito stuck in the centre of it. No words, nothing. We said "this is the European launch of Xbox".'

The mosquito was Fred & Farid's symbol of how work had come to dominate our lives, and thus ruin them. The full ad idea was to show the life of a mosquito before it became preoccupied with work – rather than endlessly sucking blood, Fred & Farid proposed that mosquitoes were once nature's musicmakers, creating joyful tunes

01-06

01-06 Stills from the Mosquito ad for Microsoft Xbox. Mosquito was one of two ads created for the Xbox launch campaign in 2002. It aired on TV, while the other film, Champagne, was initially created solely for the internet. Later Champagne proved so popular that it too was played on television.

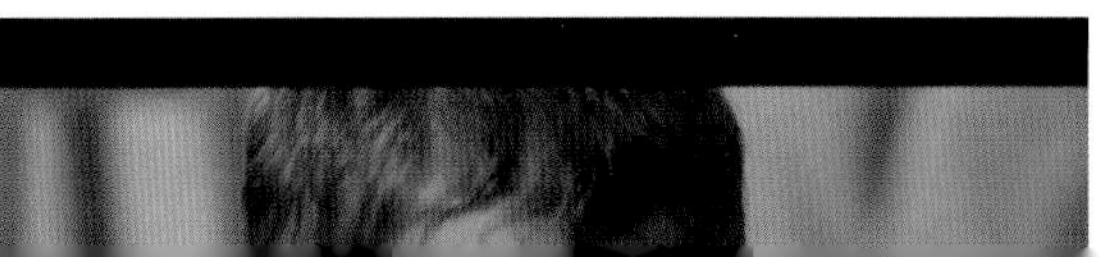

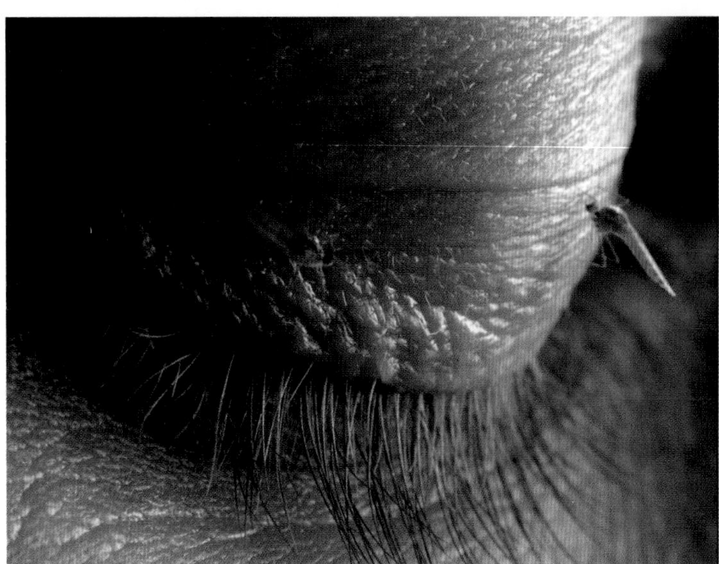

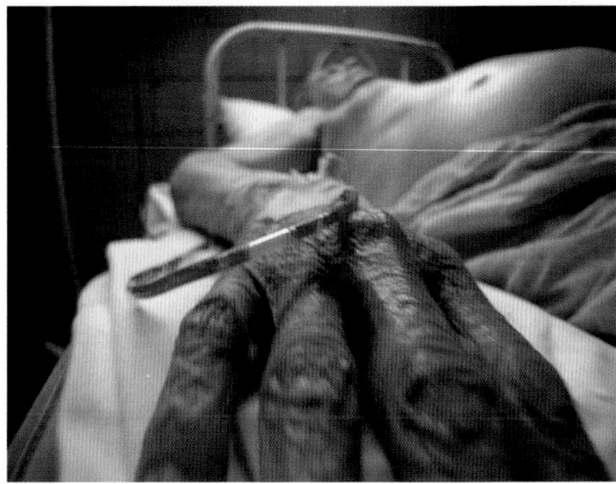

07-11

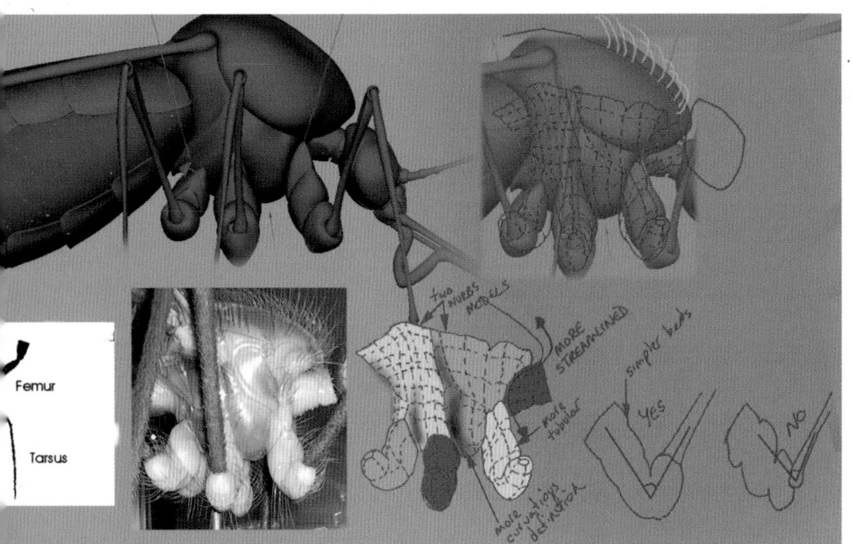

'We had to change the centre of gravity of this market. We had to shake up the rules in order to just be seen.'

12

enjoyed by all the animals of the world. The commercial opens with these scenes of happiness, before a voiceover (provided by dub poet Linton Kwesi Johnson (aka LKJ) in the final film) explains how one day the mosquitoes were compelled to get a job. The work turned the mosquitoes into pests, they became 'bad musicians', and their buzzing noise came to be hated by all. The film ends by LKJ offering a call to arms: 'Humans, you have a natural gift for play,' he says. 'Don't lose it. Work less. Play more.'

It was an audacious proposition, but Xbox saw the potential of the ad to present a powerful and almost existential idea to people, and for the brand to sell a lot of games consoles off the back of it. Fred & Farid's second idea, Champagne, was even simpler: it would show a child being born and then flying rapidly through life, before crashing into a grave as the tagline 'Life is short. Play more' appears on screen. There was less certainty from the client about this idea, so it was decided that the Mosquito ad would be the main launch spot, playing out on TV and in cinemas, while Champagne would be released online as a viral. 'They liked the two spots, but their attention was more focused on Mosquito,' says Raillard. 'Then we convinced them that we could shoot both for the same amount of money. So they said, "okay let's do it".'

Fred & Farid brought in Daniel Kleinman, a director well versed in mixing strong narratives with special effects, to work on both ads. 'We hit it off straight away, and we were all talking about the same thing, so I think we only really met once or twice before we went into proper production,' Kleinman remembers. 'I do storyboards, which map out what I'm going to do. On the shoot, Fred & Farid were great because they just stepped back and let me do it. They were much more involved in the edit process, which I think quite rightly they realize is the important bit.'

The Mosquito spot incorporated a mixture of stock footage with CGI and film shot specifically for the ad. 'The biggest challenge in it was creating the mosquito,' says Kleinman. 'That was CGI. It was a time when computer graphics were just on the edge of being believable. Up to that point, you'd always sort of been able to tell they were a bit dodgy. Framestore, who made the mosquito, really put a lot of work and research into it, and made a fantastic model with see-through parts and all sorts of stuff, but also a mosquito by its nature is quite CGI-friendly. We spent a lot of time looking at mosquitoes and what type it should be. Until you get into it, you don't realize how many different sorts there are, and they all look different – there are stripy ones, spotty ones, ones with long legs, ones with big snouts, hairy ones....'

'We sourced all the animals from lots of different places,' he continues. 'Some of it is stock footage, some of it is CG, some of it we manipulated, and some of the dancing that they do is real. Weirdly, the dancing of the giraffes is real footage – they actually do that as some mating ritual. We did shoot a model giraffe's head for the close-up, but the wide shot is real. I don't think maggots breakdance though, so that must have been CG.'

Kleinman shot a number of scenarios featuring humans being persecuted by mosquitoes for the end of the spot, but many of these ended up on the cutting room floor, so as to keep the message of the ad simple and sharp. The last shot, where a child gazes intensely into the camera (see fig. 06), proved crucial though, and was given extra time and space in the final ad. 'He just did this very intense stare at the camera that was sort of spontaneous,' says Kleinman. 'I was trying to get him to look at the camera, but it was a particular look that he did, which we all thought was really great, and wanted to hold onto for a few seconds. Which in an ad, where time is so precious, means that you have to lose other things.'

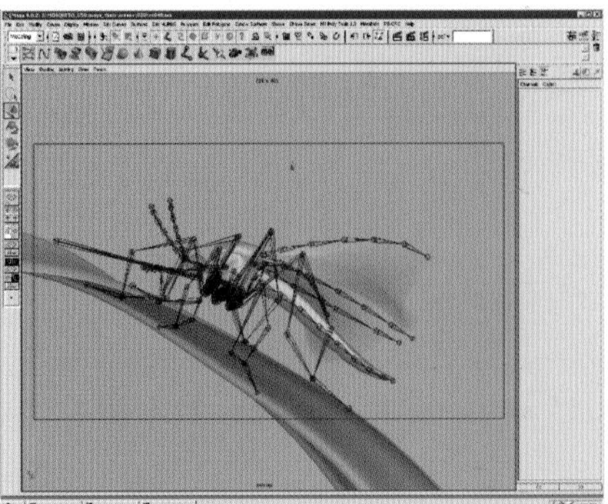

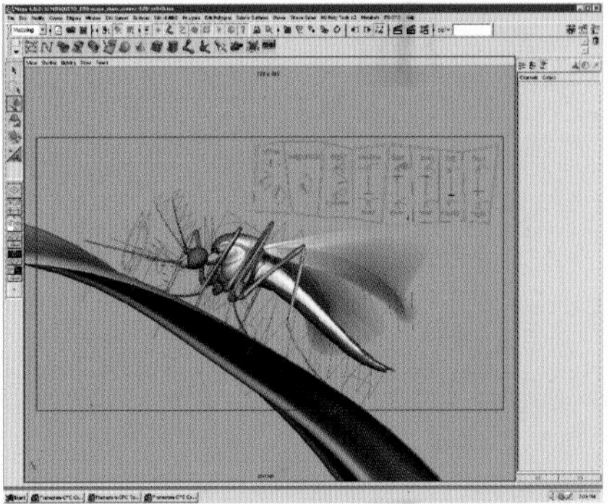

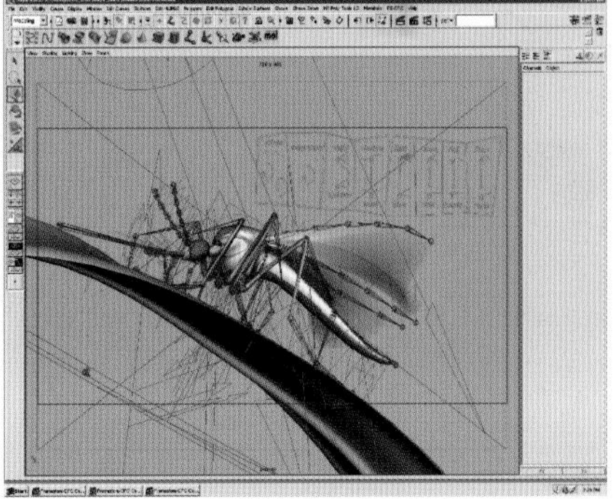

13-16

07-11 Production photographs for the Mosquito commercial show the insect hard at work.

12-16 The commercial mixed stock nature footage with computer-generated imagery. The mosquito itself was created in CGI, and these images show its development by post-production house Framestore. In image 12, early references for the mosquito are shown, while images 13-16 show the design for final insect.

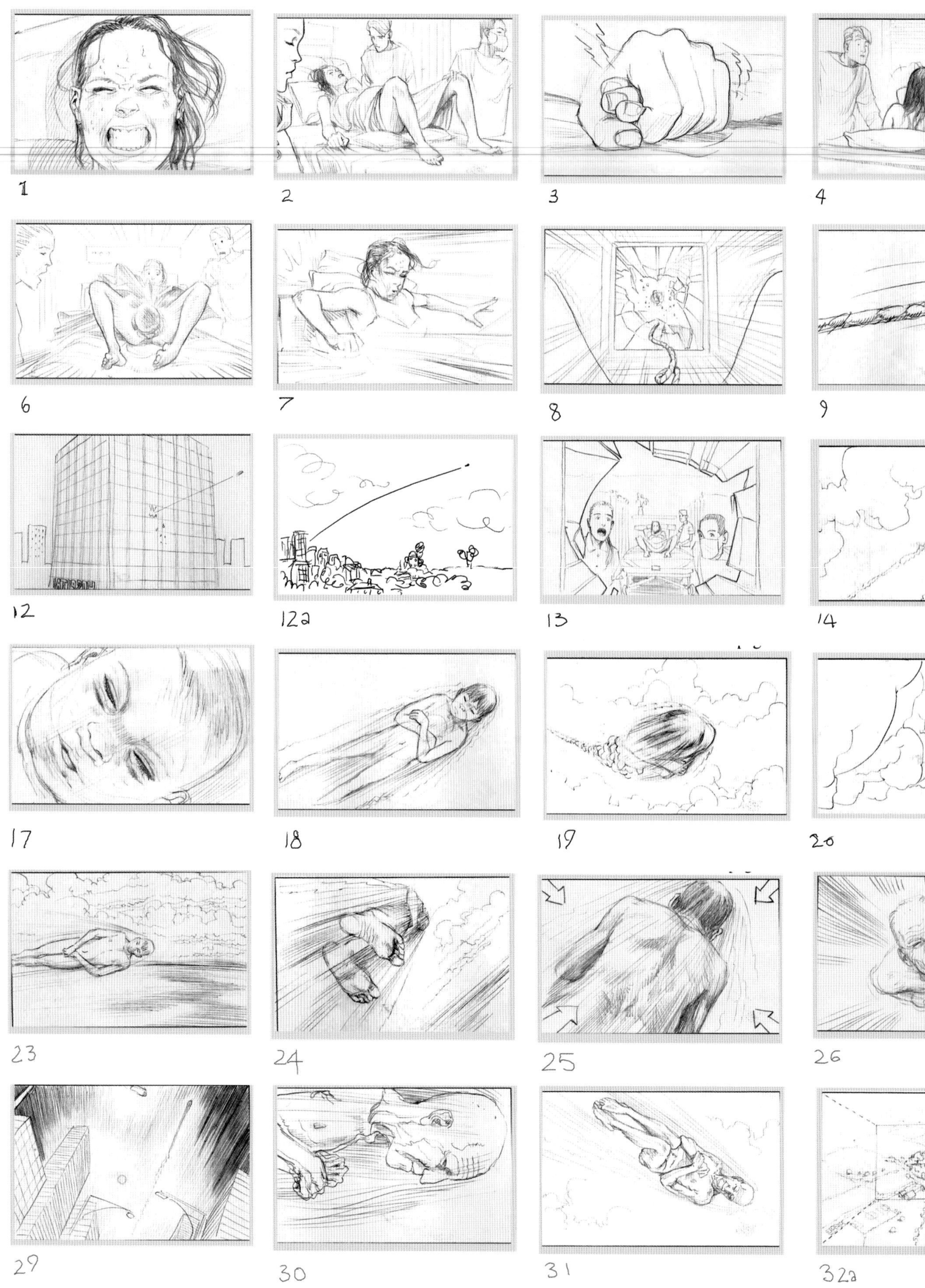
1
2
3
4
6
7
8
9
12
12a
13
14
17
18
19
20
23
24
25
26
29
30
31
32a

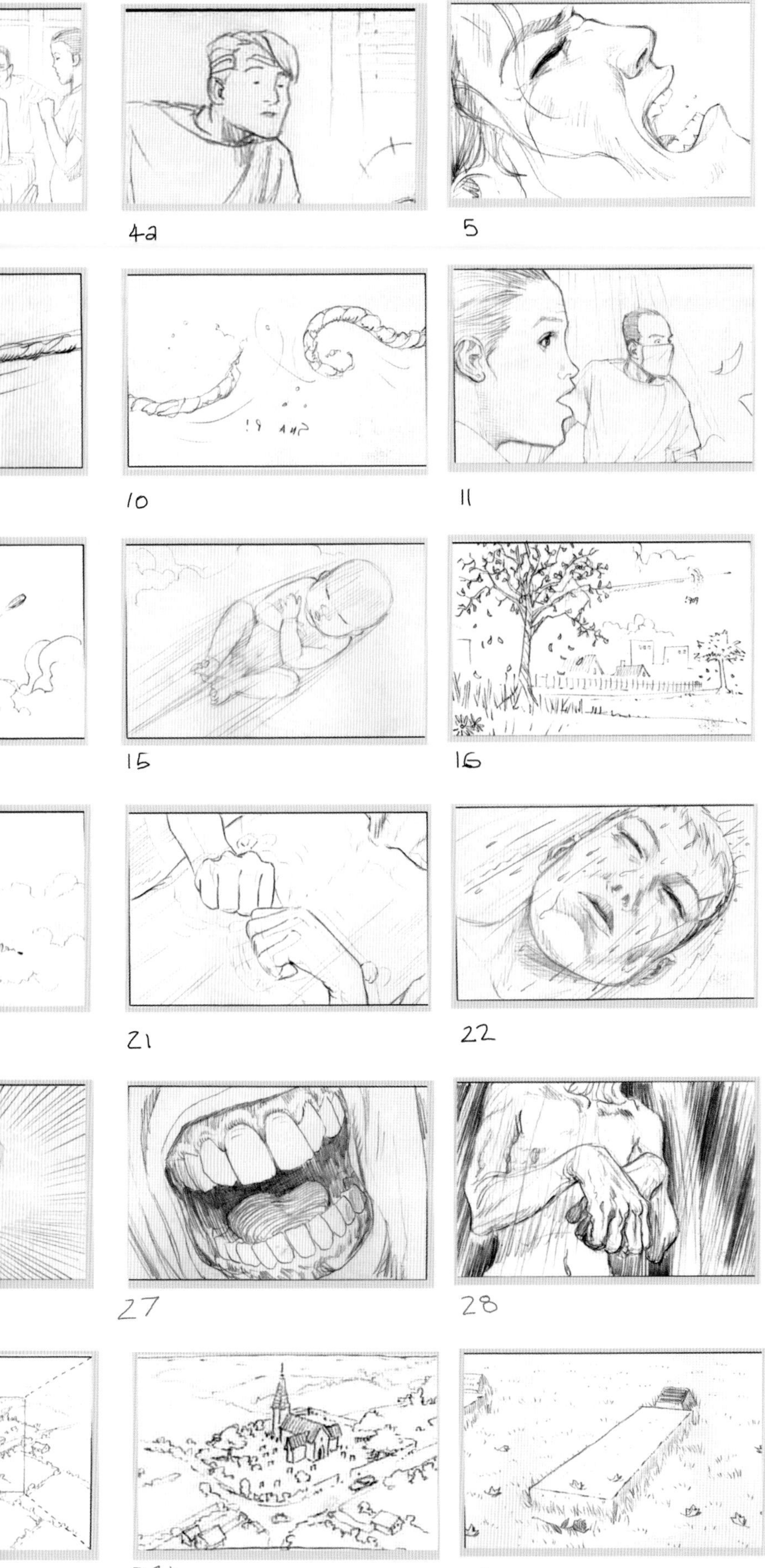

17 The Champagne film showed the life of a man dramatically sped up. We see him being born and then flying through the air while rapidly ageing, before landing violently in a coffin. These storyboards show the different shots featured in the ad.

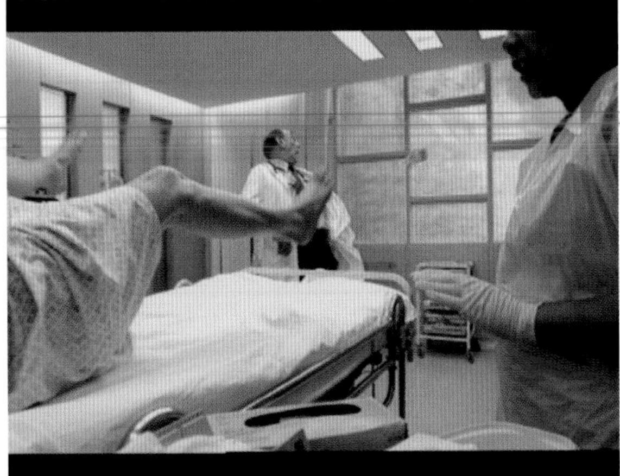

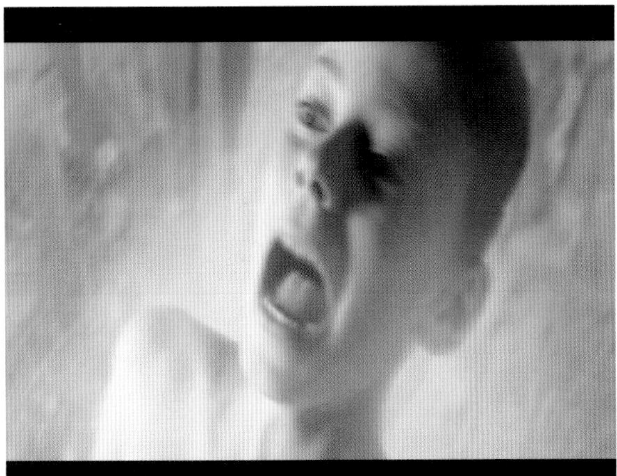

18-23

18-23 Stills from the final ad show the man's rapid journey through life.

24-29 Production photographs taken during the shoot for the Champagne film. Shown bottom is the director, Daniel Kleinman and ad creatives Fred & Farid pictured standing in the fake grave.

24-29

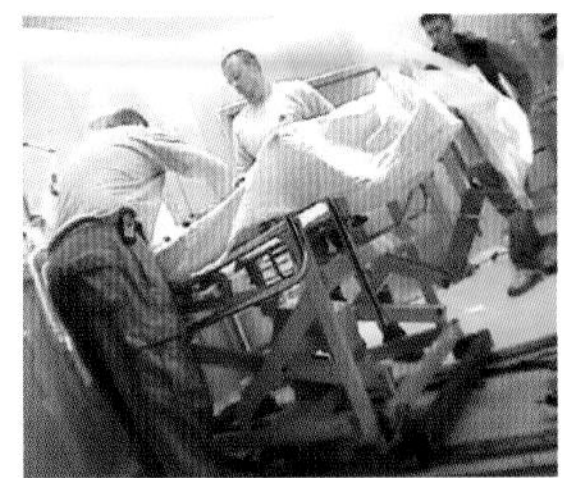

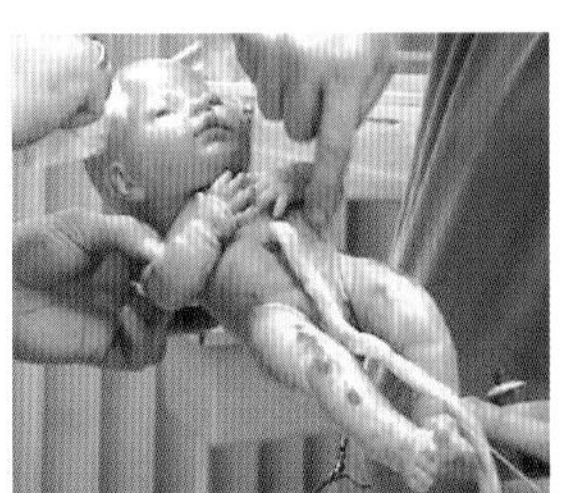

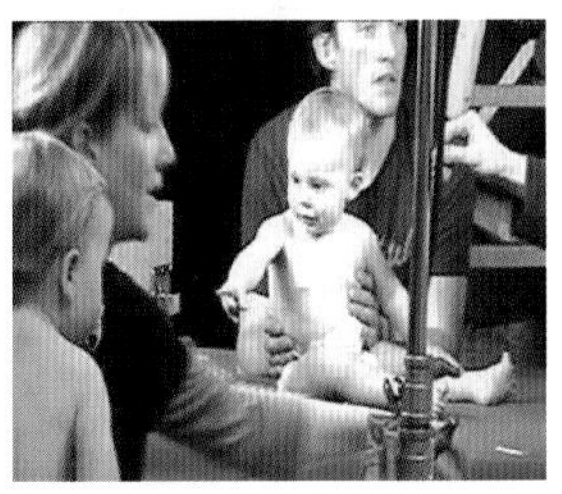

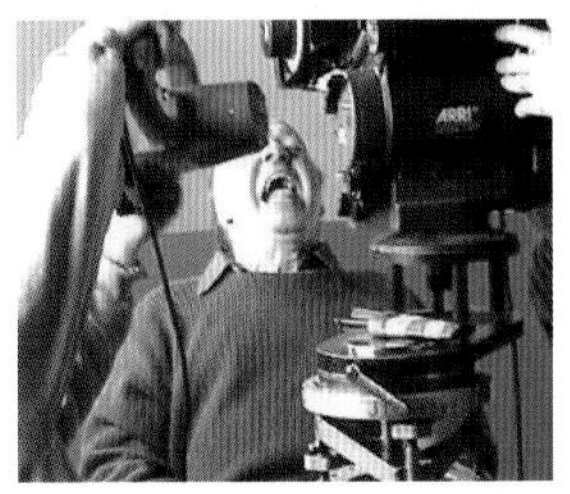

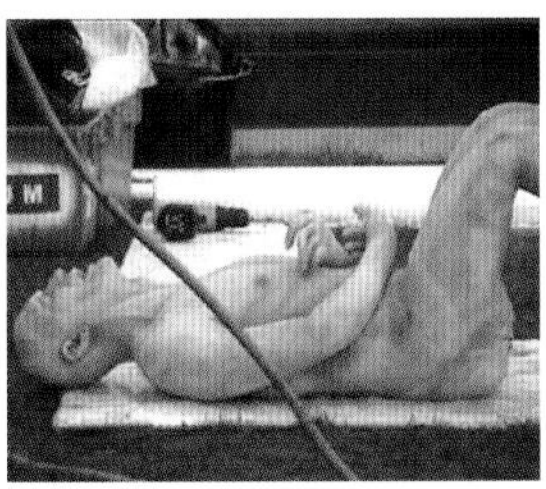

'We had this idea that the most interesting thing when you're playing video games doesn't happen inside the screen, but happens inside the room. That's the starting point.'

For Champagne, Kleinman wanted to keep the action as real-looking as possible, despite the obvious need for special effects to depict the speeded-up ageing process. 'I cast a whole line of people from a baby to an old man,' he remembers, 'who all looked vaguely similar and had vaguely similar attributes so that the transition between the various ages would be as smooth as possible. But in each shot I didn't want to just lock the camera off and have a static figure and then dissolve between the characters to make it look like the guy was getting older. What I did was have a motion-control camera, which meant that I shot one person, did a camera move and then took them out, put in another person, did the exact same camera move, and then put in the third person and did exactly the same camera move. Then in post-production they're able to selectively choose little bits and pieces from each part and meld them together so it becomes a seamless transition, but the camera is moving, which makes it more dynamic.'

'The things that I added to it are stuff like when the baby's firing out of the mother,' Kleinman continues. 'I thought "what's going to make this more dramatic?" I thought it should be like a recoil of a gun, so the whole bed jumps backwards when she fires it out. Like in a gangster film, when someone fires a gun and they get a recoil. So then the whole bed had to be on a rig that threw it backwards. You've got to get all the action coinciding at the right time, because there's a bloke working the bed, a bloke working the baby on a wire, a guy making the window smash. It's kind of tricky, but good fun. You have to experiment – until you do it, you don't know [if it will work]. It's very difficult to test beforehand, because it requires such an enormous amount of time to set the whole thing up, it's too expensive. You've got to wing it to a certain extent, and hope it works when you press the button.'

Happily, it did all work, perhaps more than either the agency or Microsoft initially expected. Mosquito on its own was a great success, and achieved Fred & Farid's aim to introduce a different kind of conversation into the video games market, while Champagne proved so popular that the client decided to show it on TV after all, a move not wholeheartedly welcomed by Kleinman. 'At that point the internet quality was not as good as it is now,' he says, 'so you didn't have to super fine-tune and do everything in really high resolution with the effects. I didn't quite finish it to the level of polish that I would have if I'd known it was going on TV. But it goes to show that if you've got a great idea, and you get a sense of the idea, really the technical polish is not important. The idea is the important thing.'

19/

Nike
Barrio Bonito

BBDO Argentina

In 2006, BBDO Argentina created the world's first football neighbourhood, on behalf of its client Nike and in honour of the World Cup. Dubbed Barrio Bonito ('beautiful neighbourhood') the project was created in La Boca, a run-down area of Buenos Aires that is famed for being the home of Boca Juniors, one of the world's most famous football clubs. Barrio Bonito formed part of Nike's global Jogo Bonito ('beautiful play') advertising campaign, though was first inspired by a localized dilemma created by the global strategy, as BBDO Argentina President Carlos Pérez explains: 'Barrio Bonito was born from the context of the 2006 World Cup in response to a little "problem" that was happening to our brand, our country and the competition.'

01 In the build-up to the World Cup in 2006, BBDO Argentina created a 'football neighbourhood' on behalf of Nike in La Boca, Buenos Aires. Barrio Bonito featured various artworks created by local artists, including this giant newspaper portrait of Argentine footballer Emiliano Insúa.

INSUA
JOY
Prueba junto al mar
llevar
Prueba junto al mar
gloria

'The concept of the global campaign that Nike planned for the most important event in soccer on a global level was Jogo Bonito,' he continues, 'a concept that speaks of the Brazilian magic and beauty of soccer. The entire campaign focused on turning the Brazilian game into an idol and making the style universally known. This is something strategically intelligent, as Brazilian soccer is admired all over the world. Everywhere except Argentina. Argentina and Brazil are friends and neighbours until it comes to soccer. Simply put, it was impossible to have a campaign in Argentina during the World Cup referring to Jogo Bonito without being classified as a traitor. Additionally it was dangerous what adidas, the historic sponsor of the Argentina team, could have done with that concept. It was clear we had to do something.'

Out of this adverse situation, an impressive piece of site-specific advertising was born. BBDO Argentina chose La Boca as the destination for its Nike football neighbourhood, both for its footballing heritage but also for its strong artistic links. 'Barrio Bonito was built in the only place on earth possible: La Boca,' says Pérez. 'Boca is the neighbourhood in which River Plate and Boca Juniors were born, two of the most important football teams in Argentina. A humble riverside town, where everything is painted in bright colours. Ancient legend says the first settlers didn't have enough money to buy all the same colour paint, so they depended on factory surplus. It is also the birthplace of most of our great artists – it is estimated that there are more than 4,000 artists living in the neighbourhood.'

While the idea of a 'Nike neighbourhood' may seem obnoxious to many, BBDO Argentina's intention was to be subtle and respectful. Rather than simply placing Nike logos all over the area, they instead wanted to bring something artistic and relevant to La Boca. A number of run-down buildings in the area were consequently renovated and

'It was impossible to have a campaign in Argentina during the World Cup referring to Jogo Bonito without being classified as a traitor. Additionally it was dangerous what adidas, the historic sponsor of the Argentina team, could have done with that concept. It was clear we had to do something.'

03

04

05-06 The La Boca neighbourhood has a strong artistic heritage, alongside its links to football. Local artists are shown here helping to create the large artworks that are displayed in the area.

05

02-03 A newspaper portrait of Argentine footballer Sergio Agüero was another of the artworks featured in the Barrio Bonito.

04 Posts in the neighbourhood were painted with images of players to encourage local footballers to practise their dribbling skills around them.

06

07 Among the artworks is a football pitch containing a number of statues of England players from the 1986 World Cup quarter-final. Visitors are encouraged to recreate Diego Maradona's controversial 'hand of God' goal from the match, using the figures as props.

10-11

08

09

'The principal intention of Barrio Bonito was to benefit the residents and leave a legacy for the city and the country. All the work included the participation of local artists approved by local residents.'

12

13

14

repainted as part of the campaign, and football-related artworks placed in the area. These include murals of Nike football stars such as Argentinean players Carlos Tévez and Sergio Agüero, as well as Brazilian player Ronaldinho (perhaps a slightly risky move in an Argentinean football stronghold).

There is also a large sculptural work that may prove uncomfortable viewing for English tourists – a courtyard filled with life-size statues of England players, around which visitors are encouraged to re-enact Maradona's notorious 'hand of God' goal from the Mexico 1986 World Cup quarter-final. 'We wanted to neutralize any negative effect [of the Jogo Bonito campaign],' continues Pérez, 'and most of all capture the essence of the brand with respect to football, which fits perfectly with the Argentine feeling towards football: a love, a passion and, most of all, a taste for beautiful football that is unmatched, even in Brazil.'

Local artists were involved in the making of Barrio Bonito, and the city government of Buenos Aires backed the project, with the site being officially opened by the mayor in May 2006. 'The principal intention of Barrio Bonito was to benefit the residents and leave a legacy for the city and the country,' explains Pérez. 'All the work included the participation of local artists approved by local residents.'

Much of the artwork is still in place today, with Barrio Bonito continuing to be a tourist attraction in the city. 'The majority of the work still remains, with the advertising things eliminated,' says Pérez. 'I feel very proud of the Barrio Bonito work, as it made La Boca a better neighbourhood.'

08 Portrait of Ronaldinho, designed to appear as if it has been created from ballprints.

09-12 Artists at work on the various murals and artworks featured in the neighbourhood.

13-14 Visitors inspect the statues of the England players, while a young footballer tries out the posts in Barrio Bonito.

20/

Oasis/City of New York
Dig Out Your Soul – In The Streets

BBH New York

To gain buzz around the launch of their 2008 album Dig Out Your Soul in the U.S., British rock band Oasis employed a decidedly unusual strategy. Eschewing the usual marketing methods, they didn't even play the music themselves, instead giving it to 30 street music acts in New York and inviting them to play it on the band's behalf. The event was the brainchild of ad agency BBH in New York, and came about after then chief creative officer Kevin Roddy put out a request to the entire agency to expand their thinking when it came to ad ideas.

'What we were saying was, we need to reinvent what advertising looks like,' Roddy explains. 'We were encouraging everybody to begin thinking a little less traditionally and a lot more broadly. With or without technology. This wasn't about "let's do things on the web"; this was about reinventing how to engage with consumers.' Two creatives at the agency, Calle and Pelle Sjönell, responded with an idea for a music launch. At this stage, Oasis was not involved, although the team knew that they needed a certain kind of act for the project to work.

'We had criteria that we needed for this idea,' says Pelle. 'It couldn't be house music, without lyrics; it couldn't be rap. It needed to be singer-songwriting, and it needed to be powerful.' Oasis seemed the perfect choice. 'Oasis' situation was fantastic because they'd been wanting to prove themselves in the U.S.,' Pelle continues. 'They'd had a really big success in the beginning, then for a couple of years they hadn't had the same success, and this was a big comeback moment for them. For them it was also important to be real, and do things that are true to their music and not be posers in any way. This was something I connected with them.'

The campaign was devised at an interesting time for the music industry; it needed to come up with fresh ways to present itself to an audience who were increasingly turning away from buying CDs in favour of downloading music online (both legally and illegally). 'This was at a time when the music industry felt very old all of a sudden,' says Pelle. 'We looked, for instance, at Radiohead, and what they did when they launched their album In Rainbows, where you could pay anything for it. It was an interesting way of launching an album in a very unique way, but it was more a comment on the industry than about the music itself. We wanted to do something that was about the music.'

02

The campaign needed to come up with fresh ways to present itself to an audience who were increasingly turning away from buying CDs in favour of downloading music online.

01-02 The U.S. launch campaign for the Oasis album Dig Out Your Soul saw street music acts in New York be the first to play the songs live in the city. The band visited rehearsals on the morning of the event to watch the musicians practising their tunes.

'If you're extremely successful, you might end up with a song that someone plays for a living on the streets. We thought that was very interesting; what if we started there? What if we had street musicians play songs that weren't out yet, and we do a backwards launch of music?'

'We thought that the most successful songs have to travel through all filters of musical success,' Pelle continues. 'You have to have a hit single, you make a video and it might be on TV, then you play in concert. Then you might, if you're really lucky, end up in karaoke, because people want to sing that song over and over again. And then, if you're extremely successful, you might end up with a song that someone plays for a living on the streets. We thought that was very interesting; what if we started there? What if we had street musicians play songs that weren't out yet, and we do a backwards launch of music?'

Another crucial component in making the campaign work was the participation of another of BBH's clients – the City of New York. The agency had a standing brief with the city for ideas that would emphasize its street life and culture. The Oasis launch idea fit this perfectly, as it highlighted the diverse and thriving music scene found on the city's streets every day. 'New York is one of the most fantastic places on earth to be a street musician because you have a huge audience – a place like Grand Central Station or Times Square has so many people passing through it,' says Pelle. 'It is very, very rare as a street musician to be able to play there. The city has a system that helped us to find those musicians and filter them through a union to get a time slot to play. To get a time slot to play in this city, you probably have to be one of the best street musicians in the world. There is a fantastic roster of talent to go to.'

The array of talent available in the city made it easier for the band, and their label Warner Brothers Records, to accept the idea. After all, their audience's first hearing of Oasis' new music wouldn't come from listening to the carefully prepared CD, but would be via interpretations from other musicians. 'There was concern on their part, before getting to the initial rehearsal,' agrees Roddy. 'It was two-fold: one was the obvious concern about releasing their music before they could control it. Even though you sort of do control its release here, once it gets played on the streets, people can record it. So there was some concern about that, but it went away. The other concern was "are these street musicians really talented? Are they going to make our music sound great?" But when they got there, they were blown away at the quality of the talent, the breadth of the talent. So that initial concern went away almost with the first person they heard.'

The street musicians were given four songs from Dig Out Your Soul, including the first single, The Shock of Lightning, which they could use in their gigs out on the streets of New York. They were given a limited amount of time to learn the material, and then spent a few hours with members of Oasis on the morning of the day the event occurred, to help fine-tune the performances. 'We said, perform them how you want, do at least one of the songs and four if you want, but it's more up to you to see what works for your sound and what works with your instrumentation,' says Pelle. 'So they took it on themselves. And when the band was there, they all talked about how to play the songs; it was all about rehearsing together

03-05 Members of Oasis shown at rehearsals with the musicians who would be performing their new album, Dig Out Your Soul, live on the streets of New York. The rehearsals were filmed by directing team The Malloys, who made a short documentary for the album launch.

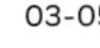
03-05

06

07

and playing for the band and making sure this was something they were okay with. It was a great meeting of musicians.'

'The interesting thing about musicians, especially performers like this, is that there's a pride in doing your thing,' Pelle continues. 'A song has so many versions if it's a powerful song. What we tried to do with all these great acts was find a multi-faceted group. We had an electronic violinist, who doesn't sing at all – he had a very different version from the a cappella group. We felt that the more diverse we can make this, the more powerful the songs are too, because then you hear how the song can be in so many different versions and still be the same.'

Thirty acts were picked to play on the day, and 20 of these were playing at any one time at different locations across the city during the afternoon and evening of the launch day. Each musician was accompanied by a board announcing that they were part of the project, and all were filmed for a documentary of the launch that was shot by The Malloys (Emmett and Brendan Malloy). The event was advertised on Oasis' fan site, and also on the street musicians' websites, but was quickly picked up by blogs and other media in the city once it began. 'It was a very multi-faceted launch,' says Pelle. 'People were filming it on the streets and posting it to other fans to hear the songs before the album came out.'

In a further twist, the city happened to be filled with Oasis fans on the day of the launch; they were in town to see a gig by the band that was unfortunately cancelled, due to injuries sustained by Noel Gallagher, who'd been pushed off the stage at a gig in Toronto the night before. 'So there were lots of Oasis fans from all over the US in New York but without an Oasis show,' says Pelle. Word got around that they could at least hear the new album out on the streets. 'That was great,' continues Pelle, 'because Warner had great contact with their fan sites and could get this information out very quickly... and it was so cool to see their reaction to the music as fans.'

The launch was a huge success on the day, garnering much coverage online and on local news channels. It then had an extended life when the documentary was released online after the album had come out. All those involved believe it was an ad campaign where the 'stars aligned'. 'When they told me the idea, it was one of those moments,' says Roddy. 'It was one of those moments of "that is a genius idea". It was one of those moments for me, it was one of those moments for New York City, it was one of those moments for Warner. Everybody just said "wow, that's fantastic, we have to do that, we have to make that happen".'

06-09 Various musicians shown in rehearsal for the Dig Out Your Soul campaign and also performing the songs live in New York. Each musician was given a sign to use that explained the project to passers-by.

08

09

10

Google Maps

Search Maps | Show search options

Get Directions **My Maps**

Create new map - Browse the directory

Created by me

- Oasis - Dig Out Your Soul - In The Streets Public
- Traverse Loop Public
- New York Places Public
- MTB Minneapolis Public
- St Paul Tour Public
- Untitled Public

RSS | View in Google Earth | Print | Send

Traffic | More... | Map | Satellite | Terrain

©2009 Google - Map data ©2009 Maponics, Tele Atlas

DIG OUT YOUR SOUL IN THE STREETS

This performance is part of the launch for Oasis' new album "Dig Out Your Soul," that releases October 7th. There are more acts spread out throughout the city playing unreleased Oasis songs today. To find out where these other acts are playing check out the map below.

If you want to upload footage or see this morning's rehearsal with the street musicians and Oasis, please visit www.nycvisit.com/oasis. For more information on the upcoming album visit www.oasisinet.com

1. **THOTH 6–8PM** "Prayformance" Central Park: Bethesda Terrace
2. **THEO EASTWIND 2–4PM** Singer/Songwriter Times Square subway – 42 St. and Broadway opposite Shuttle entrance
3. **PATRICK WOLFF TRIO 3–6PM** Jazz Astor Pl. – 6 subway platform
4. **YAZ BAND 4–7PM** Smooth Jazz Concourse between E and 6 subways at Lexington Ave. and 51st st.
5. **J. HILL & HARTLING 6–9PM** Hard Country Blues and Gospel Penn Station – Long Island Rail Road subway corridor
6. **LUKE RYAN 3–6PM** Blues Rock 59th St./Columbus Circle A,C,E subway platform
7. **MICHAEL SHULMAN 4–6PM** Shred Violin Central Park (at Columbus Circle)
8. **GABE CUMMINS 2–4PM** Jazz Guitar Grand Central Terminal
9. **LUELLEN ABDOO 3–7PM** Classical Violin Whitehall St./South Ferry – Staten Island Ferry Station
10. **NEXT TRIBE 2–3PM** World Hip-Hop/Rock Penn Station – Long Island Rail Road Subway Corridor
11. **DAGMAR 2 3–6PM** Art/Performance Rock Grand Central Shuttle platform
12. **MAJESTIC K. FUNK 2–6PM** Funk Lexington Ave. – 51st 6 subway platform
13. **JASON STUART 3–5PM** Double Bass Rock Washington Square Park
14. **SUKI RAE 2–4PM** Hard to Describe Central Park (at Columbus Circle)
15. **ELIANO BRAZ 2–5PM** Brazilian Violin 14th St. A,C,E subway platform

New York

11

'It was one of those moments of "that is a genius idea". It was one of those moments for me, it was one of those moments for New York City, it was one of those moments for Warner. Everybody just said "wow, that's fantastic… we have to make that happen".'

12

10–11 Flyers were handed out to people watching the buskers performing the new songs from Dig Out Your Soul. Each one explained the project, and also told viewers where they could see other performances in the campaign. A Google Maps page also highlighted where the musicians could be found.

12 Liam Gallagher gives an interview on a roof top in New York.

21/

Onitsuka Tiger
Made of Japan
Amsterdam Worldwide

The sports fashion world is a crowded one, so when Japanese brand Onitsuka Tiger wanted to do a brand campaign for its shoe line, it knew that it needed something unusual to stand out. Advertising agency Amsterdam Worldwide looked to the company's history for inspiration. 'Since they relaunched in 2001, they hadn't really told their story, which is really interesting,' says creative director Andrew Watson. 'It's certainly got a really interesting heritage, probably more so than most of the other brands. In fact, as a basic brand, Onitsuka Tiger pre-dates Nike, so it's really got some stories to tell. To tell those stories we needed a delivery device, or something that we could use as an icon year after year.'

01-03

01-03 Advertising agency Amsterdam Worldwide created a series of sculptures for Japanese brand Onitsuka Tiger to advertise its shoe line. The sculptures are all based on the design of the shoe, and each highlights different aspects of Japanese culture. The first in the series, shown here, featured various iconic symbols of the country.

MADE OF JAPAN

Onitsuka Tiger™

onitsukatiger.com

04-05

'At least, that's how we envisioned it', Watson continues; 'something that we could build on that embodied what the brand stood for, which we encapsulated into the line "Made of Japan".' The device the creatives chose was to focus on the shoe itself, but turn it into a work of art. Between 2007 and 2010, four shoe sculptures were made, with each one articulating a different aspect of Japanese culture. The first took the 'Made of Japan' tag literally, with a 1.5-metre-long shoe sculpture created from various iconic symbols of the country, including sushi and origami, koi carp and vinyl toys. For the second, titled Electric Shoe, Amsterdam Worldwide focused on the neon landscape of Tokyo, with the sculpture itself becoming a miniature city, complete with brightly lit highways and even a replica of Tokyo's Narita Airport contained in the shoe's tongue. The third sculpture reflected the Japanese legend of the Zodiac Race, while the fourth is inspired by the Japanese Tansu chest, a piece of furniture containing many drawers.

It was important to Amsterdam Worldwide that the shoes were real, handcrafted objects, rather than just images created in CGI. 'It would have been easier to make them in CG; it would have been easier to not make the real thing,' says executive creative director Richard Gorodecky. 'But it would have been kind of heartless – there was something about the process and the pain of actually building something that really elevated them above what they could have been just as concepts. We love to make stuff.'

'Each one's been a totally different experience, but each experience has been really fantastic in its own way,' says Watson. 'From the first one, where we were building the model in a garage, to the last one, where we were in a workshop in Osaka working with a company who are nine generations of traditional woodcrafters.

'The Electric Shoe was especially interesting because we were working with a company that was doing something quite new, which was rapid prototyping, and using that technique to create something that was going to be consumed by an advertising audience was quite unprecedented at the time.'

'Budget has always been a problem, but that problem has actually caused us to do quite incredible things.'

Fans of the shoes get the opportunity to see them in the flesh by visiting the brand's flagship stores. 'The very first one was a one-off,' says Watson, 'and it needed to be because the budget pretty much made it so. We could only afford to make one.

That became popularized by a tour that we did – we sent it around Europe and to the flagship stores, and it actually became a centrepiece for their displays for a year. It almost became an exhibition piece. Then in the years following, the popularity of the models grew, so stores wanted to have their own ones. So we had to figure out ways of creating them so we could potentially duplicate them or make scale models of them. What it meant was that more people could see the finished article and could interact with them, especially in the case of the last one, the Tansu shoe, which is the most interactive.'

06

04-05 Images showing the construction of the first shoe in the Made of Japan series.

06 Still from a film featuring the shoe, made to accompany the campaign.

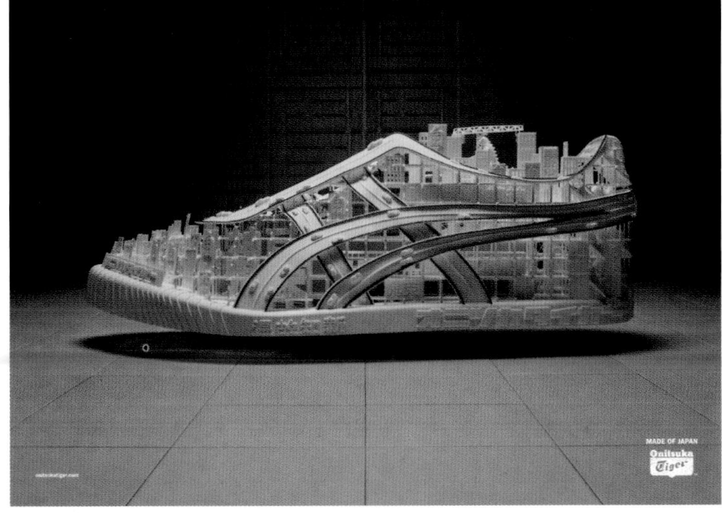

07-09

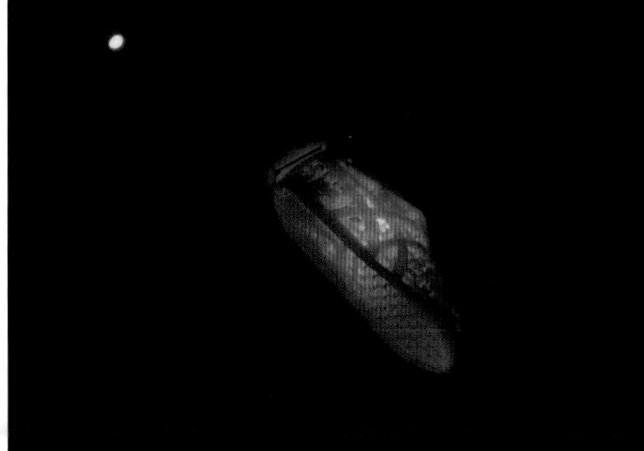

10-11

07-08 Each shoe sculpture was photographed and used in press and poster advertising for the brand. Shown here are the print ads featuring the one metre-long Electric Shoe.

09 The back of the Electric Shoe sculpture was used to display real Onitsuka Tiger shoes.

10-11 The final shoe sculptures were exhibited in Onitsuka Tiger's flagship stores. Other small accessories, including key rings and USB sticks, were also created as part of the Electric Shoe campaign.

12 A film, shot in the shoe, was created as part of the campaign. Viewers were taken on a journey through the tiny electrified streets featured in the sculpture.

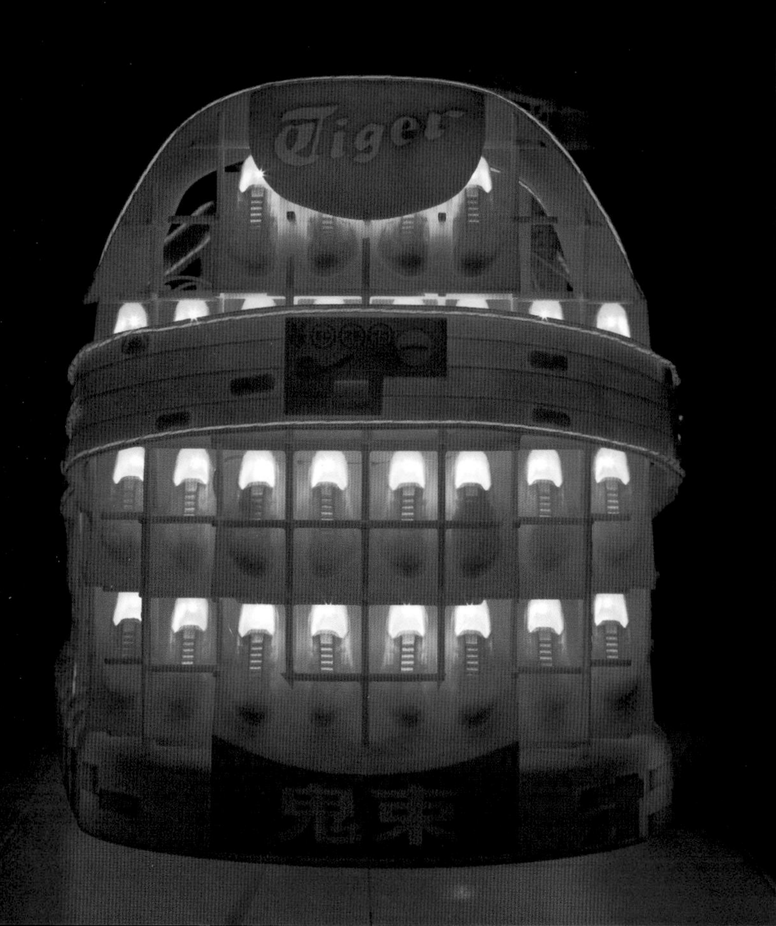

12

Onitsuka Tiger

Discover the legend of the Zodiac race at **onitsukatiger.com**

CELEBRATING 60 YEARS

Onitsuka Tiger™

MADE OF JAPAN

13 For the 2009 shoe sculpture, which also marked Onitsuka Tiger's 60th birthday, the agency created a diorama based on the Asian legend of the Zodiac Race.

14-18 The sculpture featured a race circuit, as well as several Japanese landmarks including Mount Fuji. The photographs here reveal its slow creation.

19-20 The Zodiac Race legend tells of 13 animals that race each other for a place in the Zodiac calendar. To accompany the shoe sculpture, the agency created an animated film to bring the race to life, starring various animal characters. Shown here are early character designs as well as stills from the finished film.

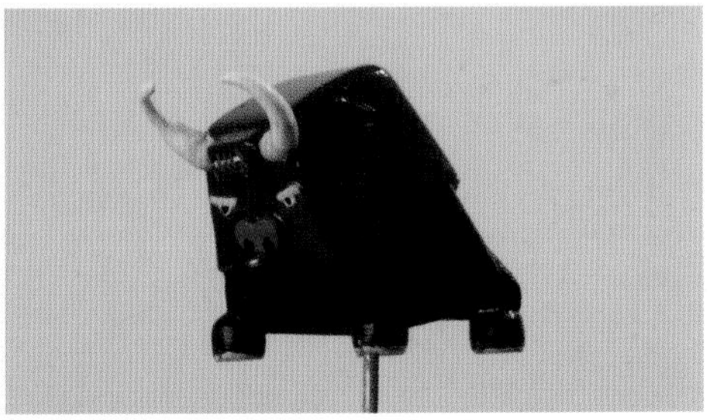

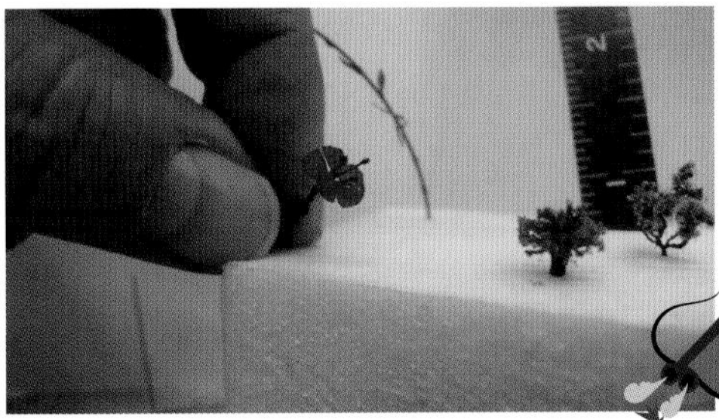

14-18

19

20

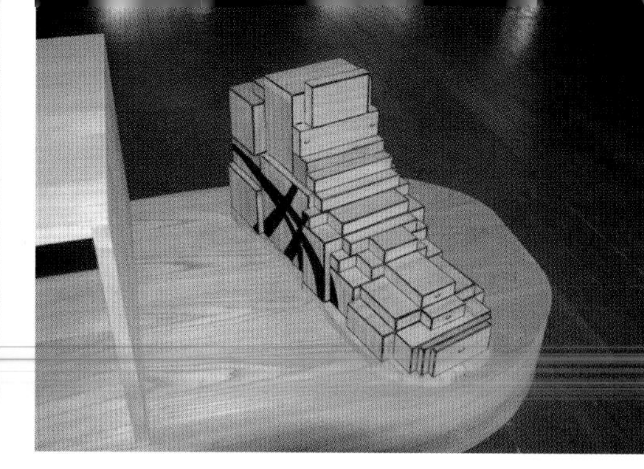

Onitsuka
Tiger

創業 江戸天明三年
伝統的工芸品
元祖 小倉タンス店

21-36

21-36 In 2010, Amsterdam Worldwide created the Tansu Shoe for Onitsuka Tiger, which contained a number of beautifully carved wooden boxes and drawers. The ad agency worked with craftsmen at a traditional woodshop in Japan to create the shoe.

37-40 A website formed part of the campaign, where viewers could open the drawers to find stories about Onitsuka Tiger's heritage, as well as films, photos and other fun stuff.

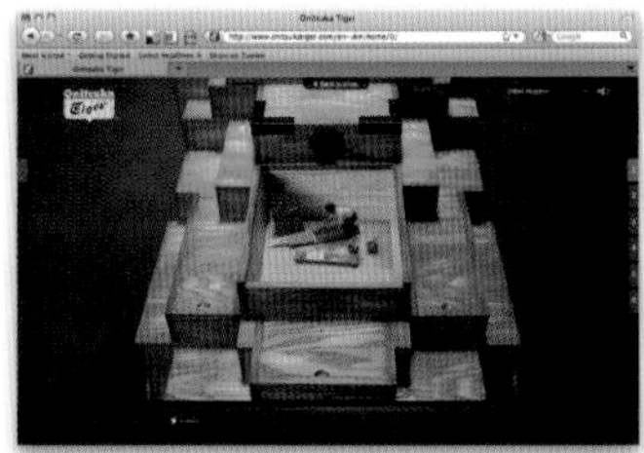

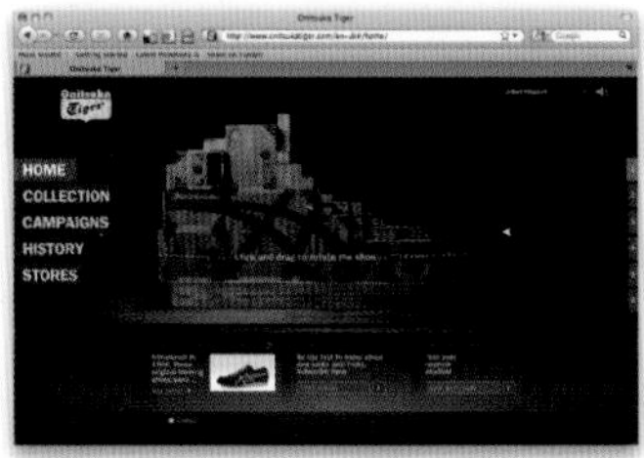

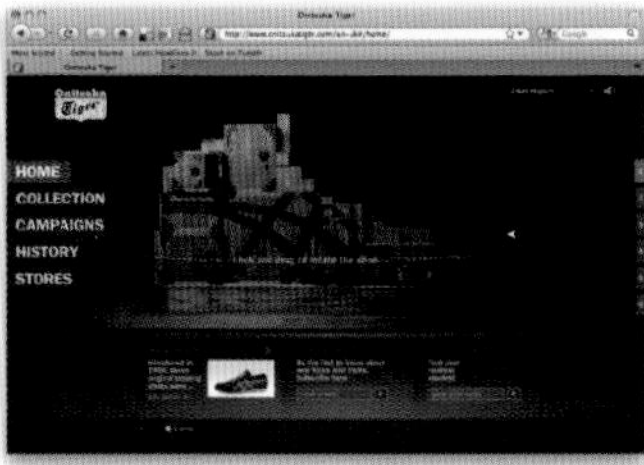

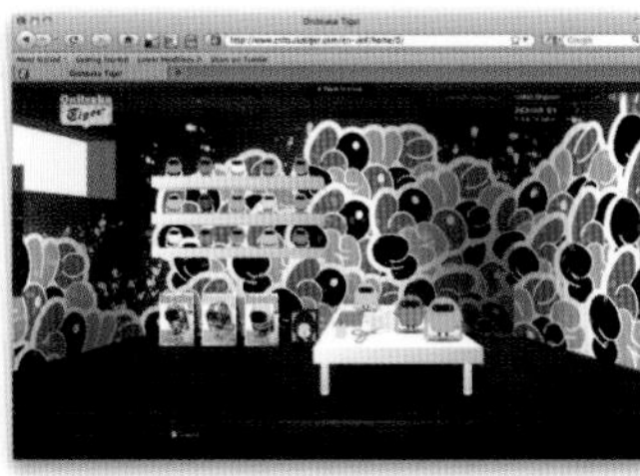

37-40

The shoes have formed the content for print campaigns, and each one has also been accompanied with a film and website. In the case of the Tansu shoe, the site allowed visitors to access the drawers of the shoe online, and find more brand-related treats. 'These campaigns from the outset were never big budget and yet they still had to transcend different nationalities and country borders, so we wanted to create something that was integrated,' says Watson. 'We knew that doing something online was important, but we needed, in a kind of mercenary way, to create as much PR as possible to back them up, because we didn't have the budget to put them in all the media. So we needed them to generate their own buzz.'

This has been successful, with bloggers and fans of the shoes eager to share the story of any new arrivals to the campaign. This word-of-mouth approach has allowed Onitsuka Tiger to carve out a niche for itself against competitors who have larger advertising budgets and a broader presence. 'Budget has always been a problem, but that problem has actually caused us to do quite incredible things,' says Gorodecky. 'So the thing that's probably worked against it all these years has actually been the thing that's advanced it, and pushed us to do things in different ways. The biggest problem has been the biggest advantage.'

'It would have been easier to make them in CG; it would have been easier to not make the real thing. But it would have been kind of heartless – there was something about the process and the pain of actually building something that really elevated them above what they could have been just as concepts.'

01

22/

Philips Carousel

Tribal DDB Amsterdam

'We were asked to do an educational website about the television. And effectively that's what Carousel is – it's an educational website about a television done in a very cinematic way.' As Chris Baylis, creative director at Tribal DDB Amsterdam suggests, the website that the agency created for the launch of the Philips cinema-proportioned 21:9 TV in 2009 is no ordinary educational site. It centres around a film directed by Adam Berg, which features a dramatic heist scene. Unlike the fast-cut, high-action style we might associate with the heist genre however, the Carousel film is still, as if the action has been frozen at the height of its intensity.

The camera moves slowly around the scene, relishing every detail. Bullets are shown hanging in mid-air, while a policeman is caught blasting through a pane of glass, having been booted there by one of the thieves, all of whom are dressed in clown suits. The camera zooms up to the ceiling and onto a new floor, gliding through an explosion and tracking past a SWAT team in the middle of a fire fight with more clowns. The film then ends back where it started, revealing the twist in the tale along the way.

The piece works in two ways for Philips. It is an entertaining narrative, but also built into the site are 'hot spots' of information about the television. As viewers watch the film on the website, they are given the opportunity to pause and click to get this information. To keep the cinematic theme, all the info is presented as if it is from the perspective of the crew, and includes speeches from a fictional director, director of photography, and VFX supervisor. The impression is that you are being taken behind the scenes of the film itself, although the intention is really to impart messages about the TV.

The aim of the site was both to launch the TV, and to give the brand a distinctive tone within the crowded television market. Prior to Carousel, the only brand in this area with unusual advertising was Sony, who had distinguished its Bravia product as having outstanding colour through commercials including Balls and Paint (see pages 172 and 178). 'Philips has always made really amazing TVs,' says Baylis. 'They win lots of technical awards – but they just hadn't managed to tell

01-02 The Philips Carousel website featured a film showing a dramatic heist scene which appeared to have been paused at the peak of its action. The actors had to hold their complex positions on set for hours at a time in order to achieve the frozen effect.

02

'Philips has always made really amazing TVs. They win lots of technical awards – but they just hadn't managed to tell the story very well. 21:9 gave us a bigger platform. In the way that Sony owned colour, Philips now owned cinema, which was an interesting territory for us to go and explore.'

03

the story very well. 21:9 gave us a bigger platform. In the way that Sony owned colour, Philips now owned cinema, which was an interesting territory for us to go and explore.'

'The original idea we had, which we talked to a lot of production companies about, was an idea of a big, looping tracking shot,' he continues. 'We thought tracking shots were cinematic and interesting, and we realized we could do a timeline-based website that you could jump off and on. So you can jump off the tracking shot, get a bit of education and then jump back in.'

Berg became involved after the agency saw a similar frozen-time-style film on his reel. 'We started exploring that with them, and started exploring how it could best be used,' says Baylis. 'We said that we wanted big cinematic things like heists or sieges. As soon as you go into frozen time, it has to be something very immediate, so we had to have a story that could be understood in shorthand. The cops and robbers story is a classic cinematic story.'

'A lot of people look at the film and think "Oh, it looks like Ronan, it looks like The Dark Knight, it's so referential",' agrees Mark Pytlik of Stink Digital, an executive producer on the website. 'It almost looks like it's stealing from those things, and it kind of is, but it was done strategically to try and help locate it in film. You don't see very many internet virals that feel like Hollywood thrillers, and that speak in the same language, so we had to do that to get into that world.'

The film was shot in Prague. 'One of the biggest challenges of the job from a location perspective was finding a place where we could do this continuous scene,' continues Pytlik. 'That location gave us everything we were looking for. There was an outside bit where we could do the tracking, we could go in through the building, go up the stairs and then come back out again and make our loop. That was a huge challenge, just finding a place that would let us do that. Our main office for the shoot was in an old Stasi listening room. We had this massive room, with this huge rectangular table, and built into the table were all these microphone decks, where people would presumably listen in on phone conversations back in the day. Now it's a college. Our art direction team in Prague converted it into a hospital in about 24 hours.'

'We cast people who had really good core body strength,' Pytlik continues. 'People look at the film and think there is a massive amount of 3D work throughout the entire piece. Truth is, there was a ton of 3D work, but it's mostly focused on the smoke, the explosions, the glass shards, the dollar bills.... But viewers think that the people who are actually frozen there are also 3D constructs and they're not. We cast former gymnasts, stunt men – people who could literally hold a position for a long time. Sometimes for hours at a time. We shot the whole thing using motion control, and it's very difficult sometimes to set up the motion control and get it right, so everybody would be waiting.'

A motion control rig allows a director to achieve the exact same camera move repeatedly, meaning that it's possible to film complicated scenes with different amounts of detail – for example, with people and without – so that everything can be knitted together neatly in post-production. While essential to this shoot, using motion control did cause some extra difficulties for the crew. 'It started raining on the first night and rain and motion control just do not go together, it's a disaster,' says Pytlik. 'We only had two days, there was no provision for any extra days, and we were already running into overtime. We were looking at ways to rethink the entire thing, but the rain just miraculously died at about four in the morning on the first day, and we got our shots, and moved inside for the second day, where things got reasonably easier.'

Shooting the 'hot spot' segments, which give info on the TVs themselves, also created problems. 'Due to a lot of complicated and convoluted reasons, we couldn't shoot the behind-the-scenes stuff at the same time as the live-action stuff,' explains Pytlik. 'We shot it all at the end, which meant that we had to go back to the set, get everybody to stand in the exact same positions and match exactly what they were doing 12 hours previously. There's no easier way to do that than to tediously set everything up and then check it against a monitor that shows what we'd already shot. We were pulling our hair out trying to match some of those shots on the second day.'

The hot spots play fast and loose with the realities of filmmaking in order to get across their messages about the TV in a simple fashion. The post-production segment, for example, makes a lengthy, painstaking job look surprisingly quick.

03 Storyboards for the Carousel film show how the action was planned.

04-08 The set allowed the director, Adam Berg, to film the narrative in one continuous scene. Many of the actors were suspended on wires, which were then removed in post-production.

'Viewers think that the people who are actually frozen there are 3D constructs and they're not. We cast former gymnasts, stunt men – people who could literally hold a position for a long time. Sometimes for hours at a time.'

09-15

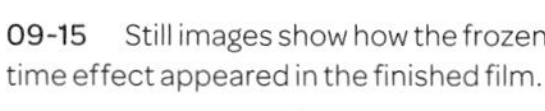

09-15 Still images show how the frozen time effect appeared in the finished film.

16 The film was showcased on a website for Philips, which allowed visitors to pause the narrative to obtain more information about the Philips 21:9 television.

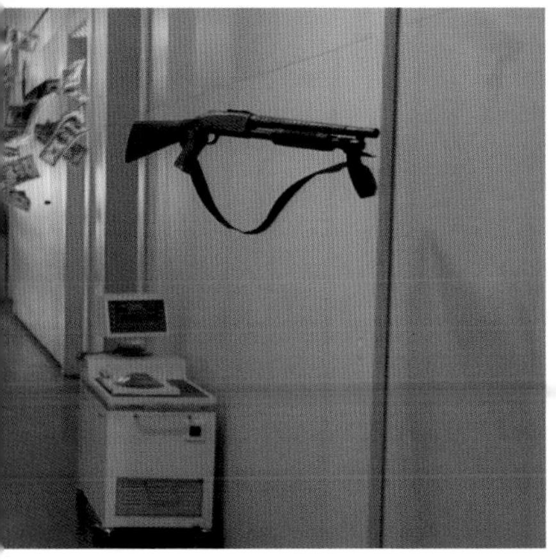

'You don't see very many internet virals that feel like Hollywood thrillers, and that speak in the same language.'

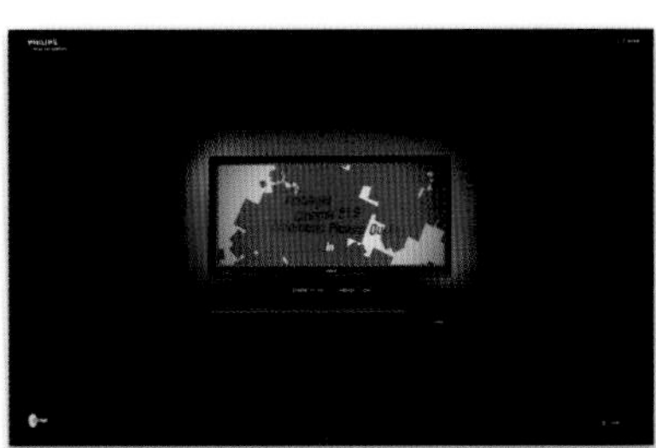

16

'We've taken a lot of poetic licence,' agrees Chris Baylis. 'It's a condensed reality really. Our director bears no resemblance to Adam Berg whatsoever. Adam Berg is a quiet, thoughtful guy and that director's played as a loud American, they're two completely different people. Our reasoning for having those people in it was about how this TV is made for cinema, and not just for cinema, for cinematographers. It's made with filmmaking in mind, so taking it back to the source in that way was a nice part of the strategy.'

The interactive element of the site, where this information is contained, is subtle but vital to fully understanding the campaign. The film did prove successful on its own, however, and was admired for its technique. 'The interactivity was fairly minimal, but it was really nicely applied,' says Pytlik. 'I think one of the things that gets lost sometimes is that people look at the film as an individual piece of content. There's no end branding on it, there's no mention of the TV, and I think when people think of the film outside the context of the site, you lose a little bit of what it's doing for the brand. The reality is the site is the destination, and the film is the central piece of content that gets people there, but it's all the stuff that's happening around it that's really doing a lot of the heavy lifting for the brand.'

The project was completed remarkably quickly – in under two months – meaning that the team working on it had little sense of what they had created while it was being made. To their pleasant surprise, it was an instant success – breaking the mould of what might be expected from an 'educational website'. 'We made it and then we realized what we had afterwards,' says Baylis. 'We were just meeting our deadline, making a website, making it as good as it could be, trying to make it cinematic... and we happened to end up with something amazing.'

23/

Skoda
The Baking Of

Fallon

'180kg of orange sugar paste. 25kg of dried apricot. 180 fresh eggs. 42kg of chocolate fudge....' Think of an advert that this list of ingredients could apply to, and it can only be one: the delicious Skoda Baking Of spot, by Fallon ad agency in London in 2007, which saw a team of chefs and home economists make a replica Skoda Fabia car entirely out of cake.

Fallon devised the unusual idea in response to a brief to celebrate the launch of the latest version of the Fabia. Unusually, there was no specific gimmick in the new car to hang the advertising around – no '0 to 60 in seven seconds', or 'the most spacious vehicle in its class' – and instead Skoda had updated it in a lot of small, if charming, ways. Rather than fight against this potential problem, the creative team decided to run with it, basing the ad around the fact that the car was 'full of lovely stuff'. The idea to use cake – because it too is full of lovely things – followed naturally.

There was a precedent for the spot in an earlier commercial for the Skoda Roomster that was also made by Fallon. This ad was set in the Skoda factory, but rather than the usual industrial soundtrack found in such a setting, the machines giggled and yelped, as if to articulate the happiness of the car plant. It ended with the tag 'Manufacturer of happy drivers'.

Despite the quirkiness that this brought to the brand, the client still needed significant persuasion from Fallon to turn their beloved Fabia into a cake. 'It was like taking medicine – "do I have to?",' says the agency's chairman at the time, Laurence Green, of the client response. 'Because any car organization expects at least the real car to be shown at some point in the commercial, and ideally shown driving speedily around bends in France and Italy – that's the expectation.'

Fallon suggested some compromises in order to sell the idea through, including an end shot that would see the cake car turn into the real one. Happily, this image didn't make the final cut. 'We shot it,' says Richard Flintham, executive creative director on the project. 'We had to go through the whole thing just to be seen to be responsible. Everyone was saying, "it would be madness to do this", and I suppose it's only because the cake car looked so good that we could. If it had looked a bit wonky, and the sponge had subsided, we would have had to show the other one. But we had amazing, amazing modelmakers.'

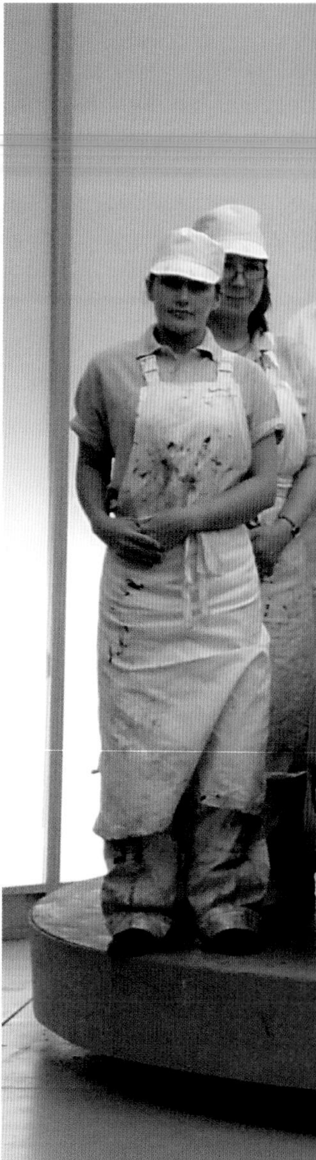

01

01 The Skoda Baking Of commercial saw a team of chefs and home economists create a Skoda Fabia car entirely from cake. The bakers all appeared in the ad, and are shown here posing alongside their creation in the final image of the spot.

02-03 Production photographs from the set of the commercial. Hundreds of biscuits and cakes were created for use in the ad.

02-03

'Any car organization expects at least the real car to be shown at some point in the commercial, and ideally shown driving speedily around bends in France and Italy – that's the expectation.'

The agency had established a reputation for making stunning ads that were all created for real, rather than using CGI or special effects. The team wanted to achieve the same surprise and awe with the Skoda ad, to create a real cake car, rather than try to fool the viewer with models. Chris Palmer was chosen to direct, in part because he felt the same way – 'I wanted to do it for real,' he says, 'which I later heard was a different approach to other treatments.'

There was also a fashion at the time for creating 'making-of' films for ads, a tendency that continues in the industry even now. This prompted the idea to make the ad in a documentary style, so the finished piece was a making-of in itself (this also gave birth to the spot's name, The Baking Of). 'There were loads of different script variants for Baking Of,' says Flintham. 'It was really sold as, we're going to make a Fabia out of cake, because cake makes you happy, and cakes are full of lovely stuff. But in the end you work through it with the director, and it ends up being the building of a cake.'

Palmer had demonstrated his skill for creating charming documentary-style advertising in spots for adidas – where David Beckham and Jonny Wilkinson were shown sharing sporting tips – and for Carlsberg, where a group of ex-England football stars were brought together to create 'the best pub team in the world'. For the Skoda ad, Palmer and Fallon hired a crack team of chefs and home economists to make the cake car and star in the ad, including a few who also had some acting experience, who 'could make something happen if it got a bit dull', says Flintham.

Perhaps inevitably, the shoot was not without its problems. 'We got through a few bakers,' remembers Palmer. 'I think it was quite tough. I remember a lot of furrowed brows and accusing eyes looking in my direction.... We did loads of tests. Some cakes turned out really badly. I remember a batch that looked like they were badly wounded. Eventually we figured out that Madeira cake was the best base. The cheapest, nastiest ingredients used in mass-market cakes created the most solid brick.'

On set, Flintham was anxious that none of the 'real moments' of the shoot were missed. 'Chris was great,' he says. 'I was angsty about it – watching people in a prep room doing all this amazing stuff and saying "my God, you've got to be shooting that, it's so exciting." But he found a really nice balance I think. He found a lovely middle ground between authenticity and performance. It was nice that he delivered something where you could see his hand in it, slightly more than we set out to do.'

Part of the solution to keeping Flintham calm was to encourage him to contribute to the making of the car cake. 'I had an idea that we could make a headlight out of Foxes Glacier Mints,' he says. 'So they gave me a glue gun and said "you'll never be able to do that". Which was a masterstroke really – it got me out of the way, sitting there doing this headlight.'

Such inventiveness in the cake's design adds enormously to the final ad's charm, which, alongside the Glacier Mint headlights, includes panels made from Rice Krispies, a Battenberg engine block, liquorice fan belts and jelly tail-lights. Even the oil that is shown being poured into the car is golden syrup. These touches were at times a headache for the team of chefs, however.

04-06

04-13 The ad was shot as if it was a fly-on-the-wall documentary recording the baking of the giant cake. In fact, it was a mixture of real scenes with performance: some of the chefs also had acting experience. But the ad's charm lies in its authentic feel, and a real cake car was built. Production images from the set shown here document the design of various details of the car, including the speed dials and battery.

07-13

'We did loads of tests. Some cakes turned out really badly. I remember a batch that looked like they were badly wounded.'

14-16 Bricks of Madeira cake were used to create the car's basic form. Perhaps unsurprisingly, it turned out that the cheapest ingredients made the most solid and durable blocks of cake.

17-21 Part of the delight of the Skoda ad lies in its attention to detail. Instead of simply creating the external shell of the car, the team sculpted all its internal machinery too. Shown here is the cake engine, alongside other production photographs taken during the shoot.

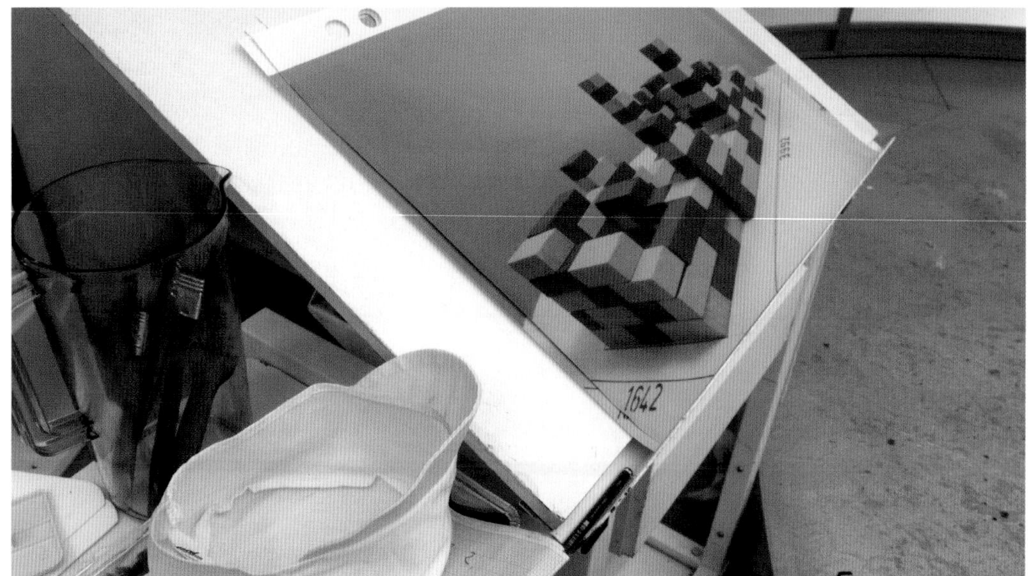

14-16

17-21

'The toughest problem to crack was probably creating a realistic-looking windscreen for the pack shot,' says Palmer. 'Initially the concept of doing it for real horrified the technical experts. At times I felt like the Antichrist, but we were all mates again in the end.'

The shoot took place over four days and resulted in a spectacular, if inedible (due to being under the heat of the studio lights) cake car. All that was left to resolve was the music. As their dream soundtrack, the team had chosen Julie Andrews singing My Favourite Things from The Sound of Music, a song that fitted perfectly with the clean-cut, feel-good tone of the spot. But Andrews had never consented to her voice being used in an ad before. 'The music was the scariest bit,' says Flintham. 'Half an hour before play out we had to wait for Julie Andrews to give her consent, otherwise we had [BBC talent show winner] Connie Fisher. Again good, but when you've just built a bloody Foxes Glacier Mint headlight, you want Julie Andrews to go with it.' In the end, Andrews acquiesced. 'She liked it because of how well Chris had done it, I think,' says Flintham.

Despite the joy of this success, the song did have an impact on the film's length, as Palmer remembers. 'We had so much more footage and a really good longer cut,' he says, 'but the track only really worked for 60 seconds. For some reason, when Julie repeated a verse your inclination was to kick the TV in.'

'We had so much more footage and a really good longer cut, but the track only really worked for 60 seconds. For some reason, when Julie repeated a verse your inclination was to kick the TV in.'

22-24

22-24 The director, Chris Palmer (shown bottom left in fig. 24) was the one who insisted on making the cake car for real. His resolve tested the skills of the bakers and technical experts on set, but they produced an impeccable model of the Fabia by the end.

25-30 Stills from the finished commercial, which was set to a soundtrack of Julie Andrews singing My Favourite Things. It was the first time ever that she had consented to her voice being used in a commercial.

ŠKODA

24/

Sony Bravia Balls

Fallon

One of the most memorable commercials of the 2000s, Sony Balls is a simple proposition. Hundreds of thousands of coloured balls are launched down a hill in San Francisco to create a film that radiates joy, playfulness and a love of colour. In advertising terms though, the film is unusual. It was created to launch Sony's Bravia high-definition television line in 2005, but the product is nowhere to be seen – instead, the audience is offered a feeling. They are invited to connect an emotion with the brand, rather than be wowed by the product's technical capabilities. This strategy ultimately proved highly successful, although it required considerable persuasion by the ad agency, Fallon in London, and bravery by the client to exist at all.

'We wanted to harness a point about colour, so it was important to not just show colour, but to feel colour as well.'

01-02 For the Sony Balls commercial, hundreds of thousands of coloured balls were thrown down the hilly streets of San Francisco. The aim of the ad was to emphasize the Sony Bravia television's superior colour.

01-02

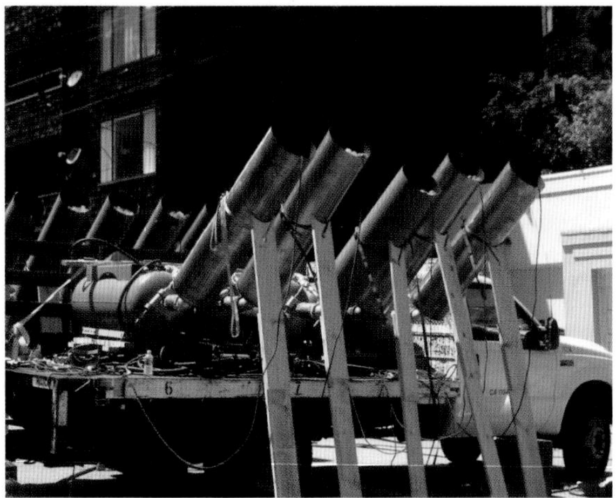

03-08

'Even though it is a brilliant piece of advertising, it could be seen as an original and conceptual piece of art as well.'

03-11 Photographs taken during the shoot for the Sony Balls commercial reveal the crude cannons that were initially used to launch the balls, and the large nets that were set up to try and catch them. Surprisingly little damage was caused during the shoot, although some untested 'rogue balls' did result in a few breakages.

09-11

The initial concept for the spot was born out of the endline that Sony had instructed should be used on all of its advertising: 'Like No Other'. 'It was a global edict,' explains Laurence Green, then chairman of Fallon. 'The great irony was "Like No Other" was written by Y&R in North America, imposed on everything globally that month, and then they lost the business about a month later. We were the first people to carry "Like No Other"; we said, we don't really like that on its own, but let's attach it to the specifics or premise or benefits of the Vaio, or the Walkman, or, in this case, Bravia – which was colour. So we knew the commercial was going to conclude with "Colour Like No Other".'

Another early problem that the creative team identified was that they were trying to sell a new television to an audience via their old sets. This provoked the idea of the ad expressing an emotion, rather than technical prowess, as they would then have a piece of branding that would resonate beyond the specifics of where the ad was being viewed. 'It's a funny head-screwer,' says Richard Flintham, then executive creative director at the agency, 'you're going to be demonstrating how good this is on a different television. We wanted to harness a point about colour, so it was important to not just show colour, but to feel colour as well. That was the big leap – that it would be nice if you really felt this. So we put that in the brief, and Juan [Cabral, creative at Fallon] came back with "let's chuck some bouncy balls down a hill".'

This was pretty much the idea the agency presented to Sony, who liked it but were uncertain, in part because of the proposal's simplicity. 'They were used to more words,' says Flintham, 'but no matter how you try... Juan and I sat there and tried to make it sound longer, but we really struggled to get to a quarter of a page.'

The budget required was also a worry, alongside a concern over the lack of product that would be on show in the film and the fact that it was focusing on just one quality of the television. In early feedback, the client proposed that the piece should showcase sound as well as colour. But Fallon held firm to the original idea, despite it being 'bought and un-bought, pre-produced and un-pre-produced,' according to Green. 'There were moments where we had to say

'I think Sony loved it not just because it worked, but because it elevated marketing and what advertising could do for their business.'

"honestly, this will be the best piece of work we've ever done, you have to do this",' continues Flintham. 'From a script, there's a lot of trust involved in that, a lot of money. It's a big call.'

After many meetings the go-ahead was given and Fallon sought a director. Nicolai Fuglsig was chosen, and from the start he recognized the film's potential to be something startlingly different from the average ad. 'Even though it is a brilliant piece of advertising, it could be seen as an original and conceptual piece of art as well,' he wrote in an early treatment. 'There is no doubt that a very entertaining and colourful film like this could easily end up in galleries like Tate Modern and the Museum of Modern Art. I think it's such a great idea that for the main spot we don't focus on anything but the fantastical journey of the balls.'

Fuglsig was also adamant that the action in the ad be real, rather than a computer-generated concept, which chimed with the creatives' ambitions too. 'There is something so goddamn cool and honest about that,' he wrote in the treatment. 'From the whole shoot and PR point of view it's so great that yes, we are in fact going to drop loads of colourful bouncing balls down some steep streets in a huge city. And I promise you that so much totally unexpected and surprising footage evolves when you actually do things in camera and for real.'

The team settled on hilly San Francisco as the ideal location for the shoot and then spent considerable time sourcing the right, and the most affordable, balls. Fuglsig was keen that the balls be small – 'I feel it is really important that we stay far away from the Ronald McDonald playground-sized balls and even more important that we stay away from football-sized balls,' he wrote at the time. A launching device was also required.

'We saw projection devices, and different cannons, and lorry-mounted cannons, and building-mounted cannons... all this sort of stuff,' says Flintham. Tests were done on virtually everything, before the shoot began.

When viewing the finished film, it is easy to imagine that the launching of the real balls would be spectacular, romantic even. In reality, it was quite shocking. 'We thought it would be beautiful,' says Flintham. 'I took my little boy, Tom – he was five then – and thought it would be a lovely, beautiful thing for him to see. Then we were on a balcony, having been given helmets and some sort of riot shield, and they get released and you just hear the most deafening car alarms, and the odd window smashing.'

Surprisingly, despite the capacity for chaos, the shoot largely went to plan, aside from the impact of some 'rogue balls' that had been sourced at the last minute and missed the tests. 'I think there was one story of someone who came home from holiday and found a perfect hole in his window and a bouncy ball on his floor,' says Flintham. 'But it's America – it's all been completely sorted out. There were giant nets and every drain's been covered, there was nothing that could go wrong... apart from when those balls did start to break windows and we weren't allowed to use cannons anymore. We had to drop them from skips, from big dumper trucks. This meant the balls went down before they went up, rather than up before they went down.'

In the finished film, the balls appear like coloured pixels, bouncing through space. The effect is startling, and emotional. Certain moments ground the scenes in reality though – a woman is shown watching the balls go by through a window, dustbins are knocked over, and, most notoriously, a frog is shown leaping from a drainpipe. This last touch was introduced by Fugslig. 'That one jumped completely out of my head,' he says. 'We cut up a drainpipe, stuffed the fat frog in there, and gently looped five colourful balls into the pipe. We'd already rigged a little lid with some fishing wire on it that we yanked right before impact.'

The atmosphere of the final ad is created in part by its music, which is a gentle, folksy track written by Swedish musicians The Knife, and performed by José González. It was initially suggested by Flintham. 'There was a theory that we might use something like that, because it felt nice, it was honest, the brand was being warm,' he says. When they played it alongside the rushes, it worked perfectly, and the music in fact led to the ad achieving a wider showcase than could have first been imagined. González bought out a single of it, and appeared on UK music television show Top of the Pops with the ad playing behind him. By serendipity, the music ended up fulfilling Sony's original desire for the ad to contain an emphasis on sound too. 'You'd suddenly hear conversations about the way

'I think there was one story of someone who came home from holiday and found a perfect hole in his window and a bouncy ball on his floor.'

that you can hear the strings,' says Flintham, 'the little moments when José touches the string, brushes the string. That ticked the sound brief – and of course we meant that as well....'

Sony Balls as an individual ad is immensely striking, but the making of it also unexpectedly signalled a sea change in the way that advertising is shared with the public. At the time, advertising was still an extraordinarily secretive world – the suggestion that an idea for a launch campaign could be leaked in advance was catastrophic. 'The rules of campaigns, and especially product launches, were that you go away and you privately shoot something, plan something, plot something, and then when it's all perfectly polished and honed, you present it to your internal people, then you present it to the trade, then, on a certain day, it appears. People see it for the first time on the air date,' explains Green. 'It seems kind of sweet now that that's how it used to work.' By throwing 250,000 balls down a hill though, it was difficult to keep the idea under wraps, and the agency discovered that photographs and videos of the balls were popping up all over the internet even before the shoot was over.

The news was initially terrifying, although Flintham now describes it as 'the

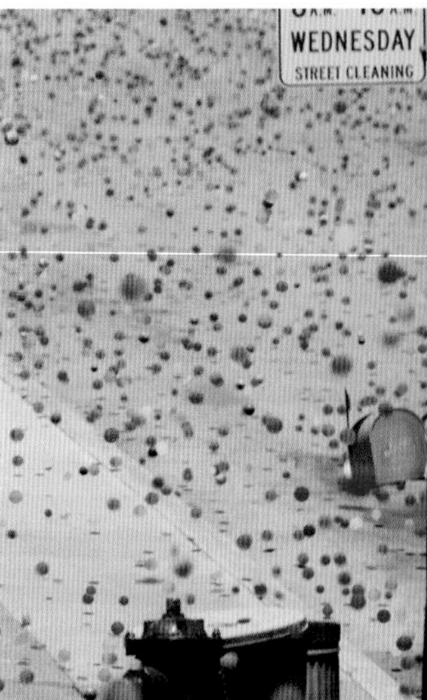

12-16

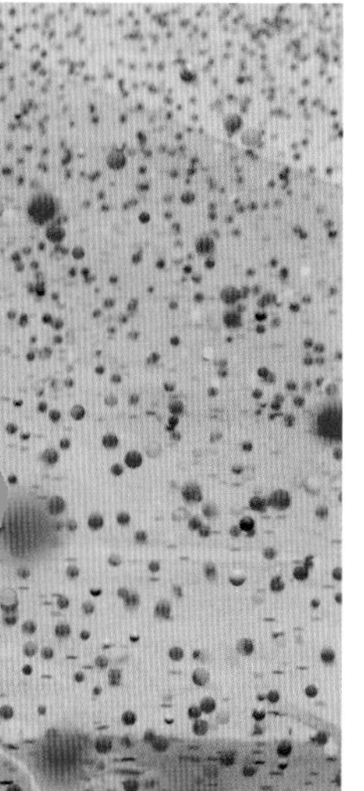

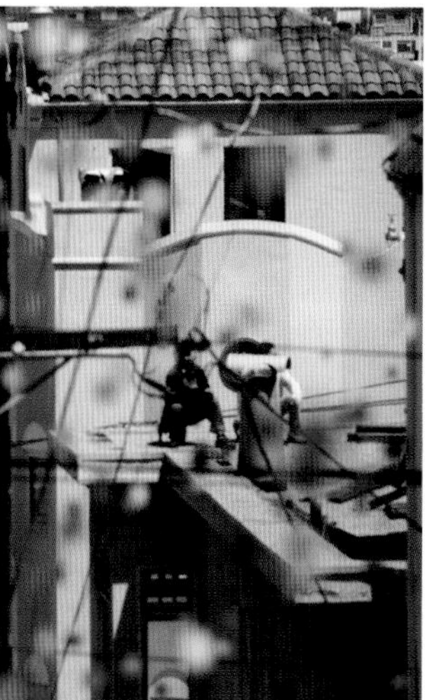

12-16 Stills from the final commercial. The visuals were set to José González's folksy cover version of The Knife track 'Heartbeats', which gave the commercial a warm, almost hypnotic feel.

day we woke up as an agency,' as they began to realize that such unsolicited enthusiasm for the enterprise could only be a good thing. The leaked imagery also served as a teaser for the final film, which of course was quite different. 'What they didn't know is that what was coming is slow motion, and they don't know the music,' says Flintham. 'Literally we had wave after wave of news.' The rest of the ad industry watched this occur, and realized its power. Controlled leaks prior to an ad's release and making-of films have now become standard in the industry, with agencies these days longing for their audiences to be interested enough to share this information with their friends.

By the time that Sony Balls was finished, both the agency and the client knew that they had something astonishing, so they aired it with great confidence – first in a two-and-a-half-minute version that played out in the UK in the middle of a Chelsea versus Manchester United football match, a sporting event that guaranteed a huge audience.

Fallon had set a tone for the brand that would continue in its advertising for many years. 'I think Sony loved it not just because it worked,' says Green, 'but because it elevated marketing and what advertising could do for their business. It elevated it back to a level it had been maybe 10 years previously, maybe 20 years previously. For big projects, it wrote a new model for how Sony would go about marketing stuff.'

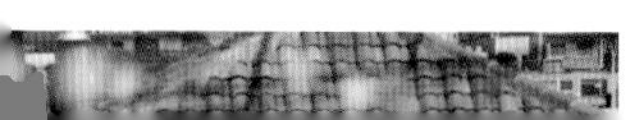

25/

Sony Bravia Paint

Fallon

Following up a successful piece of work, whether it be an album or a piece of great advertising, is never easy. Yet this was the situation that the London-based Fallon advertising agency faced when they began work on Sony Paint, which was the second ad in the Colour Like No Other series of ads for Sony Bravia. The spot followed Balls (see page 172), an ad that startled both the public and the ad industry, and began a trend for warm, folksy ads that continues to this day. Fallon knew that they needed to do something different with the second ad, to create something new that would prove as striking as Balls.

01-03

'We shot nothing else that day – nine hours of preparation under dark storm clouds, and four seconds of shooting in about ten seconds of sun at six in the evening. And not a single barrel failed to detonate. Perfect.'

01-03 The Sony Paint ad was filmed using a condemned tower block in Glasgow. The production team look on as hundreds of barrels of paint are detonated up the building to achieve the 'rainbow sequence' that is at the core of the film.

04-05

'I think everyone was saying, "you've got to do another one now, are you scared?"' remembers Richard Flintham, then executive creative director at the agency. 'You shouldn't be scared – you've got a really good company who's sponsoring you to think of something else that no-one's seen before. It's a great thing. It wasn't the second album, it was the second single, it was fun still.'

The agency came up with the idea of doing a 'daytime fireworks display', and quickly brought in director Jonathan Glazer, who helped refine the idea. 'I'm trying to work out what was on the table before Jonathan was in the room,' says Flintham. 'I think there was an idea around a building spewing colour, and there were loads of fire engines squirting different coloured paints to put out the colours. We talked to Jonathan about it, and he quite rightly said that it was trying a little bit too hard.

Although the ball thing felt quite free, we wanted it to feel a bit more constructed; within something like that you'd have to manufacture every stage of it. There would be very little room for God, if you know what I mean. We were trying to explain to Jonathan that it wanted to feel like a daytime fireworks display, and then he said "let's do that then. Let's forget the fire engines, let's just turn it into the most amazing daytime paint fireworks display." Which is great, that chopped away so much stuff we didn't need.'

After the sunny San Francisco setting of Balls, the team decided to film Paint in the somewhat more sombre environs of an estate in Glasgow, Scotland. They received permission to film on a condemned tower block that was due to be pulled down in the Toryglen district of the city, and testing began. 'There were so many obstacles,' says Glazer. 'Paint is heavy. Mimicking a fireworks display with gallons of paint instead of grams of gunpowder was incredibly challenging. We spent months and months testing ways to get the paint 22 storeys high. Obviously, because of the paint left on every surface, we had to shoot chronologically and there was no opportunity for a second take on anything, so the planning had to be absolutely meticulous. Nevertheless, with miles and miles of wiring, exactly timed explosives and thousands of barrels filled with very precise shades of colour – filled by an army of art students – it was remarkable that actually everything, apart from the weather, did go to plan.'

According to Glazer, the fireworks were constructed using 'vast quantities of paint – coloured food thickener that wouldn't mix to brown or poison the water table; substantial quantities of explosive from black power charges to TNT; and truly heroic amounts of ingenuity, passion and problem-solving from Mark Mason at Asylum [post house] and Chris Oddy, the art director.'

'The rainbow sequence up the height of the building relied on hundreds of barrels of paint suspended and wired to detonate precisely in time to the music track,' he continues. 'The whole sequence was one shot lasting 4.5 seconds, all achieved in camera. For the airborne explosions we basically rigged the sky using cranes that needed cranes to build them, and each of the enormous ground-shaking paint eruptions on the lawn was a one-tonne container full of paint buried and rigged with TNT.'

Alongside heckles from the onlooking locals, the major issue that the team faced on the shoot was the weather, and a stubborn lack of sun. This made for a nerve-racking time for all, as they sat waiting for a section of sunshine to break through in order to capture the rainbow sequence, a shot that could only be done once. 'I remember sitting there and going "that's our budget",' says Flintham. 'We could recreate all the other ones. But that's taken days and days to rig. You've got a grey sky, and you don't really want greyness. It's fine to have a grey backdrop, but we wanted lightness to hit the colour of the paint, because it would have been a flat colour otherwise.'

The team were only blessed with a tiny window of sunshine to capture the rainbow moment, but achieved it, with Glazer now remembering it as his favourite part of the shoot. 'It was just such a fantastic four seconds to witness after all the months of

06

07

04-05 A hard-hat souvenir from the shoot; Director Jonathan Glazer (left) discusses progress on set with members of the production team.

06-07 The buildings on the estate covered with barrels of paint prior to detonation; cranes were used to put all the paint barrels in place.

08-15 Stills from a short computer-generated film that Jonathan Glazer created to help plan how the ad was shot.

16 The mysterious clown, who appears towards the end of the spot, on set.

'There was an idea around a building spewing colour, and there were loads of fire engines squirting different coloured paints to put out the colours. We talked to Jonathan about it, and he quite rightly said that it was trying a little bit too hard.'

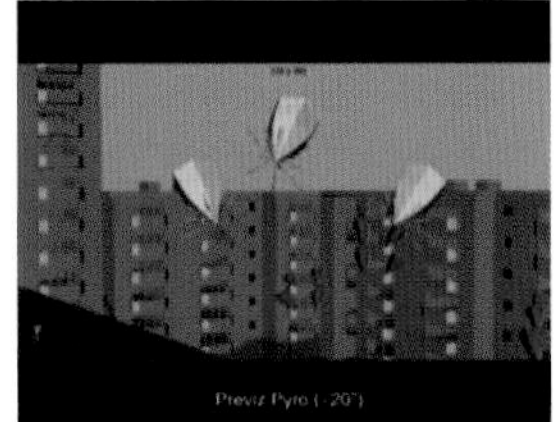

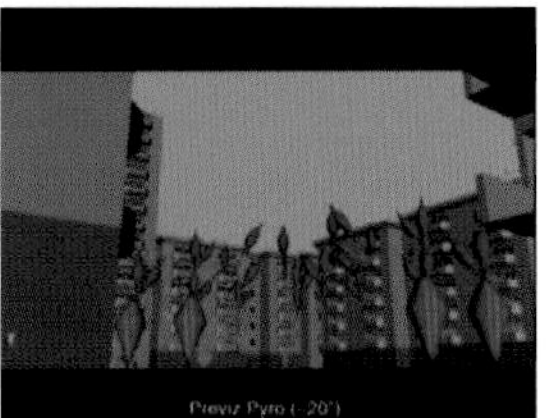

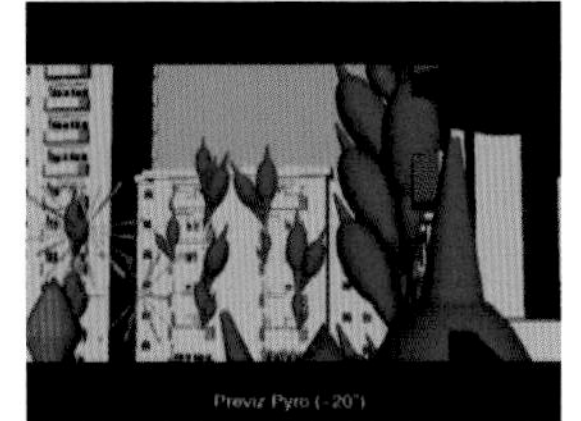

08-15

16

13

'We spent months and months testing ways to get the paint 22 storeys high. Obviously, because of the paint left on every surface, we had to shoot chronologically and there was no opportunity for a second take on anything, so the planning had to be absolutely meticulous.'

13-14 The crew attempt to protect themselves and the cameras against the showers of paint.

15-17 The aftermath of the shoot shows the rainbow-coloured paint that covered the buildings and the park in the Toryglen estate, which was demolished as planned after the filming.

14

work,' he says, 'and such a perfect distillation of everything the ad was about. We shot nothing else that day – nine hours of preparation under dark storm clouds, and four seconds of shooting in about ten seconds of sun at six in the evening. And not a single barrel failed to detonate. Perfect.'

Much of the post-production for the ad revolved around removing the cranes and other structures used to set the fireworks from the shot. What is left is the magical sight of paint exploding magnificently up the grey tower block. In the first version of the ad, the team chose to enhance the sense of the triumphant by setting the imagery to the overture to The Thieving Magpie by Gioachino Rossini. A later version uses just the sounds of the paint explosions themselves – which in many ways is more powerful, due to its simplicity. As with Balls, where a frog is unexpectedly shown leaping across one shot, Paint has its own quirky moment, introduced by Glazer. In a surreal scene, a clown is shown running across the frame, giving the film a narrative twist – was he the one who set the explosions?

Due to the success of Balls, there was already much anticipation surrounding Paint before it came out in 2006. Fallon decided to capitalize on this to generate more PR for the ad. The team learnt from the experience on Balls, where onlookers at the shoot shared photos and films of the event online, and realized that giving the audience a taste of what was to come could prove an advantageous strategy. 'By the time we were doing Paint, we'd had a million views of the making-of film of Balls, not just the commercial, so we built a micro-site [to build interest around the new ad],' says Laurence Green, then chairman at Fallon. 'All we said was that we'd upload details of the shoot and early edits... so people did know where it was, and were checking on the site to see what had been uploaded.' This proved successful, for by the time the ad came out, the media and the public were desperate to see the results. The awkward second album (or single, according to Flintham) more than lived up to expectation, and was eagerly shared, written about and discussed all over the world.

26/

Sony PlayStation
The History of Gaming; The Future of Gaming

Johnny Hardstaff

Traditionally, an advertising campaign is developed in a fairly formulaic fashion. A client will brief its agency, the agency will devise a campaign, and – for TV commercials at least – a director will be commissioned to bring the idea to life in film. Occasionally, however, a project will follow a less ordinary path, as is the case with two brand films that were created for Sony PlayStation back in 2000–01. The films are unusual firstly in their content: rather than advertising a specific aspect of PlayStation to customers, they convey a general message about gaming itself, and its significance to our lives. The first film depicts gaming's past, while the second is a meditation on what gaming's future may look like.

The development of the films was unconventional too, for rather than being made to a brief, they were conceived entirely by director Johnny Hardstaff, who, upon finishing his first short film, decided to pitch it directly to a client. He chose Sony, who immediately recognized the potential of his work. This first film had developed out of a combination of creative experimentation and tenacity. Having studied graphic design at Central St Martins College of Art and Design in London, Hardstaff was determined not to enter a dead-end design job on graduation. Instead, he worked in a variety of places – including a mortuary and at Billingsgate Fish Market – and toiled away on his own projects at night. 'I'd been keeping sketchbooks and amassing

01 Director Johnny Hardstaff's first film for Sony is a nostalgic look at gaming's past, with imagery from old computer games set to a soundtrack of Minnie Ripperton's soul track Les Fleurs. Stills from the finished film are shown here, while two pages from Hardstaff's sketchbooks for the film are overleaf.

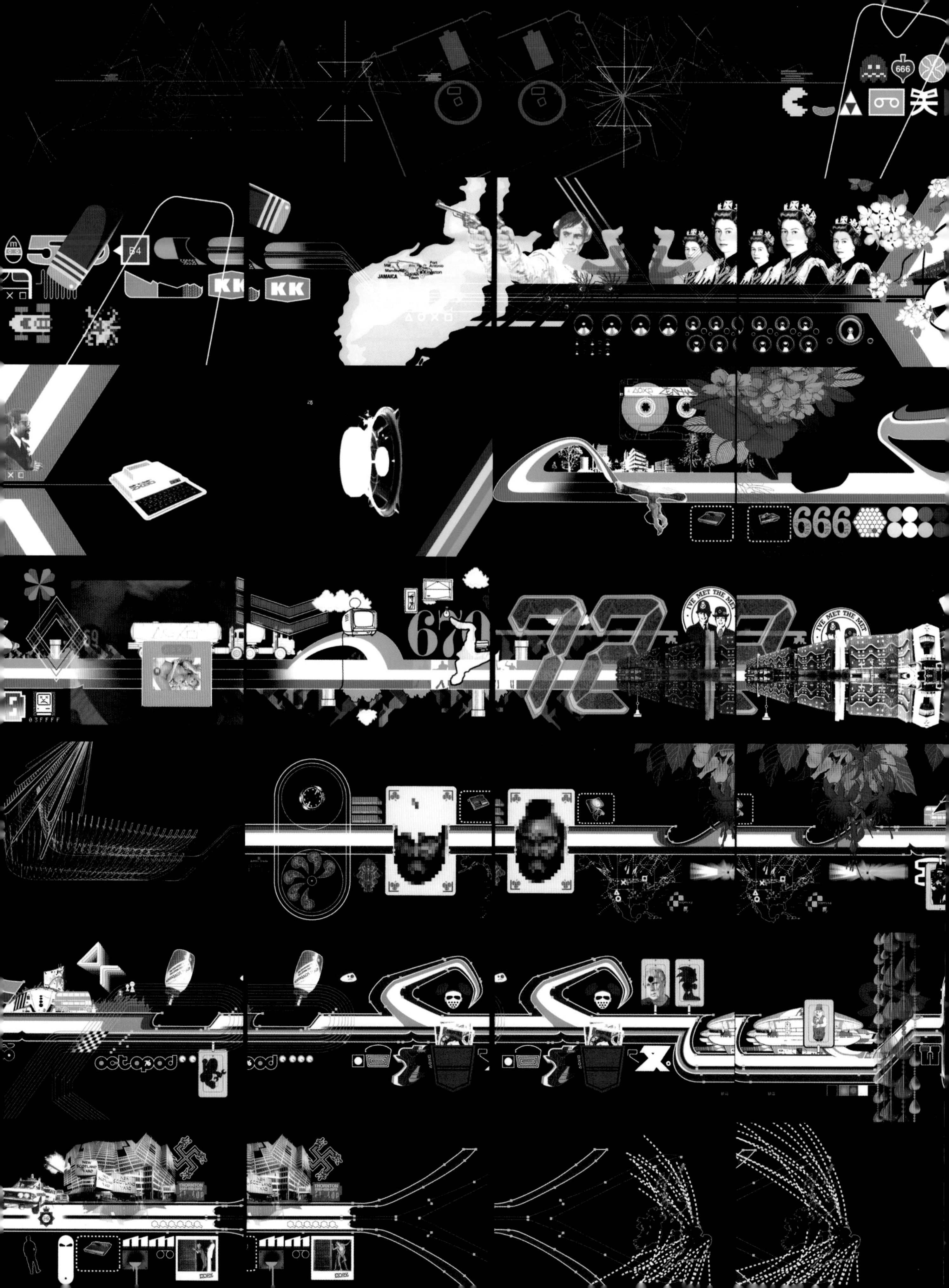

Baby Defenceman - Urban Police Operational Unit.
Infrared Stadium:
Motorsport race arena.
Rough number 5: Infrared Stadium: Copyright
Johnny Hardstaff @ Tudor 1998.

Roulette
Roulette
A-team van
Crack
FIRE
His Hers
'Kunt'
Skirt up-
Grasp knickers + turn
'k' down-
in blue + orange + pink
DANGER
Red line builds up obscuring car wash with colour sweep-
Miss Matched identical stripes
black slides up to reveal girl on white
Drops back to obscure pussy-
'HAPPY DAYS'
60345
Avoids spills for Mums
'Killy'
Blood spatt
Car wash brushes slides in: spring to life-
Kent
love
V. IMPT- static for 5 seconds- then kicks off-
pauses on lilac redraw
'Milk bikini'
KY
Strap on-
DG
everyone stops-
all eyes blink then on spit dripping down- then look to camera-
ABSORBERS

02

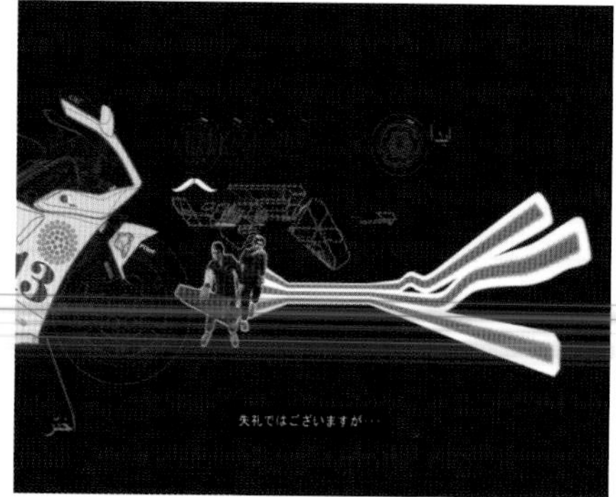

03

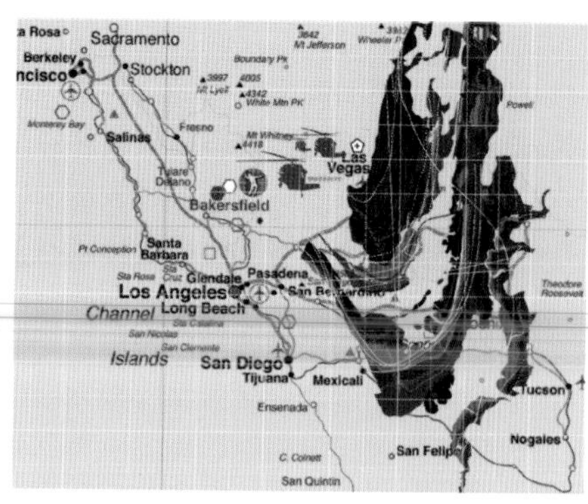

04

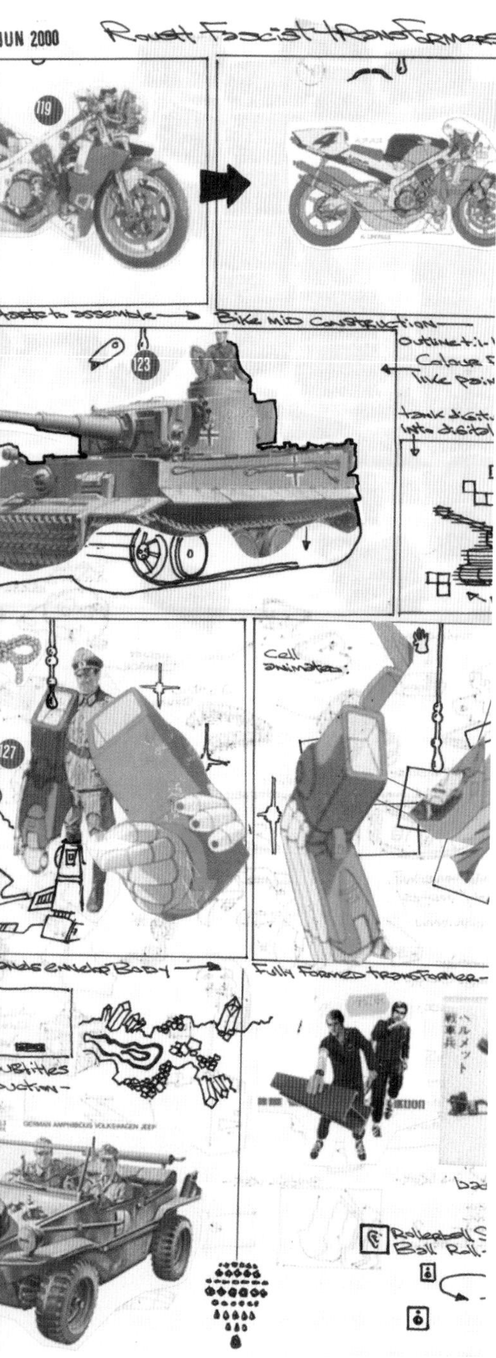

05

all this information,' he says of this time. 'Then the sketchbooks got to a point where I started to do drawings and develop these graphic freeforms. I thought it would be really nice to make them move. There was no rhyme or reason. I thought I'd build a narrative out of these sketches, put it all together and show people.'

Hardstaff chose the laborious process of using Photoshop to make his first moving-image piece. 'I didn't have any training in anything, and I'd taught myself to use Photoshop,' he explains. 'It was the worst way of working, but I wasn't even aware that there was a program called After Effects. So I made it in Photoshop, which means you save a frame and go on to the next, it's like cell animation.' After months of work, Hardstaff took all the frames to Lux, an arts centre in London, where a technician put them together with the music that Hardstaff had chosen. 'I saw the film, which was kind of emotional – I cried,' he says.

With the encouragement of those who'd seen it, Hardstaff decided to approach Sony PlayStation with the film. It was a successful meeting. The film featured a number of game motifs, and was set to the nostalgic but joyous tones of Minnie Ripperton's song Les Fleurs; Sony saw that it could become a homage to computer gaming's past. 'They saw some chronology within it, and said "could you modify it and call it The History of Gaming?",' says Hardstaff. 'They felt they could use it for some kind of subversive purpose.'

To many young directors, such an opportunity might seem like a dream come true, yet Hardstaff was uncomfortable about the company's intentions from the outset. 'In the meeting I took such a dislike to them and this marketing nonsense,' he admits. 'I took a dislike to the idea that their agenda was creeping so heavily into something I was making.' But alongside this disquiet, Hardstaff was aware of the potential of the connection. 'Already they were talking about another one,' he says. 'I thought, I'll do this, but I wonder what we can do on the next one....'

Hardstaff modified the film and Sony was delighted with it, releasing it with the PlayStation 2 console when it launched, and showing it at film festivals and events. Hardstaff gained attention as a result and signed to RSA Films for representation. On the back of the success, Sony was indeed keen for another film from him, this time on the theme of The Future of Gaming. There was little budget on offer, however, so Sony came to an unusual arrangement with Hardstaff and RSA: they agreed to sign a contract that gave the director full ownership of the film, meaning he would be allowed to show it wherever he liked. This gave Hardstaff just the freedom he'd been after, along with ample opportunity for mischief.

Hardstaff set about looking for a narrative that would prove provocative. 'I heard about a brilliant conference call that had gone on in [Sony's] office, because I'd got to know one of the secretaries there,' Hardstaff says. The conference call related to a UK marketing campaign for the brand that had gone horribly wrong. 'Legend has it there was this amazing call between Mr PlayStation in Japan and the PlayStation marketing manager in the UK, where he just ripped the life out of them,' he continues. 'I thought that was too tasty to miss, so I thought I'd use that as the basis for this film. I thought that would really annoy them.'

'It was exciting because I could see already that the commissioning opportunities in the UK within advertising and music videos were challenged,' he continues. 'It was really tricky to make anything that one wanted to make.... I felt that the commissioning opportunities were such that one needed to try to explode a hole in it, or explode a hole for yourself. I was feeling spunky enough to just have an agenda and put it out there, to see what

'It was really tricky to make anything that one wanted to make.... I felt that the commissioning opportunities were such that one needed to try to explode a hole in it, or explode a hole for yourself.'

people would say. I wasn't clamouring to work in advertising.' And if you annoy a huge corporation, Hardstaff believes, 'they're so big that they don't care, they'll just come back one day.'

The second film that Hardstaff created for Sony PlayStation is dark in tone, featuring shocking imagery overlaid with a spoof of the conference call. It is stylistically utterly in opposition to the feel-good atmosphere of the first short. 'I thought we'd been really clever in getting a corporation to pay for essentially an anti-corporate piece of work,' says Hardstaff now. 'We went in there and played it to them – and there were cakes and stuff, it was a really nice setting – and basically they never spoke to us again. There was absolute silence. People walked out and we were left with a film that they just wouldn't touch.'

'We'd kept the copyright though, so we could go and put it wherever we wanted,' he continues. 'So we did – we put it everywhere we possibly could. The film festivals just loved it, went mad for it, showing it globally. It's gone everywhere – even Tate Modern.'

Such a viral response to a film prior to the launch of websites such as YouTube or Vimeo is impressive. Hardstaff's film was an early precursor, albeit a risqué one, to the short films that brands have begun to sponsor in recent years, which are intended to be viewed and shared online. Yet his film was spreading without the benefits offered by the internet. Despite this, looking back on the experience, he is not as happy with the outcome as might be expected. 'I knew I'd pulled some punches with it, in a way,' he says; 'because as much as it's an anti-corporate piece, it kind of aggrandises PlayStation as well. I had a very negative view of their product. I never play, and have never really played computer games, because I can't imagine wasting that amount of time. For kids it's brilliant, but I really resent what they're doing to people. But I pulled my punches.'

06

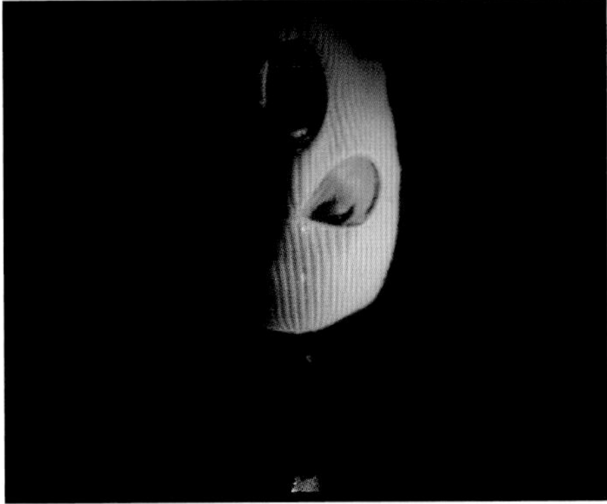

07

02-07 Hardstaff's second film – which had the future of gaming as its theme – was deliberately a much darker affair. Stills from the finished film are shown here, alongside a detail from one of Hardstaff's sketchbooks (05), within which he collated imagery and ideas related to the film.

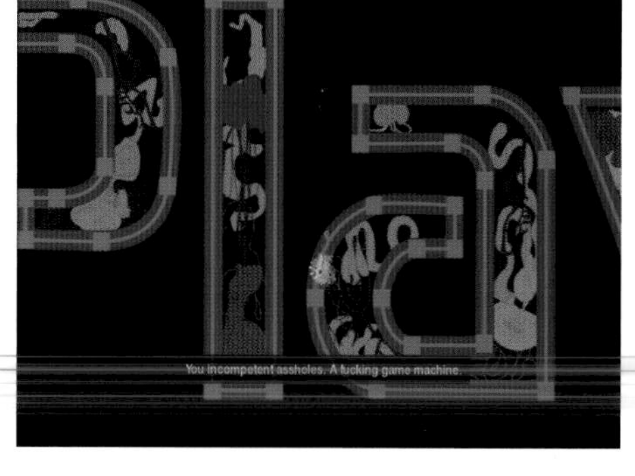

09

10

11

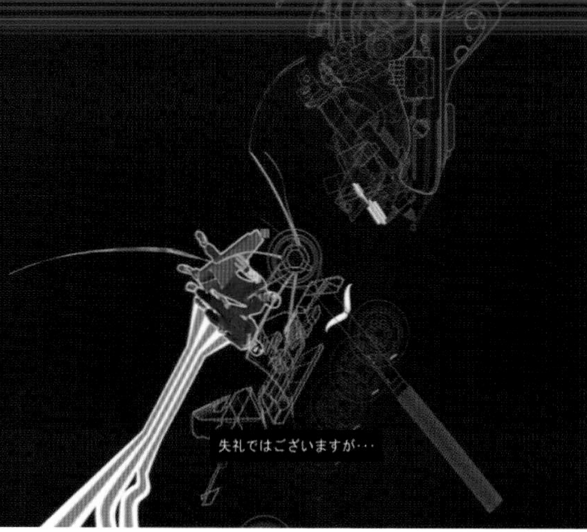

08

'It made them look fabulous. People couldn't believe this had been made for PlayStation. Their caveat, their get-out-of-jail card was that they had nothing to do with it. They didn't endorse it, but they were happy to leave their logo on it.'

Even more frustratingly, Hardstaff now feels that, despite his intentions, he played directly into Sony's hands, creating a film that in fact boosted the brand rather than humiliating it. Though the corporation couldn't be seen to have commissioned something so provocative, they undoubtedly benefited from its success.

'It made them look fabulous,' Hardstaff concludes. 'People couldn't believe this had been made for PlayStation. Their caveat, their get-out-of-jail card was that they had nothing to do with it. They didn't endorse it, but they were happy to leave their logo on it. They're big enough, they could have crushed the whole thing if they'd wanted. They could lock you down into years of legal dispute. They didn't. They let it go everywhere.'

Both The History of Gaming and The Future of Gaming still enjoy regular attention via the internet more than ten years after their first release. And despite his mixed feelings about them now, the films kick-started a fruitful career for Hardstaff, who has since created films and music videos for a number of artists and brands. Somewhat ironically, these clients still include Sony, who, as he prophesized, did indeed eventually come back for more.

08-14 Pages from one of Hardstaff's sketchbooks for The Future of Gaming film are shown, overlaid with stills from the finished film. In the end, The Future of Gaming proved too risqué for Sony to officially endorse, although as Hardstaff owned the rights, it appeared in film festivals around the world regardless.

12

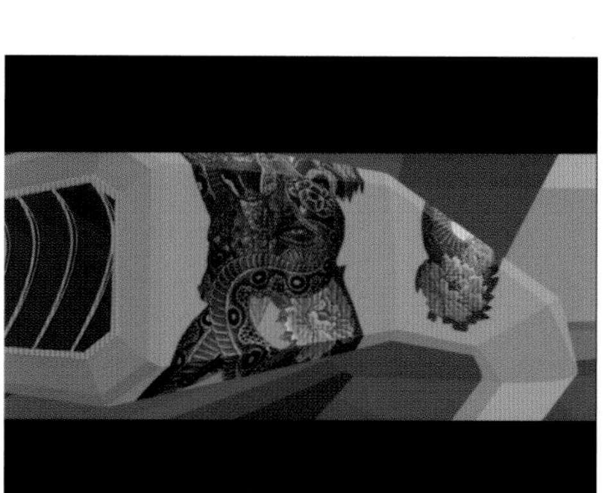

13

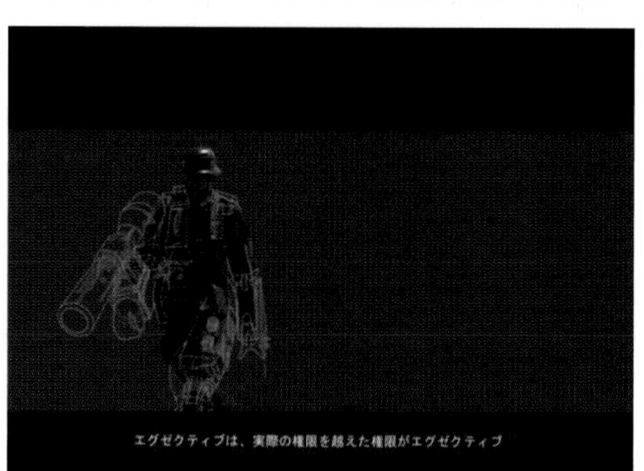

14

QUEEN'S GARDENS
FOR PAVILION LEISURE CENTRE CAR PARKS
LEVEL 2
LEVEL 1
FOR CAR PARKS
FOOD COURT
DEBENHAMS BASEMENT
DEBENHAMS
ENTRANCE ELMFIELD ROAD
OTTAKAR'S
OTTAKAR'S MEZZANINE LEVEL ABOVE REGENT ARCADE
MARKS & SPENCER MENSWEAR
MARKS & SPENCER
BROMLEY SOUTH ENTRANCE
.M113
Scale up + Blur on Sound
Uncovering Horns: Rollerball test Horn:
Strobed
Crunchy Flame Morph — Extended Duration:
v.impt – Both morph objects in view
Shatter
Rollerball
Navigational Device — at end of each trooper
Camera Zooms in
Walking in Jap characters
Computer coding fighting each other – subtitles – chimming each almost mini film in film
animate arrows etc
Get Laurie Anderson not voiceover – v.american – arab voice – japanese voice – subtitles transfer languages – pauses – when jap voice speaks = no subtitles – talk of future of gaming = alarm – gradually reaches admission of unlimited potential of future gaming = fear –
we simply will not be able to control what these machines
with fuzzy static
brief pixellated flashes of army footage
Zoom
أحلامك الاقتصادية هي كابوسنا
إحدى عشر خطوة للقتال
احميني بشدة
لا تحتاج لتعليمات
Is this something I need to worry about?

27/

Stella Artois
La Nouvelle 4%

Mother

'Ask anyone and they'll probably say that they'd love to have been in their twenties in the 1960s. Even now, it's cool. There is stuff that happened then, and stuff that was designed and created then, that is just cool. The furniture still looks modern now, the cars are beautiful, everything looks beautiful. There was a certain innocence, but it's when the world changed.' As John Cherry, a creative at advertising agency Mother in London suggests, the 1960s contained a certain aura of style and sophistication that remains highly desirable today. So when Stella Artois was launching its new 4% variant in 2009, they looked to the decade for inspiration.

01-02

01-06 Robert McGinnis's early sketches for one of the Stella Artois La Nouvelle 4% posters, with the finished ad shown right. The drawings show McGinnis's different ideas for the characters in the ad.

03-05

La Vie
TRÈS SMOOTH
STELLA ARTOIS
STELLA ARTOIS
4%
TRIPLE FILTERED
smooth lager
Triple filtered.
Smooth taste.

07-11 Drawings and early paintings created by McGinnis for another poster. Each painting shows subtle differences in the characters' hairstyles and clothing.

12

13

12 Robert McGinnis working on the pool poster in his studio in the U.S.

13 The final poster sees the girl presented with her hair up, rather than flowing down her shoulders as in many of the test paintings.

'Robert McGinnis is undoubtedly the best film poster illustrator of the 1960s, and probably one of the best poster designers ever, so it wasn't a hard choice.... He was retired, but to our surprise he told us he was willing to come out of retirement to do this project.'

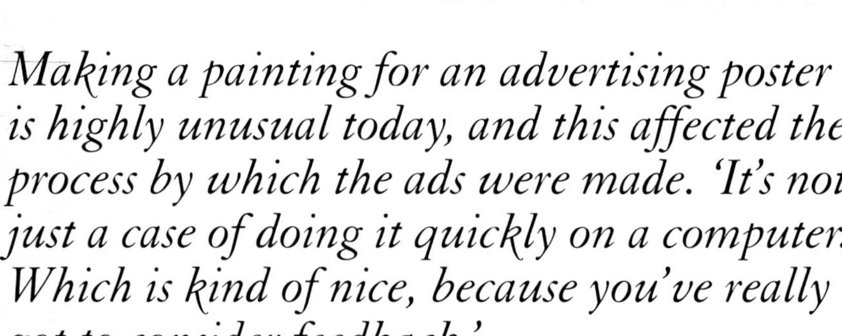

14-15

Making a painting for an advertising poster is highly unusual today, and this affected the process by which the ads were made. 'It's not just a case of doing it quickly on a computer. Which is kind of nice, because you've really got to consider feedback.'

The team wanted to achieve an authentic 1960s look for the poster campaign, and in looking at illustrators that would offer this, they discovered the work of Robert McGinnis, who created classic posters for films including Breakfast At Tiffany's and Barbarella, as well as the Bond movies Live and Let Die and Thunderball. 'We tried to make the work look as genuine as possible, so it becomes a homage to that era, rather than just a parody of it,' say Gustavo Sousa and Rodrigo Saavedra, creatives on the project. 'Robert McGinnis is undoubtedly the best film poster illustrator of the 1960s, and probably one of the best poster designers ever, so it wasn't a hard choice. In fact, we had been referencing his posters when we started looking for illustrators, but we thought he was retired. Eventually we thought "what if we try it?" and decided to give him a call. As we expected, he was retired, but to our surprise he told us he was willing to come out of retirement to do this project.'

'When you see his imagery, it defines that era,' continues Cherry. 'It was before photomontages were used – it was still painted stuff.' Making a painting for an advertising poster is highly unusual today, and this affected the process by which the ads were made. 'It's not just a case of doing it quickly on a computer,' says Cherry. 'Which is kind of nice, because you've really got to consider feedback. It's not unusual now to say, "let's see it" before you make a judgement on an image, rather than using your imagination.' These images required a leap of faith by Mother, who would send McGinnis a rough outline of what they wanted in the poster, and then let him develop it. 'I mean, he knows what the 1960s were like better than we do,' says Cherry. 'He painted a lot of Riviera stuff, so we'd just send him references. We'd prowl the internet for the right kind of 1960s furniture and clothing and stuff like that. But it was very much a collaborative thing, and we'd always bow down to his judgement, because he was there.'

McGinnis made early sketches for the posters and would consult the agency over some specific points, but then sent back actual paintings for Mother to view and approve. Often these would be more or less finished when the agency first saw them, which caused some anxiety among the creatives on the project. 'The first thing he'd supply to us was a painting, with a lot of colour and detail in there, and we'd say "don't – because you're going to have to do more work if it's not right!",' says Cherry. 'Obviously we were going to have a few things to feed back and we didn't want him to do it all again.'

Despite these concerns, the experience of working with McGinnis was a pleasure for all involved. 'It was all very easy,' remembers Cherry. 'I know I shouldn't say that, but it was very smooth. He's an artist and I think the clients were very appreciative that he actually accepted to do it. He is very much the guy that knows that world.'

McGinnis also drew the product image for the posters, which was placed separately onto the painting after it was completed. The type for the project was handpainted in-house at Mother, and again positioned after the central painting was finished. Otherwise, the posters remained largely true to their source images, with little correction made. 'There was a little bit of jiggery-pokery going on, but there wasn't a lot,' says Cherry. 'But it was quite funny because we would spend a lot of time doing that, because everything else had taken a long time, and we didn't want to spoil it.'

14-16 Drawings for the seaplane poster, including a selection of different potential faces for the characters.

17-19 The slow development of the poster can be seen through these sketches and an early painting. The finished poster is shown centre.

Mans costume
Maybe brown Leather
Jacket?
alternate
Hair-dos

16-19

LA NOUVELLE 4%
STELLA
ARTOIS
4%
TRIPLE FILTERED
smooth lager
Triple filtered. Smooth taste.

20-22 The piano poster features the female figure reading her book, while the man stares intently out at the viewer.

ELLE 4%
STELLA ARTOIS
STELLA ARTOIS
4%
TRIPLE FILTERED
smooth lager
iple filtered. Smooth taste.
www.drinkaware.co.uk ©2009 InBev UK Limited, all rights reserved.

28/

Uniqlo
Uniqlock
Projector Inc

Uniqlock took an age-old invention, the clock, and reinterpreted it for the digital age. Designed by Koichiro Tanaka at Projector Inc in Tokyo as a piece of branding and marketing for the Japanese clothing brand Uniqlo, Uniqlock is a downloadable digital clock that can be placed onto blogs or used as a screensaver. It mixes films of Uniqlo-clad dancers with a digital clock face that counts down each second. The clothes worn by the dancers change depending on the time of day and the season, with polo shirts worn in the summer, jumpers in the winter. At midnight, the dancers are shown asleep. By mixing charming and constantly changing visuals and music with the usefulness of a clock, Tanaka created a piece of advertising that customers in their droves sought to engage with.

From the beginning, Tanaka intended to attract the attention of bloggers. 'I wanted to create a new circuit, or a new path, to connect Uniqlock and consumers across the world; that's how I started,' he says. 'I focused on the blog, because I read blogs every day. One thing I realized while I was observing various blogs, is that when there is interesting information, and interesting content, it spreads across the world very, very quickly.'

'However, it is not sufficient just to create blog content that is entertaining,' Tanaka continues. 'Because if there is something else interesting on the blog, the initial content will disappear very quickly. So I thought what was needed was not just interesting blog content, but something that would remain as a fixture on the sidebar, something that has utility. Unless it has utility, people don't want to see it for a long time. We always wear a watch, so that's why I came up with the idea of the clock. The clock is useful, it has utility, but it goes beyond mere utility – it has an entertaining element too. At the same time, I wondered how I could translate Uniqlo into an entertainment. Almost instinctively, it came to me that the physical movements of people who are wearing Uniqlo clothes, in a dance, could be the simplest, most universal expression of the brand.'

01-04 The Uniqlock screensaver and app intercuts a digital clock face with footage of dancers dressed in Uniqlo outfits performing short rhythmical set pieces. The dancers are clothed in outfits relevant to the season of the country where the clock is being viewed.

05 Teaser films showing the auditions for Uniqlock were released on YouTube in advance of the campaign's launch.

06 Users can download the Uniqlock app to feature on blogs via the Uniqlo website.

UNIQLOCK MUSIC DANCE CLOCK

MUSIC FANTASTIC PLASTIC MACHINE
DANCE WHO WILL? ←
CLOCK GET FREE

6 15 START

'I thought what was needed was not just interesting blog content, but something that would remain as a fixture on the sidebar, something that has utility.'

01-04

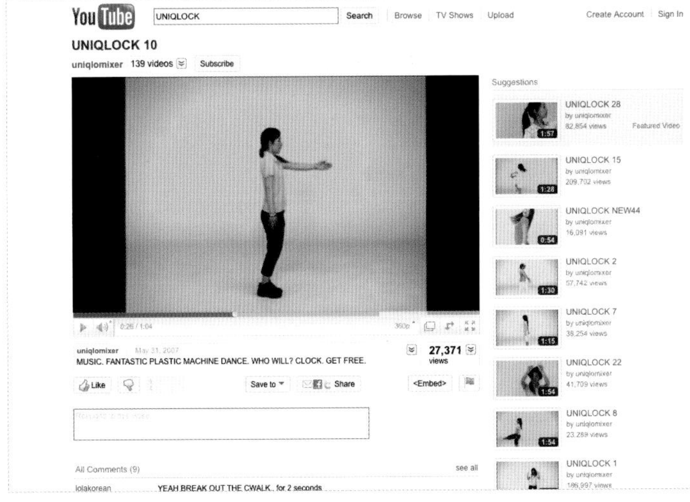

05

06

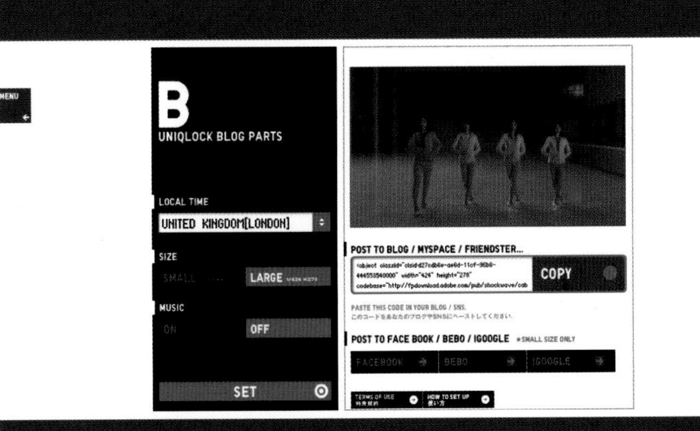

'I overwhelmed the web development team with a vast number of development briefs, so the team leader was frightened of me. He said that he was so frightened that for about a week before the launch he was not able to sleep.'

07

Tanaka realized that the rhythm of the dancers would combine well with the time beats of a clock, and Uniqlock was born. To execute the concept, he teamed up with a commercial production company to create the films of the dancers, and worked with a freelance web development team to implement the technology. He also brought in a PR team very early in the process, to propose ideas for how Uniqlock could be seeded into various media. Unusually, he oversaw the entire production process personally, as this deep involvement by one person is a core element of Projector's working practice. 'If you are to carry out a project in a completely innovative way, I think it is very important that there is one person who is completely committed to the project,' Tanaka says. 'I think the important thing is not to have a large number of staff, but one person who is completely committed.'

'My brief for the video production team was to produce a dance video that would go on and on forever, 24 hours a day, 365 days a year,' he continues. 'We made about 100 clips for various seasons – we had to create them in two days, so we only had a very short amount of time to create each clip.' Tanaka decided to alternate each five-second dance clip with a five-second clock interface, a decision that contributed to the smooth running of Uniqlock. 'The insertion of a clock between dance clips has the hypnotic effect of making viewers want to see the next clip, and also technically speaking it was possible to use the five-second clock display for pre-loading the dance footage,' he says. 'So it was a kind of breakthrough that we were able to make the loading invisible to viewers. Also the clock cut up the visual timeline, making it possible to reshuffle the dance clips and play them endlessly and completely at random.' The music for Uniqlock was designed to endlessly loop as well.

Such an intense working process was not without its difficulties. 'I overwhelmed the web development team with a vast number of development briefs,' says Tanaka, 'so the team leader was frightened of me. He said that he was so frightened that for about a week before the launch he was not able to sleep' – but this attention to detail is what makes Uniqlock so compelling. The team allowed users to set Uniqlock to the local time of any one of 282 cities across the world, and on the website there is a map showing all those people using Uniqlock at any one time.

Prior to its launch, teaser films of the dancers were placed on YouTube, leading to intrigue about the site. These, and the website itself, quickly spread around the world, proving that Tanaka had judged his target audience of bloggers well. In just six months, 175,000 screensavers and 27,000 blog widgets were downloaded, with the Uniqlock website receiving 68 million viewers from 209 countries around the world.

07 Uniqlock is also available for use on the iPhone.

08 The Uniqlo website allows visitors to see where the Uniqlock blog app is being used in the world at any one time.

09-16 Images of the Uniqlock dancers performing their moves. At midnight, instead of dancing, they are shown asleep.

08

MENU
134435
LONDON / UNITED KINGDOM

MENU

UNIQLOCK
MUSIC.
DANCE.
CLOCK.
BLOG PARTS
WORLD.UNIQLOCK
DOWNLOADS
HEAT TECH INNER
PRESENT & TRY

UNIQLOCK
MUSIC.
DANCE.
CLOCK.
BLOG PARTS
WORLD.UNIQLOCK
SCREENSAVER
CASHMERE KNIT

MENU

UNIQLOCK
MUSIC.
DANCE.
CLOCK.
BLOG PARTS
WORLD.UNIQLOCK
DOWNLOADS
HEAT TECH INNER
PRESENT & TRY

UNIQLOCK
MUSIC.
DANCE.
CLOCK.
BLOG PARTS
WORLD.UNIQLOCK
SCREENSAVER
DRY POLO SHIRTS

09-16

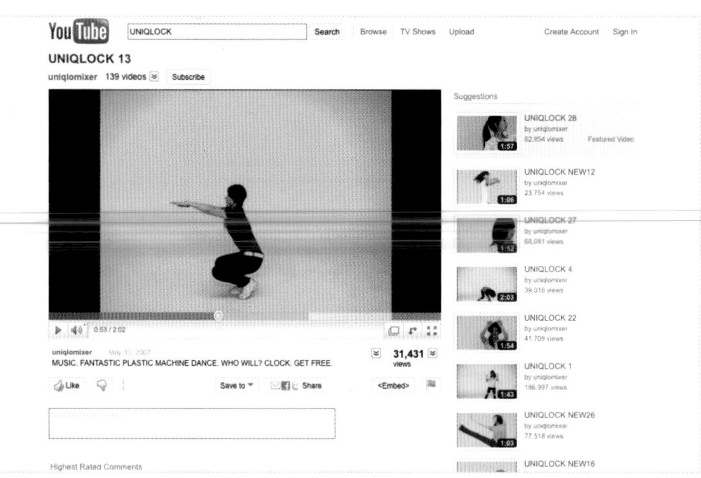

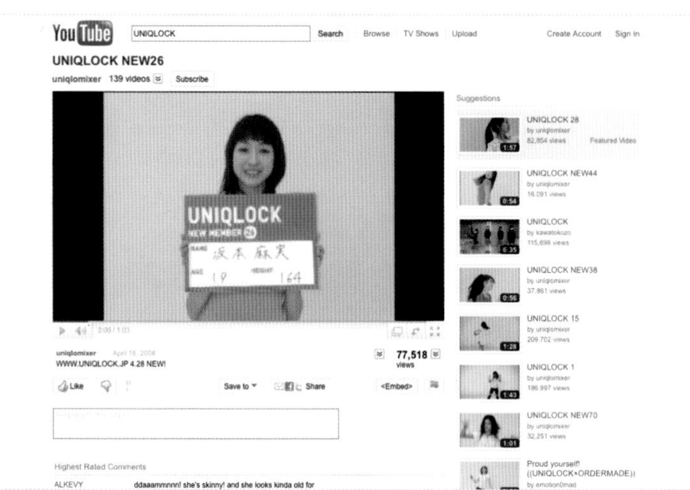

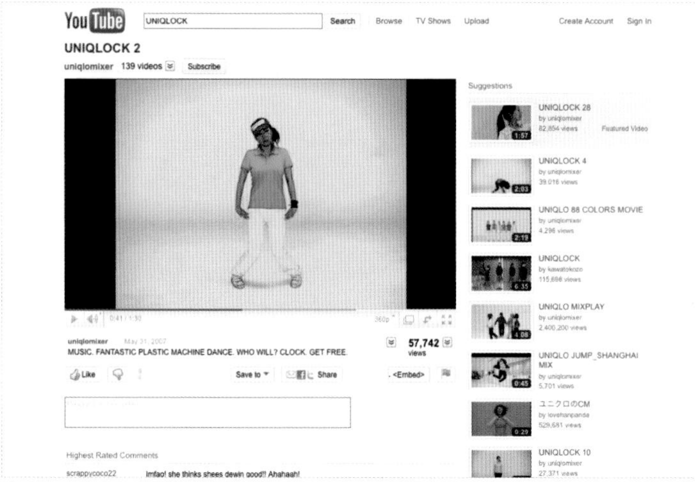

17-19

17-19 Uniqlock audition films, as shown on YouTube.

20-23 Imagery from the Uniqlock website.

24-26 The Uniqlock website allows visitors to see who is using the app around the world via different infographics.

UNIQLOCK MUSIC. DANCE. CLOCK.
BLOG PARTS
WORLD.UNIQLOCK
DOWNLOADS
HEAT TECH INNER
1000 HEAT TECH PRESENT & TRY

05 17 04

TOKYO / JAPAN

20

21-23

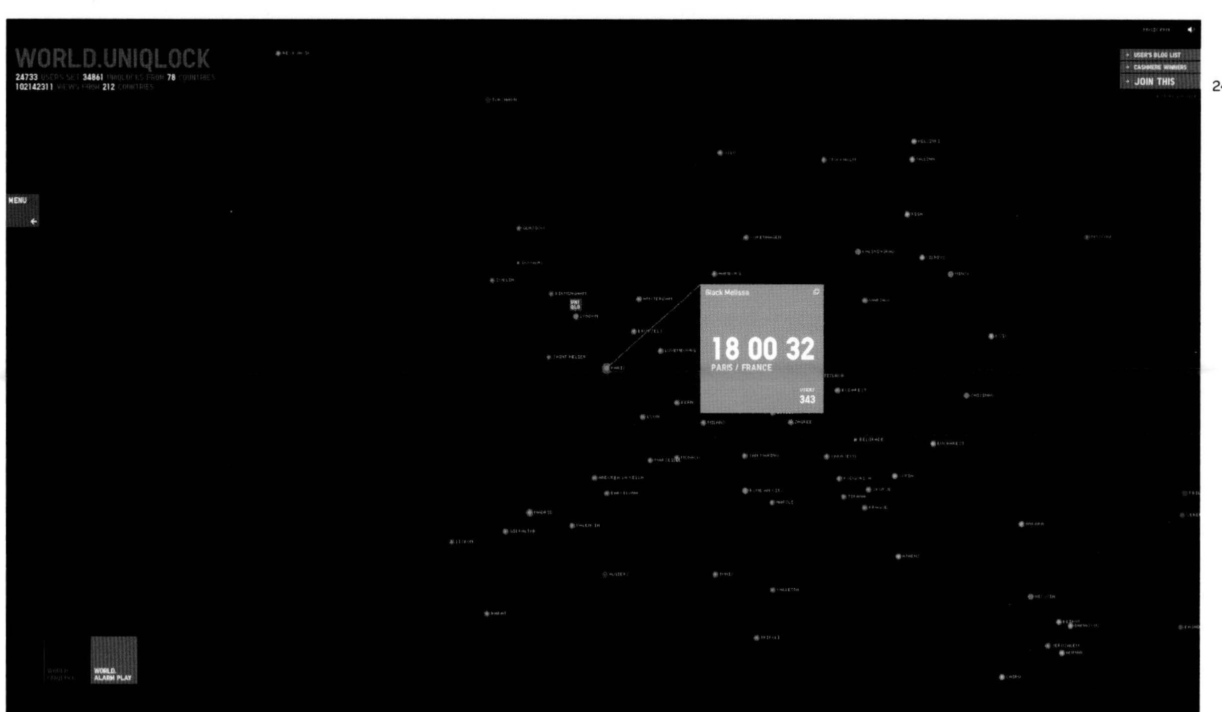
WORLD.UNIQLOCK
24733 USERS SET 34861 UNIQLOCKS FROM 78 COUNTRIES
102142311 VIEWS FROM 212 COUNTRIES
USER'S BLOG LIST
CASHMERE WINNERS
JOIN THIS
MENU
Black Melissa
18 00 32
PARIS / FRANCE
343
WORLD.
ALARM PLAY
24

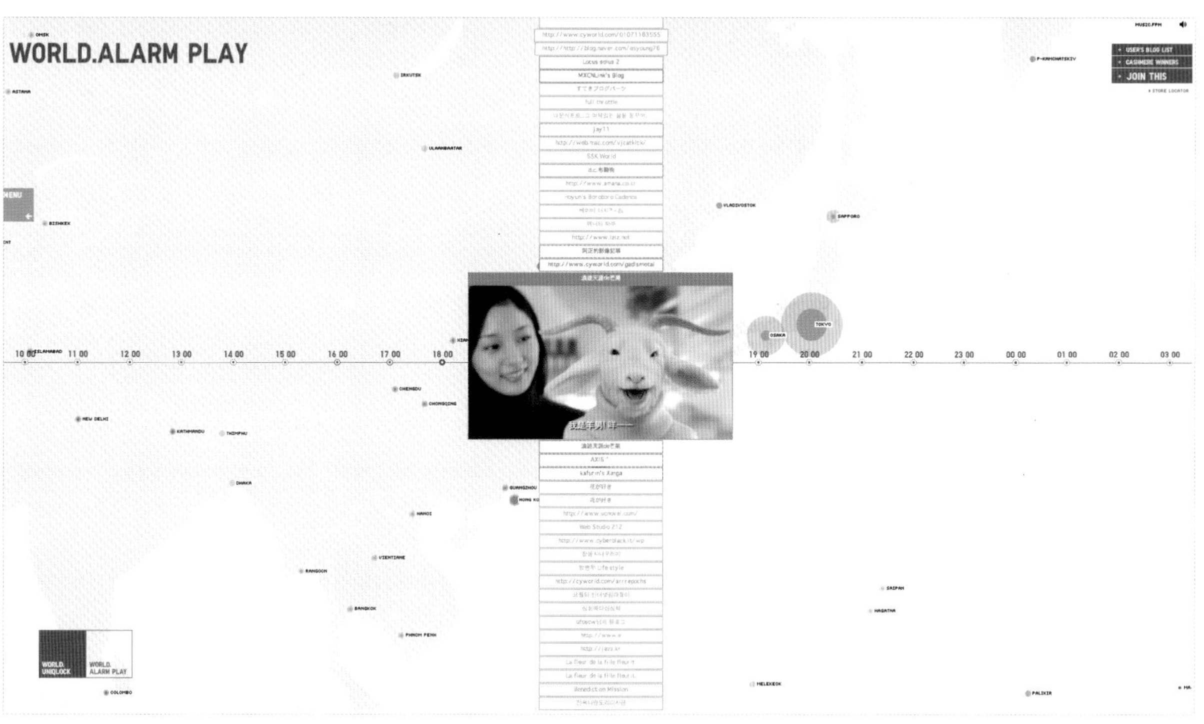
WORLD.ALARM PLAY
USER'S BLOG LIST
CASHMERE WINNERS
JOIN THIS
MENU
10 00
11 00
12 00
13 00
14 00
15 00
16 00
17 00
18 00
19 00
20 00
21 00
22 00
23 00
00 00
01 00
02 00
03 00
WORLD.
UNIQLOCK
WORLD.
ALARM PLAY
25

WORLD.UNIQLOCK
10061 USERS SET 13821 UNIQLOCKS FROM 67 COUNTRIES
33264658 VIEWS FROM 197 COUNTRIES
17:09:06 KUALA LUMPUR / MALAYSIA
17:09:06 PERTH / AUSTRALIA
17:09:06 SHANGHAI / CHINA
USER'S BLOG LIST
18:09:06 TOKYO / JAPAN
CLOSE
RED G-SHOCK WINNERS
JOIN THIS
MENU
26

29/

Wrangler
We Are Animals

Fred & Farid

In 2008, clothes company Wrangler put out a pitch to advertising agencies asking for help to reinvigorate the brand within the European youth market. It faced a specific image problem. 'The problem was that Wrangler is an American brand, 125 years old, associated with middle America,' explains Fred Raillard of Parisian agency Fred & Farid. 'So the perception of Wrangler was very much linked to the cowboy.... But the cowboy in Europe was negative, because the cowboy means old, white America. It's Marlboro, it's John Wayne, it's the people behind the Indian genocide. It's George Bush, who was hated in Europe.'

Despite this, Fred & Farid, which won the pitch, felt it was important not to stray too far away from the brand's roots in its new advertising. 'You cannot start from scratch with the communication of a brand that is 125 years old,' continues Raillard. 'You cannot. Especially as in America the communication about the cowboy was to carry on. So we tried to extract the values of the rodeo – the wildness, being on an animal, roughness. Also, the positive aspects of cowboys – environment, nature, living with animals. Living in synch with nature, having courage. We tried to extract some values that would connect with young people in Europe. Then we thought, "maybe we could just move from the cowboy to the animal". To the horse, in fact.'

This concept tied in with an old logo for the brand that the creative team found during their research. The logo from the 1970s saw the letters of the Wrangler name forming the shape of a horse. It may have been what Raillard describes as 'cheesy', but it meant that Fred & Farid's idea of focusing on the brand's associations to animals had a heritage. They then tested the concept on the target audience, and connected the idea with the culture of the time. 'It was a period when we were facing a crisis,' says Raillard. '... everything was collapsing, the banks were collapsing, and in that period of time we all had the feeling that our human society had reached a limit. So it was relevant to highlight that maybe we'd lost something when we lost our animality.'

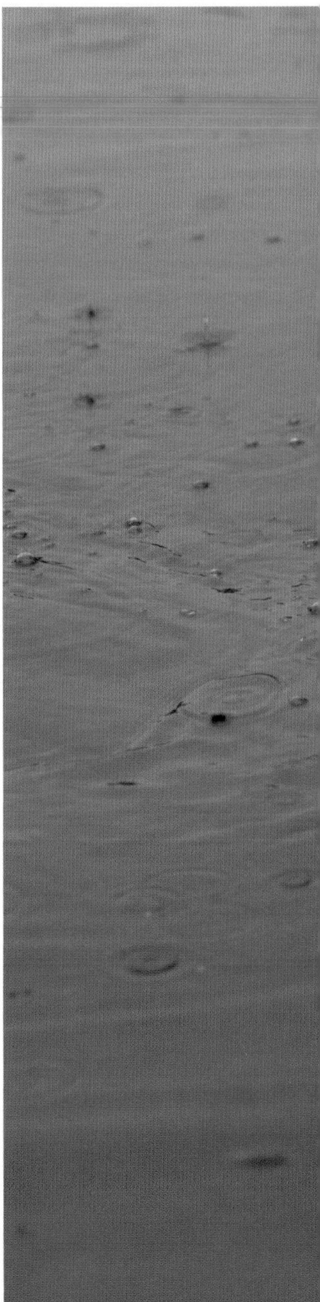

01

01 The We Are Animals press and poster campaign for Wrangler features a series of striking photographs shot by Ryan McGinley. The ads aimed to give the brand a new attitude, rather than showcase the clothing.

'The first thing we decided was to never show any animals. To not create confusion – we're talking about human animality, so the big mistake would be to show an animal.'

02

03

The slogan 'We Are Animals' was decided upon, though Fred & Farid realized that this high concept ran the risk of backfiring if the execution of the ads was too heavy-handed. The key was to emphasize the animal instincts of humans, but in an unexpected way. 'The first thing we decided was to never show any animals,' says Raillard. 'To not create confusion – we're talking about human animality, so the big mistake would be to show an animal. Then we thought with such a strong statement, we couldn't play around, we had to really do it. The whole background had to be animalistic – spontaneous, not too intellectual. So we decided to set up a way of working on Wrangler that was more spontaneous and creative.'

The team decided to avoid too much planning and over-thinking before the shoot, and to employ a photographer who was skilled in attaining a raw, natural quality to their work. 'We looked at photographers not from the ad industry but from art,' says Raillard. 'People who in their personal work are passionate about showing human animality, celebrating animality in humans. We chose Ryan McGinley, as already in his personal work he was really driven by the whole idea of our animality.'

McGinley's shooting style is loose, and his work follows a tradition of documentary photography begun by artists such as Nan Goldin and Larry Clark. He developed his style in the late 1990s by documenting his friends and acquaintances in New York engaging in parties, sex and general hedonism. When he moved to more formal shoots, using models, he retained this naturalistic approach. A shoot of McGinley's, even a commercial one, will usually involve setting up loose parameters and scenarios but otherwise letting events evolve naturally, with everything captured on camera.

'Clients want to show their product, but we really fought to convince them, to get them on board with us that it is more important to bring back the Wrangler attitude and make a connection with a new generation.'

Fred & Farid wholeheartedly embraced this style of working for the Wrangler shoot, which took place in the New Jersey countryside over two nights. Twelve models were selected to take part, drawn not from professional agencies but from street-casting. Actors and performance artists were also among those chosen, and the shoot, when described by Raillard, has the feel more of an art performance than a commercial exercise. 'It was a crazy shoot,' he says. 'People made love in front of us.... Everybody got crazy for two nights. It was freezing like hell, we were wearing North Face jackets, and they were naked in nature! Everybody was amazing, everybody went for this art experience. We experimented with any idea that anybody had on set.'

McGinley, and his assistant, Tim Barber, took thousands of photographs over the two nights, according to Raillard. 'So you don't even have time to think about anything – any idea that anyone has you experiment with. It's chaos, complete chaos... and inside this chaos some pearls pop up.' The shoot resulted in a set of arresting images, which were used to create the posters that stood at the centre of the We Are Animals campaign. Beyond the impact of the images themselves, what is striking about the posters is the lack of overt branding. The brand's logo appears at the bottom, alongside the tagline, but otherwise the photographs are given room to breathe, a highly unusual approach in billboard advertising today, where brands have a tendency to shout their messages.

Even the product itself is absent from many of the shots. 'We had to convince them,' says Raillard. 'Clients want to show their product, but we really fought to convince them, to get them on board with us that it is more important to bring back the Wrangler attitude and make a connection with a new generation. They would never have done it by showing the denim, because even if it's great denim, denim is not a surprising product. We all wear denim now.'

The We Are Animals print and poster campaign is a great example of pure branding. Fred & Farid used other media to do the less exciting work of the ad campaign – using the Wrangler website to provide the vital product information, for example – but insisted that the posters be more ambiguous. It was a risky strategy that ultimately paid off for the jeans brand, injecting it with an edge and attitude that allowed Wrangler to stand out within an extremely crowded market.

02-03 Finished posters in the campaign. The images were shot in the countryside in New Jersey over two nights, in freezing temperatures.

04-06 Images of the New Jersey shoot, showing the make-up artists, the photography crew and the models posing by a lake. According to the ad creatives, thousands of photographs were taken during the shoot, which were then edited down to a final set that was used in the campaign.

07-08 More final posters from the campaign.

04-06

'The perception of Wrangler was very much linked to the cowboy.... But the cowboy in Europe was negative, because the cowboy means old, white America. It's Marlboro, it's John Wayne, it's the people behind the Indian genocide. It's George Bush, who was hated in Europe.'

07-08

WE ARE ANIMALS
Wrangler®

30/

The Zimbabwean
The Trillion Dollar Campaign
TBWA\Hunt\Lascaris

Every now and then an advertising campaign becomes news. For modern ad agencies, having a piece of advertising picked up by the mainstream media can be a holy grail, giving a brand massive coverage at a very low cost. It's a risky strategy to intentionally embark on, however – newspapers and magazines can be fickle and unpredictable beasts, and a story that may seem perfectly constructed back at the agency can be simply ignored when released into the world, or worse, heavily criticised in the press for all to see. But come up with an approach that works, and your campaign will be discussed by journalists and bloggers all over the world.

TBWA\Hunt\Lascaris in Johannesburg achieved one such media breakthrough with its unusual outdoor ad campaign for The Zimbabwean newspaper.

The newspaper is produced by a group of exiled Zimbabwean journalists, and sold in South Africa, the UK and Zimbabwe. On entering its home country, however, it is charged an import duty of 55 per cent, rendering the paper unaffordable to the average Zimbabwean. The newspaper wanted to draw attention to this, and raise awareness of the newspaper generally, so approached TBWA\Hunt\Lascaris for help.

'The Zimbabwean approached us for a campaign to boost sales and subscriptions,' explain the creative team on the campaign, which consisted of copywriters Raphael Basckin and Nicholas Hulley, and art directors Shelley Smoler and Nadja Lossgott. 'The business was being aggressively targeted by a despotic government, and the "luxury tax" the Mugabe regime had imposed was making life incredibly difficult for them to operate and deliver the news. We needed to come up with a campaign that raised awareness quickly and powerfully for the paper that simultaneously told people about the plight of the paper, and the plight of freedom of speech in Zimbabwe.'

The creatives came up with an ingenious solution – to create a series of wall murals, billboards and flyers out of real Zimbabwean banknotes, specifically the Z$100 trillion dollar note, which had become a symbol of the country's world-record inflation. Despite its enormous face value, the note was in fact worth less than paper, so TBWA\Hunt\Lascaris turned it into advertising. 'Their media budget was limited, because their operating costs had soared on account of having to subsidize their own distribution,' continue the creatives, 'and

01

'We realized that the most succinct thing we could do was to use their worthless money to break through to consumers about the situation in Zimbabwe and the fearlessness of The Zimbabwean in reporting it.'

02

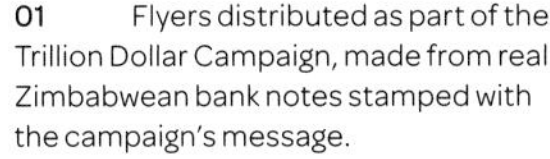

01 Flyers distributed as part of the Trillion Dollar Campaign, made from real Zimbabwean bank notes stamped with the campaign's message.

02 Billboard advertisement for The Zimbabwean newspaper on display in Johannesburg. The ad is made of hundreds of defunct Zimbabwean bank notes.

03 A member of the team sticks the bank notes to a wall for another of the ads.

04-05 Members of the public read and photograph one of the ads on the streets of Johnannesburg.

03

04

05

MAIL
THANKS TO
MUGABE THIS
MONEY IS
WALLPAPER
TheZimbabwean

06-09

10

11

06-09 The ad creatives used a grid to create the posters of money, and the notes were stuck together using tape. The flyers – made of individual bank notes – were all stamped by hand.

10-13 Examples of the finished posters, displayed on walls in Johannesburg. While it only ran locally, the campaign drew huge attention in the media, and was covered in newspapers and blogs across the world.

12

'Our clients have been persecuted and forced into exile for reporting the news, so they were very excited and not the least bit fazed by our idea.'

also because [Zimbabwe's ruling party] ZANU-PF had run the economy into the ground – people were buying their newspaper with money that had become worthless before the next edition was released. We realized that the most succinct thing we could do was to use their worthless money to break through to consumers about the situation in Zimbabwe and the fearlessness of The Zimbabwean in reporting it.'

The client loved the idea. 'Our clients are brave people,' say the creatives. 'They've been persecuted and forced into exile for reporting the news. And they are resourceful – managing to keep a paper alive under extreme conditions. So they were very excited and not the least bit fazed by our idea.'

To accumulate enough money to create the various ads, Basckin, Hulley, Smoler and Lossgott called everyone they knew. 'We took to the streets, scoured our phonebooks for Zimbabweans, met people in gloomy parking lots... but the reality is, Jo'burg is awash with this defunct currency. We just had to gather it up.' This low-fi approach to the campaign was continued in the making of the posters, with everything made by hand – 'we literally stuck all the notes together,' say the team. Once the posters were finished, a printmaker silkscreened a simple message on top of the notes, which proclaimed 'Thanks to Mugabe this money is wallpaper', above The Zimbabwean logo. Flyers made of single notes printed with the same slogan were also distributed around Johannesburg.

Unsurprisingly, the campaign caused a stir. And, despite only being displayed locally in Johannesburg, news of the billboard and flyers spread rapidly around the globe. 'Our campaign became the news,' say the team, simply. 'We've been reported on in the traditional media all around the world, as well as extensively on the web. In fact, we even received footage of one of our posters being displayed in South Korea (we have no idea how it got there). In terms of the public reaction, we have evidence of a massive surge in visits to the website and a strong increase in revenue and sales. Anecdotally, there is strong evidence that it caught the public's imagination having been told about the campaign from the unlikeliest sources.'

In many ways, The Trillion Dollar Campaign was a very simple idea, despite the unusual materials that were employed in its creation. The art direction was minimal but striking, and its message was clear and direct. This transparency of approach contributed to the campaign becoming a significant news story, capturing the imagination of editors and bloggers alike. What began as a local, fairly low-key ad campaign was therefore spread all over the world, giving The Zimbabwean coverage and attention that could never have been bought.

13

Picture credits

01/ adidas Originals
House Party

Agency: Sid Lee
Production agency: Jimmy Lee.tv
Production company: Partizan, Los Angeles; Radke Film Group
Director: Nima Nourizadeh
Post-production: Peep Show, Method NY
Music licensing: Massive Music, LA, NY and Amsterdam
Music composer & company: Pilooski, Boogie Studio, Montréal, Quebec
Music: Beggin', Frankie Valli & The Four Seasons, Pilooski Re-edit
Photographer: RJ Shaughnessy
Web studio: Hue Web Studio, Popcode Studio
Application Architecture: Ergonet

02/ Axe Dark Temptation
Chocolate Man

Client: Unilever
Agency: Ponce Buenos Aires
Executive creative director: Hernan Ponce
Brand planning director: Diego Luque
Art director: Martin Ponce
Copywriter: Mario Crudele
Client services director: Vanina Rudaeff
Brand group director: Nestor Ferreyro
Brand executive: Constanza Vanzini
Responsible for client: Pablo Gazzera/ Tomas Marcenaro/Hernan de Majo/ Fernando Laratro
Head of TV: Roberto Carsillo
Agency producer: Jose Silva
Production company: MJZ
Director: Tom Kuntz
Executive producer: Jeff Scruton, David Zander
Director of photography: Harry Savides
Editorial house: Final Cut LA
Editor: Carlos Arias
Post-production facility: The Mill LA
Music: Allen Toussaint: A Sweet Touch of Love
Sound: La Casa Post Sound

03/ Budweiser
Wassup

True (original)
Writer/Director/Editor: Charles Stone III
Director of photography: Stacey Harris

True: Change (2008)
Director: Charles Stone III
Writers: Chris Fiore, Charles Stone III
Director of photography: Shane Hurlbut
Editor: Nico Alba (Union Editorial)

04/ Burger King
Subservient Chicken

Agency: Crispin Porter & Bogusky
Executive creative director: Alex Bogusky
Creative director: Andrew Keller
Associate creative director: Rob Reilly
Art director: Mark Taylor
Copywriter: Bob Cianfrone
Interactive creative director: Jeff Benjamin
Executive producers: Rupert Samuel, David Rolfe
Agency producer: Terry Stavoe
Interactive production company: The Barbarian Group

The BURGER KING® trademarks and image are used with permission from Burger King Corporation

05/ Cadbury's Dairy Milk
Eyebrows

Client: Lee Rolston, Director of Marketing – Blocks & Beverage
Creative agency: Fallon
Executive creative director: Richard Flintham
Creative directors: Chris Bovill, John Allison
Art director: Nils-Petter Lovgren
Agency producer: Olivia Chalk
Production company: MJZ
Director: Tom Kuntz
Director of photography: Mattias Montero
Executive producer: Debbie Turner
Editor: Steve Gandolfi, Leo King @ Cut + Run
Post-production: The Mill

06/ California Milk Processor Board
Get The Glass

Agency: Goodby, Silverstein & Partners
Co-chairman, Executive creative director: Jeff Goodby
Creative director: Pat McKay
Creative director: Feh Tarty
Interactive creative director: Will McGinness
Associate interactive creative director: Ronny Northrop
Senior art director: Jorge Calleja
Senior copywriter: Paul Charney
Copywriter/Art director: Jessica Shank
Copywriter/Art director: Katie McCarthy
Art director: Brian Gunderson
Creative coordinator: Asya Soloian
Director of interactive production: Mike Geiger
Senior interactive producer: Heather Wischman
Associate interactive producer: Kelsie Van Deman
Broadcast producer: Michael Damiani
Account director: Martha Jurzynski
Account manager: Ashley Weber
Production: North Kingdom

California Milk Processor Board © 2007. All rights reserved. Get The Glass and the logo are registered trademarks of California Milk Processor Board

07/ Canal +
The March of the Emperor

Agency: BETC Euro RSCG
Creative director: Stéphane Xiberras
Copywriters: Pierre Riess, Luc Rouzier
Art directors: Romain Guillon, Eric Astorgue
TV producer: David Green
Production: @radicalmedia
Directors: Glue Society (Gary Freeman and Jonathan Kneebone)

08/ Carlton Draught
Big Ad

Client: Fosters Australia
Agency: George Patterson Partners, Melbourne
Creative director: James McGrath
Writer: Ant Keogh
Art director: Grant Rutherford
Producer: Pip Heming
Group communications director: Paul McMillan
Director: Paul Middleditch/Plaza Films
Executive producer: Peter Masterton/ Plaza Films
VFX supervisor: Andrew Jackson/ Animal Logic
Senior compositor: Angus Wilson/ Animal Logic
VFX producer: Caroline Renshaw/ Animal Logic
Editor: Peter Whitmore/The Editors
Music: Cezary Skubiszewski

09/ Coca-Cola
Happiness Factory

Agency: Wieden + Kennedy Amsterdam
Executive creative directors: Al Moseley, John Norman
Creative directors: Rick Condos, Hunter Hindman
Copywriter: Rick Condos
Art director: Hunter Hindman
Agency producers: Darryl Hagans, Tom Dunlap
Production company: Psyop
Director: Psyop
Psyop creative directors: Todd Mueller and Kylie Matulick
Executive producer: Justin Booth-Clibborn
Producer: Boo Wong
Assistant producers: Kate Phillips, Viet Luu
Lead flame artist: Eben Mears
Flame artist: Jaime Aguirre
Lead 3D artist: Joe Burrascano
Animation director: Kevin Estey
Technical director: Josh Harvey
3D animators: Kyle Mohr, Miles Southan, Boris Ustaev, Dan Vislocky
3D artists: Chris Bach, Clay Budin, David Chontos, Tom Cushwa, Josh Frankel, Jonathan Garin, Scott Hubbard, Jaye Kim, Joon Lee, Paul Liaw, Joerg Liebold, David Lobser, Dylan Maxwell, Naomi Nishimura, Ylli Orana
Storyboard artist: Ben Chan
Matte painter: Dylan Cole
Editor: Cass Vanini
Music: Human
Sound design: Amber Music

10/ Coca-Cola
Yeah Yeah Yeah La La La

Creative agency: Mother
Director: Dougal Wilson
Production company: Blink Productions

11/ Guinness
noitulovE

Client: Georgina Meddows-Smith, Marketing manager for Guinness beer
Creative agency: AMV BBDO
Copywriter: Ian Heartfield
Art director: Matt Doman
Production company: Kleinman Productions
Director: Danny Kleinman
Editor: Steve Gandolfi, Cut & Run
Post-production: Framestore
Audio post-production: Wave

Images courtesy of AMV BBDO, Rattling Stick and Framestore

12/ HBO
True Blood

Creative agency: Digital Kitchen

13/ HBO
Voyeur

Agency: BBDO New York
Production company: RSA Films Ltd
Director: Jake Scott
Digital agency: Big Spaceship

Stills photographer: Gusmano Cesaretti (figs 02-05, 9)
Getty Images/Bryan Bedder (fig. 01)

14/ Honda
Cog

Agency: Wieden + Kennedy London
Executive creative directors: Tony Davidson, Kim Papworth
Creatives: Ben Walker, Matt Gooden
Production company: Partizan
Director: Antoine Bardou-Jacquet

15/ Honda
Grrr

Agency: Wieden + Kennedy London
Executive creative directors: Tony Davidson, Kim Papworth
Creatives: Michael Russoff, Sean Thompson, Richard Russell
Production company: Nexus Productions
Design, animation, direction: Smith & Foulkes
Digital production company: Unit9

16/ Johnnie Walker
The Man Who Walked Around The World

Agency: BBH
Creative director: Mick Mahoney
Copywriter: Justin Moore
Agency producer: Ruben Mercadal
Production company: HLA
Director: Jamie Rafn
Producer: Stephen Plesniak
Actor: Robert Carlyle
Bagpiper: Chris Thomson

Greta Garbo image: © 2011 Harriet Brown & Company, Inc. All Rights Reserved
Hitchcock image: Courtesy of the Alfred J. Hitchcock Trust
(both shown in figs 02 + 09)

17/ Microsoft Xbox
Halo 3

Agency: TAG (now agencytwofifteen)/ McCann Worldgroup San Francisco
Production company: MJZ
Director: Rupert Sanders
Executive producers: Lisa Rich, David Zander
Director of photography: Chris Soos @ Radiant Artists
Editor: Andrea MacArthur @ Peep Show
VFX: Method
Music: Stimmung

18/ Microsoft Xbox
Mosquito; Champagne

Mosquito:
Agency: BBH London
Creative team: Fred & Farid
Production company: Spectre, UK
Director: Daniel Kleinman
Music: Etienne de Crecy

Champagne:
Agency: BBH London
Creative director: John Hegarty
Creative team: Fred & Farid
Agency producer: Andy Gulliman
Account supervisor: Derek Robson
Production company: Spectre, UK
Director: Daniel Kleinman
Producer: Johnnie Frankel
Lighting cameraman: Ivan Bird

Images courtesy of BBH London, Rattling Stick and Framestore

19/ Nike
Barrio Bonito

Agency: BBDO Argentina

20/ Oasis/City of New York
Dig Out Your Soul - In The Streets

Client: NYC & Company/Warner Brothers Records
Creative agency: BBH New York
Creative directors: Kevin Roddy, Calle Sjönell, Pelle Sjönell
Account director: Alex Lubar
Group account director: Chris Wollen, Shane Castang
Head of Broadcast: Lisa Setten
Director of Business Development: Ben Slater
Senior Editor: Mark Block
Agency Producer: Julian Katz

Photographer: Seth Smoot (figs 01-02, 04-05)

21/ Onitsuka Tiger
Made of Japan

Creative agency: Amsterdam Worldwide
Executive creative director: Richard Gorodecky

Made of Japan shoe:
Producer: Miranda Kendrick
Executive producer: Circus Family
Creatives: Al Kelly, Andrew Watson, Erik Holmdahl, Mark Chalmers
Director: Wonter Westen, Circus Family
Camera: Peejee Doorduin, Circus Family
Edit: Peejee Doorduin, Circus Family
Post-production: Maurits Venekamp, Circus Family

Electric Tigerland - Night and Day:
Creative director: Andrew Watson
Art directors: Mathieu Garnier/ Joy-Ann Bouwmans
Copywriters: Mathieu Garnier/ Joy-Ann Bouwmans
Agency producer: Nicolette Lazarus
Production company: B-Reel

Photographer: Satoshi Minakawa (figs 07, 08)

Zodiac race shoe:
Creative director: Andrew Watson
Copywriter: Gillian Glendinning
Art director: Jasper Mittelmeijer
Planner (creative agency): Simon Neate-Stidson
Senior producer (creative agency): Samantha Koch
Production company: Panda Panther

Tansu shoe:
Creative director: Andrew Watson
Copywriter: Dan Goransson
Art director: Rickard Engstorm
Planning director: Jonathan Fletcher
Planner: Ben Jaffe
Producer: Samantha Koch
Business development director: Nicolette Lazarus
Account director: Paula Ferrai
Account manager: Romain Lauby (working with ASICS Europe communications manager Sandra Koopmans)

Photographers: Rene Bosch (fig 36); Ogura Tansu Ten (figs 23, 25, 27, 29-35)

22/ Philips
Carousel

Creative agency: Tribal DDB
Production company: Stink Digital
Director: Adam Berg

23/ Skoda
The Baking Of

Client: Mary Newcombe, Head of Marketing, Skoda
Creative agency: Fallon
Executive creative director: Richard Flintham
Creative directors: Chris Bovill, John Allison
Agency producer: Nicky Barnes
Production company: Gorgeous Enterprises
Director: Chris Palmer

Photographer: Nadia Marquard Otzen (figs 01, 04-06, 08, 14-15, 20-21, 22-24)

24/ Sony Bravia
Balls

Client: David Patton, Senior vice-president marketing communications, Sony Europe
Creative agency: Fallon
Group account director: Chris Willingham
Senior planner: Mark Sinnock
Creative directors: Richard Flintham, Andy Mcleod
Copywriter/Art director: Juan Cabral
Media agency/OMD media planner: Christina Hesse
Production company: MJZ
Director: Nicolai Fuglsig
Executive producer: Debbie Turner
Directors of photography: Joaquin Baca-Asay, Jim Frohna
Editor: Russell Icke
Editing company: The Whitehouse
Post-production company: The Mill
Audio post-production company: Wave sound studios

25/ Sony Bravia
Paint

Client: David Patton, Senior vice-president marketing communications, Sony Europe Creative agency: Fallon
Writers: Juan Cabral, Richard Flintham, Jonathan Glazer
Director: Jonathan Glazer
Production company: Academy
Editor: Paul Watts, Quarry
Post-production: MPC
Audio Post-production: Soundtree and Wave
Agency planner: Mark Sinnock
Media agency: OMD International

Location stills: Lucy Gossage, Academy Films

26/ Sony PlayStation
The History of Gaming;
The Future of Gaming

Director/designer: Johnny Hardstaff
Producer: John Payne
Editor: JD Smyth
Production company: RSA Films Ltd

27/ Stella Artois
La Nouvelle 4%

Creative agency: Mother

28/ Uniqlo
Uniqlock

Creative agency: Projector Inc

29/ Wrangler
We Are Animals

Client: VF Europe Wrangler
Agency: Fred & Farid, Paris
Creative directors: Fred & Farid
Copywriters: Fred & Farid
Art directors: Fred & Farid, Juliette Lavoix, Pauline De Montferrand
Advertiser's supervisors: Giorgio Presca, Marc Cuthbert, Gary Burnand, Carmen Claes
Agency supervisor: Fred & Farid, Daniel Dormeyer
Account managers: Paola Bersi, Vassilios Bazos, Branimira Branitcheva

Photographer: Ryan McGinley

30/ The Zimbabwean
The Trillion Dollar Campaign

Agency: TBWA\Hunt\Lascaris, Johannesburg
Clients: Liz Linsell, Wilf Mbanga, Trish Mbanga at The Zimbabwean
Executive creative director: John Hunt
Art directors: Shelley Smoler, Nadja Lossgott
Copywriters: Raphael Basckin, Nicholas Hulley
Account director: Bridget Langley

Photographers: Chloe Coetzee, Des Ellis, Michael Meyersfeld, Rob Wilson

Acknowledgements

A huge thanks to all the contributors and everyone who helped to put this book together, in particular to Jo Lightfoot, Melissa Danny and Ida Riveros at LKP; & SMITH; and Patrick Burgoyne, Gavin Lucas and Mark Sinclair at CR. Also to Thierry Albert, William Bartlett, Raphael Basckin, Chris Baylis, Damien Bellon, Jeff Benjamin, Todd Brandes, John Cherry, Rick Condos, Mario Crudele, Brian DiLorenzo, Matt Doman, Daniel Dormeyer, Scott Duchon, Eric Eddy, Richard Flintham, Fred & Farid, Gary Freedman, Piero Frescobaldi, Nicolai Fuglsig, Jonathan Glazer, Matt Gooden, Richard Gorodecky, Laurence Green, Greg Hahn, Johnny Hardstaff, Ian Heartfield, Hunter Hindman, Héloïse Hooton, Nicholas Hulley, Ant Keogh, Daniel Kleinman, Jonathan Kneebone, Tom Kuntz, Bella Laine, Nicolette Lazarus, Nadia Lossgott, Ryan McGinley, Will McGinness, Darlene Mach, Kris Manchester, Emily Mason, Kylie Matulick, Justin Moore, Todd Mueller, Nima Nourizadeh, Benjamin Palmer, Chris Palmer, John Patroulis, Carlos Pérez, Mark Pytlik, Jamie Rafn, Tom Ramsden, Patricia Reta, Kevin Roddy, Natalia Rodoni, Michael Russoff, Tom Sacchi, Rodrigo Saavedra, Rupert Sanders, Stephen Sapka, Calle & Pelle Sjönell, Jake Scott, Jose Silva, Shelley Smoler, Mike Smith, Taylor Smith, Smith & Foulkes, Gustavo Sousa, Shannon Stephaniuk, Roger Stighall, Charles Stone III, Koichiro Tanaka, Ben Walker, Andrew Watson, Dougal Wilson, Sara Woster, and Stéphane Xiberras. And finally, thanks to Sean and to Mum for all their support.